W9-AGP-936

Get Those Guys Reading!

Get Those Guys Reading!

Fiction and Series Books that Boys Will Love

**Kathleen A. Baxter and
Marcia Agness Kochel**

 **LIBRARIES UNLIMITED**

AN IMPRINT OF ABC-CLIO, LLC
Santa Barbara, California • Denver, Colorado • Oxford, England

Library of Congress Cataloging-in-Publication Data

Baxter, Kathleen A.
  Get those guys reading! : fiction and series books that boys will love /
Kathleen A. Baxter and Marcia Agness Kochel.
    pages cm
  Includes bibliographical references and indexes.
    ISBN 978-1-59884-846-5 (pbk.) — ISBN 978-1-59884-847-2 (ebook) (print)   1. Boys—Books and reading—United States.   2. Children's stories, American—Bibliography.   3. Children's literature in series—Bibliography.   I. Kochel, Marcia Agness.   II. Title.
  Z1039.B67B377   2012
  028.5'5—dc23   2012005430

ISBN: 978-1-59884-846-5
EISBN: 978-1-59884-847-2

16 15 14 13 12   1 2 3 4 5

This book is also available on the World Wide Web as an eBook.
Visit www.abc-clio.com for details.

Libraries Unlimited
An Imprint of ABC-CLIO, LLC

ABC-CLIO, LLC
130 Cremona Drive, P.O. Box 1911
Santa Barbara, California 93116-1911

This book is printed on acid-free paper ∞

Manufactured in the United States of America

Contents

Introduction

Due to a series of fortunate events, which led me to the realization that an extremely effective way to get boys interested in reading was to promote nonfiction, I spent several years writing about and talking about that topic. Then the Bureau of Education and Research asked me to put together an all-day seminar called "Connecting Boys to Books," and that, of course, had to include fiction.

I started reading fiction aimed at boys. I may be the only woman you will ever encounter who has actually read *Sir Fartsalot Hunts the Booger.* And, no, it was not my thing. But then again, most of what my husband reads is not my thing either. In fact, a lot of the books that boys love are not often read by women. When I talk about the *Wimpy Kid* books, I am always surprised at how few women in the room have ever read even one of them. Then I read one of my favorite excerpts and the whole room dissolves in laughter. I *love* the *Diary of a Wimpy* kid series and have read them all. I grab them the minute I see them and anticipate every single new one. Once, a flight attendant spotted me reading one on a plane. She grinned, approached me and said, "You look like you're having a really good time with *that* book!"

I have read that most young boys have their lives controlled by women. If a parent stays home with a baby, it is usually the mother. Day care providers? Usually female. Preschool teachers? Usually female. Children's librarian at the public library? Usually female. Kindergarten teachers, school librarians, almost all elementary school teachers? Mostly female. And guess what we females would love you boys to read? We would love you to read the books we loved when we were your age. And many boys do love those books, but they yearn for something that speaks directly to them.

Remember the general dismay that erupted when the *Captain Underpants* books by Dav Pilkey came out? Many were appalled that such gross, tasteless books were so beloved by boys in particular. Mercifully, we seem to have gotten over it, and years after their initial appearance, boys still read and love *Captain Underpants*. And people seem resigned to it, at least most of the time.

Adult women and men do not often read and enjoy the same books. Boys and girls, as we all observe all of the time, enjoy many different activities, some together and some not. But we have a crisis in boys' reading in this country, and I believe that one possible solution to the problem is providing enough different kinds of books to make sure that there is something there that will appeal to every kid.

Boys do read fiction. We see it all of the time. What Marcia and I hope to provide here is a list of some well-reviewed and/or popular books with plenty of guy appeal. Series books right now are big, as we all know. Get a kid interested in one book in a series and he may happily read every book in it.

Our book focuses on books published in the last few years but includes many with enduring appeal from the past. We hope it will help you select the books you need to entice those reluctant boys to stick their nose in a good book!

Kathleen Baxter, 2012

A NOTE ABOUT THE ORGANIZATION OF THIS BOOK

We have divided this book into thematic chapters, making it easier to locate books on a particular topic of interest such as adventure or sports. Within each chapter we divided the recommended books by age group. "Younger Guys" means that the book works for kids in third and fourth grades (and often older boys, as well). "Older Guys" indicates that the book's interest and appropriateness level begins at fifth grade or higher. Individual titles and series books are listed together, alphabetized by author. Series book citations are in bold print to help you find them more easily. If a publisher numbers a series, we have numbered it here. If they do not number it but it is in a particular order, we have ordered it correctly here (usually by year of publication). Occasionally series books have no discernable order or numbering system, and in these cases the books are alphabetical by title. We have occasionally used Library of Congress descriptions for the books, and when this is the case we have put the book summary in quotes followed by LC. All other annotations are our own.

Chapter 1

Action, Adventure, and Spy Books

It used to be that adventure books meant outdoor survival stories such as *My Side of the Mountain* by Jean Craighead George, *Hatchet* by Gary Paulsen, and just about anything by Will Hobbs. As we put together this chapter we found our definition of adventure expanding to include some more high-tech adventures and lots of books dealing with intrigue and spies. There's a real mix of books here, but they all share the fast-paced action that makes them winners with boys—particularly reluctant readers.

YOUNGER GUYS

Arnosky, Jim. *The Pirates of Crocodile Swamp*. Putnam Juvenile, 2009. 230 p. Grades 4–8.
> "Brothers Sandy and Jack Casperin flee from their abusive father into the remote swamplands of the Florida Keys, and after they learn how to survive on their own amongst the dangerous wildlife, they encounter a young girl and an old sailor who teach them how to begin anew." LC

Bosch, Pseudonymous. *Secret* series, illustrated by Gilbert Ford, published by Little Brown, Grades 4–7.
> Mystery, adventure, and fantasy combine to make an entertaining series featuring a boy and a girl protagonist.

1. *The Name of this Book is Secret,* 2007
2. *If You're Reading This, It's Too Late,* 2008
3. *This Book is Not Good for You,* 2009
4. *This Isn't What It Looks Like,* 2010
5. *You Have to Stop This,* 2011

Brown, Jeff. *Flat Stanley's Worldwide Adventures* series, published by HarperCollins, by various authors and illustrated by various artists, Grades 2–5.

The hugely popular character created by Jeff Brown appears in these geographically themed chapter books. They're fun and educational.

1. *The Mount Rushmore Calamity,* by Sara Pennypacker, 2009
2. *The Great Egyptian Grave Robbery,* by Sara Pennypacker, 2009
3. *The Japanese Ninja Surprise,* by Sara Pennypacker, 2009
4. *The Intrepid Canadian Expedition,* by Sara Pennypacker, 2010
5. *The Amazing Mexican Secret,* by Josh Greenhut, 2010
6. *The African Safari Discovery,* by Josh Greenhut, 2011

Buckley, Michael. *NERDS* series, published by Amulet, Grades 4–7.

When a cool kid gets ugly new braces, he becomes one of the kids he used to make fun of and bully. Now he is recruited by their secret agency, NERDS. Comic book–style illustrations. Fun and exciting.

1. *NERDS: National Espionage, Rescue, and Defense Society,* 2009
2. *M is for Mama's Boy,* 2010

Clements, Andrew. *Benjamin Pratt and the Keepers of the School* series, published by Atheneum, Grades 3–6.

"Ben and his friend Jill find themselves in danger when they discover the secret history of their Massachusetts school and set out to derail a developer's plan to level the building to make way for an amusement park. Ben is drawn into an effort to keep the school from being destroyed." LC

We the Children, 2010
Fear Itself, 2010
Whites of their Eyes, 2011

Garretson, Dee. *Wildfire Run.* HarperCollins, 2010. 272 p. Grades 3–7.

The hero of this book is Luke, the son of the president of the United States. When a wildfire follows an earthquake at Camp David, he and his friends must struggle to survive. Fans of *Hatchet* will like this one. It is the first in the *Danger's Edge* series.

Korman, Gordon. *Dive* trilogy, published by Scholastic, Grades 4–7.

"Four adolescents interning as research divers for the summer find themselves searching for a centuries-old treasure and fending off killer sharks. Interweaves their story with that of Samuel Higgins, a boy who died in a shipwreck in the same waters in 1665." LC

1. *The Discovery,* 2003
2. *The Deep,* 2003
3. *Danger,* 2003

Author Spotlight: Gordon Korman

Gordon Korman wrote his first published novel as his seventh grade English project. From there he has gone on to write many humorous and action-packed books for kids. It is no surprise that he was a big reader as a boy and that his first love was humor books. He also loved survival and adventure books, and later fantasy and science fiction. As an adult he began reading nonfiction in order to research his own adventure series. His influences include Jack Gantos, Jerry Spinelli, old-school heist movies, and adult nonfiction.

Gordon Korman Recommends

The Great Brain series: Okay, 19th-century Utah may not seem all that glamorous to today's reader, but these were my favorite books as a kid. So much of what I know about telling a middle-grade story comes from *The Great Brain*.

Percy Jackson: I had a chance to work alongside Rick Riordon during *The 39 Clues* series, and I've been working to "channel" him ever since. No one has a better instinct for what's cool.

The Hitchhikers Guide to the Galaxy: Okay, it's not for everybody. But those who love it do so to the nth degree. (And I'm one of them.)

Jack Gantos: Whenever I start to lose touch with a middle-grade audience, I reread his "Jack Henry" books. He's one of the authors who gets it.

The Mad Scientists Club: Another old-school choice, but this novel really defines that middle-school-boy sweet spot.

Chris Crutcher: Even when dealing with the heaviest, most intense YA topics, he always manages to tell a story with honesty, simplicity and, amazingly, humor. The current "golden age" of teen books would not exist without him.

Korman, Gordon. *Everest* trilogy, published by Scholastic, Grades 4–7.
    "Four climbers, winners of an American Junior Alpine Association contest, vie to become the youngest person ever to reach the peak of Mount Everest." LC

1. *The Contest*, 2002
2. *The Climb*, 2002
3. *The Summit*, 2002

Korman, Gordon. *Island* **trilogy, published by Scholastic, Grades 4–7.**
"Six children try to survive on a desert island in the Pacific Ocean after a storm destroys their boat." LC

1. *Shipwreck,* 2001
2. *Survival,* 2001
3. *Escape,* 2001

Korman, Gordon. *Kidnapped* **series, published by Scholastic, Grades 4–7.**
"Aiden teams up with the FBI to track down his sister Meg who was kidnapped while they were walking home from school." LC. These are the same kids who are in Korman's *On the Run* series.

1. *Abduction,* 2006
2. *Search,* 2006
3. *Rescue,* 2006

Korman, Gordon. *On the Run* **series, published by Scholastic, Grades 4–7.**
It is *The Fugitive* all over again as Aiden and Meg Falconer must escape from a juvenile detention center in order to prove their parents innocent of charges of treason that would put them in jail for life. The story continues in Korman's *Kidnapped* series.

1. *Chasing the Falconers,* 2005
2. *The Fugitive Factor,* 2005
3. *Now You See Them, Now You Don't,* 2005
4. *The Stowaway Solution,* 2005
5. *Public Enemies,* 2005
6. *Hunting the Hunter,* 2006

LaFevers, R. L. *Nathaniel Fludd, Beastologist* **series, published by Houghton Mifflin, Grades 2–5.**
"Ten-year-old Nate is sent to live with a family cousin, the world's last beastologist, after his parents are declared lost at sea, but danger mounts when he is brought on an expedition to the Arabian desert, gets lost, and must protect a newly hatched phoenix egg and rescue his guardian." LC

1. *Flight of the Phoenix,* 2009
2. *The Basilisk's Lair,* 2010
3. *Wyvern's Treasure,* 2010
4. *The Unicorn's Tale,* 2011

Lord, Gabrielle. *Conspiracy 365* **series, published by Kane-Miller, Grades 4–7.**
An Australian series about a 15-year-old kid who is chased on December 31 by a man who warns him that he must survive the coming year. Lots of action and adventure.

1. *January,* 2010
2. *February,* 2010
3. *March,* 2010
4. *April,* 2010
5. *May,* 2010
6. *June,* 2010
7. *July,* 2010

    8. *August,* 2010
    9. *September,* 2010
  10. *October,* 2010
  11. *November,* 2010
  12. *December,* 2010

Malaghan, Michael. *Greek Ransom.* IPG/Anderson, 2010. 272 p. Grades 4–7.

"Callie and Nick embark on a dangerous adventure after their archaeologist parents are kidnapped on a Greek island, and they battle deadly tombs, a lion-headed monster, and the schemes of a psychotic millionaire while trying to obtain a Mycenaean treasure that could cover their parents' ransom." LC

Mone, Gregory. *Fish.* Scholastic, 2010. 256 p. Grades 3–5.

"Eleven-year-old Fish, seeking a way to help his family financially, becomes a reluctant cabin boy on a pirate ship, where he soon makes friends—and enemies—and is asked to help decipher clues that might lead to a legendary treasure." LC

Morpurgo, Michael. *Kensuke's Kingdom.* Scholastic, 2003. Grades 4–7.

Eleven-year-old Michael is washed overboard off his family's yacht and awakens on what he believes is a deserted island in the Pacific. In this riveting survival story, Michael discovers he is not alone.

Nelson, N.A. *Bringing the Boy Home.* HarperCollins, 2008. 216 p. Grades 4–8.

When an Amazonian tribal boy is thrown out because of a deformed foot, he is adopted and taken to Miami by an American anthropologist. Now nearing age 13, he is hearing the voices of his ancestors and wants to go back and become a man by tribal standards. An exciting good read.

Paulsen, Gary. *Masters of Disaster.* Random House, 2010. 112 p. Grades 4–6.

"Twelve-year-old Henry Mosely, having decided his life is boring, ropes his friends Riley and Reed into a series of hair-raising adventures, including trying to break world records, visiting a haunted house, and solving a century-old murder." LC

Petersen, P. J. *Wild River.* Delacorte, 2009. 121 p. Grades 3–7.

There's plenty of adventure in this story of two brothers on a camping trip who get into trouble when they set off in a kayak. Nominated for multiple state young reader awards.

Richards, Justin. *Agent Alfie* series, illustrated by Jim Hansen, published by IPG/Harper-Collins UK, Grades 3–5.

Alfie is mistakenly enrolled in a school that trains future British spies and secret agents. Funny, fast-moving, and with lots of illustrations.

    1. *Thunder Raker,* 2010
    2. *Sorted,* 2010
    3. *License to Fish,* 2011

Rogan, S. Jones. *The Daring Adventures of Penhaligon Brush.* Illustrated by Christian Slade. Alfred A. Knopf Books for Young Readers, 2007. 230 p. Grades 3–6.

"When Penhaligon Brush the fox is summoned by his step-brother to the seaside town of Porthleven, he finds immediately upon arrival that his brother is incarcerated in the dungeon at Ferball Manor." LC. Lots of adventure and excitement. The sequel is *The Curse of the Romany Wolves,* 2009.

Rylander, Chris. *The Fourth Stall.* Walden Pond, 2011. 320 p. Grades 4–7.
"Sixth-graders Mac and Vince operate a business charging schoolmates for protection from bullies and for help to negotiate conflicts peacefully, with amazing challenges and results." LC. *The Fourth Stall Part II* came out in 2012.

Selfors, Suzanne. *Smells Like Dog.* Little, Brown, 2010. 368 p. Grades 4–7.
"When farm boy Homer Pudding's explorer-uncle dies and leaves him a droopy dog with a mysterious coin hidden on its collar, it leads him to The City, where they meet Madame La Directeur, the conniving head of the Natural History Museum, who is trying to steal the coin and take Homer's place in a secret society of adventurers." LC. Starred review in *Kirkus*; may be the first in a series.

Small, Charlie (pseudonym of Nick Ward). ***Charlie Small Journals* series, published by Random House, Grades 3–6.**
Charlie Small, age eight but alive for 400 years, keeps journals about his exciting adventures.

1. *Gorilla City,* 2007
2. *Perfumed Pirates of Perfidy,* 2007
3. *The Puppet Master,* 2007
4. *The Daredevil Desperados of Destiny,* 2008
5. *Charlie in the Underworld,* 2008
6. *The Barbarous Brigands of Frostbite Pass,* 2008
7. *The Mummy's Tomb,* 2009
8. *Forest of Skulls,* 2009
9. *Planet of the Gerks,* 2010
10. *Land of the Remotosaurs,* 2010
11. *The Hawk's Nest,* 2011

Stilton, Geronimo. ***Geronimo Stilton* series, published by Scholastic, Grades 2–4.**
Geronimo Stilton, the editor of *The Rodent's Gazette* in New Mouse City, and has numerous exciting adventures. The pages are graphically lively, and this is a popular series.

1. *Lost Treasure of the Emerald Eye,* 2004
2. *Curse of the Cheese Pyramid,* 2004
3. *Cat and Mouse in a Haunted House,* 2004
4. *I'm Too Fond of My Fur,* 2004
5. *Four Mice Deep in the Jungle,* 2004
6. *Paws Off, Cheddarface,* 2004
7. *Red Pizzas for a Blue Count,* 2004
8. *Attack of the Bandit Cats,* 2004
9. *A Fabumouse Vacation for Geronimo,* 2004
10. *All Because of a Cup of Coffee,* 2004
11. *It's Halloween, You 'Fraidy Mouse,* 2004
12. *Merry Christmas, Geronimo,* 2004
13. *Phantom of the Subway,* 2004
14. *The Temple of the Ruby,* 2004
15. *The Mona Mouse Affair,* 2005
16. *A Cheese-Colored Camper,* 2005
17. *Watch Your Whiskers, Stilton!* 2005

The Karate Mouse by Geronimo Stilton.

18. *Shipwreck on the Pirate Islands*, 2005
19. *My Name Is Stilton, Geronimo Stilton*, 2005
20. *Surf's Up!* 2005
21. *The Wild, Wild West*, 2005
22. *The Secret of Cacklefur Castle*, 2005
23. *Valentine's Day Disaster*, 2005
24. *Field Trip to Niagara Falls*, 2005
25. *The Search for Sunken Treasure*, 2006
26. *The Mummy with No Name*, 2006
27. *Christmas Toy Factory*, 2006
28. *Wedding Crasher*, 2006
29. *Down and Out Down Under*, 2007
30. *Mouse Island Marathon*, 2007
31. *Mysterious Cheese Thief*, 2007
32. *Valley of the Giant Skeletons*, 2008
33. *Geronimo and the Gold Medal Mystery*, 2008
34. *Geronimo Stilton, Secret Agent*, 2008
35. *Very Merry Christmas*, 2008
36. *Geronimo Valentine*, 2009
37. *Race Across America*, 2009
38. *Fabumouse School Adventure*, 2009
39. *Singing Sensation*, 2009
40. *The Karate Mouse*, 2010
41. *Mighty Mount Kilimanjaro*, 2010
42. *Peculiar Pumpkin Thief*, 2010
43. *I'm Not a Supermouse*, 2010
44. *The Giant Diamond Robbery*, 2011
45. *Save the White Whale!* 2011

Stone, Rex. *Dinosaur Cove* **series, illustrated by Mike Spoor, published by Scholastic, Grades 2–4.**

Tom and Jamie find a secret entrance to a prehistoric world filled with dinosaurs. There are at least 10 more of these books published or to be published in England. It is unclear if they will make their way to North America.

1. *Attack of the Tyrannosaurus*, 2008
2. *Charge of the Triceratops*, 2008
3. *March of the Ankylosaurus*, 2008
4. *Flight of the Quetzalcoatlus*, 2008
5. *Catching the Velociraptor*, 2008
6. *Stampede of the Edmontosaurus*, 2008
7. *Saving the Stegosaurus*, 2008
8. *Swimming with the Plesiosaur*, 2008
9. *Tracking the Diplodocus*, 2009
10. *Escape from the Fierce Predator*, 2009

Voelkel, Jon, and Pamela Craik Voelkel. *Jaguar Stones* **series, published by Egmont, Grades 4–8.**

Indiana Jones–type adventures about a 14-year-old with archaeologist parents whose profession takes them into interesting and sometimes dangerous places.

1. *Middleworld*, 2010
2. *The End of the World Club*, 2010

Wilkins, Kay. *Ripley's Believe It or Not!* **series, published by Ripley, Grades 4–7.**

Ripley High School now houses students with special powers—and the best ones go on dangerous missions around the world. Lots of graphics here, and lots of appeal to reluctant readers.

1. *A Scaly Tale*, 2010
2. *The Dragon's Triangle*, 2010
3. *Running Wild*, 2010
4. *Secrets of the Deep*, 2010
5. *Wings of Fear*, 2010
6. *Sub-Zero Survival*, 2010

> 7. *Shock Horror,* 2010
> 8. *The Lost Island,* 2010

Wilson, N. D. *Leepike Ridge.* Random House, 2007. 224 p. Grades 4–7.
   "While his widowed mother continues to search for him, eleven-year-old Tom, presumed dead after drifting away down a river, finds himself trapped in a series of underground caves with another survivor and a dog, and pursued by murderous treasure-hunters." LC

Wurge, B. B. *The Last Notebook of Leonardo.* Leapfrog, 2010. 152 p. Grades 4–6.
   "Jem is led on an adventurous journey to find the final resting place of Leonardo da Vinci after his scientist father turns himself into a nine-foot-tall orangutan." LC

OLDER GUYS

Adam, Paul. *Max Cassidy: Escape from Shadow Island.* Walden Pond, 2010. 295 p. Grades 5–up.
   "British fourteen-year-old Max Cassidy calls on his skills and training as a professional escape artist when he attempts to clear his mother of murdering his father, who disappeared two years earlier in the Central American country of Santodomingo." LC

Blackwood, Gary. *Around the World in 100 Days.* Dutton, 2010. 368 p. Grades 5–9.
   Philas's Fogg's son takes a bet that he cannot drive around the world in 100 days— though he can take it on ships. Action and adventures!

Bowler, Tim. *Blade* series, published by Philomel, Grades 5–8.
   Lots of action and adventure in these stories about a young tough guy who is constantly getting into trouble while trying to flee his past.

> 1. *Playing Dead,* 2009
> 2. *Out of the Shadows,* 2010
> 3. *Fighting Back,* 2011

Bradford, Chris. *The Young Samurai* series, published by Hyperion, Grades 6–9.
   Jack Fletcher, an English teenager in the 1700s, starts training as a samurai at his foster father's school. But his real father was murdered by a ninja leader named Dragon Eye, and he remains a threat. Lots of action and adventure.

> *The Way of the Warrior,* 2009
> *The Way of the Sword,* 2010
> *The Way of the Dragon,* 2011

Briceland, V. *The Cassaforte Chronicles* series, published by Flux, Grades 8–up.
   "On his first sea voyage, seventeen-year-old Nic Dattore faces vicious pirates then, with a motley crew of castaways, decides to commandeer the pirate ship to return home, racing against time to save the magical city of Cassaforte from a diabolical plot." LC

> 1. *The Glassmaker's Daughter,* 2009
> 2. *The Buccaneer's Apprentice,* 2010
> 3. *The Nastenza Conspiracy,* 2011

Carman, Patrick. *Trackers* series, published by Scholastic, Grades 6–9.
   Another new series that requires looking at videos on the web. "Adam, Finn, Lewis, and Emily use their computer coding skills and high-tech equipment to catch criminals, but

when they begin to track Shantorian, a dangerous hacker, things do not play out as easily as the four Trackers predict. Includes passwords for Web content." LC

Trackers, 2010
Shantorian, 2011

Colfer, Eoin. *Airman.* Hyperion, 2008. 412 p. Grades 5–up.
Conor Broekhart, born in a balloon, is falsely imprisoned and vows to escape and seek revenge on the evil man who hates him. His determination always to fly makes for an engrossing, action-packed story.

Collard, Sneed B., III. *Double Eagle.* Peachtree, 2009. 247 p. Grades 4–8.
"Michael and Kyle's discovery of a rare Confederate coin near an old Civil War fort in 1973 turns into a race against time as the boys try to find more coins before a hurricane hits Alabama's Gulf coast." LC. Nominated for multiple state young reader awards.

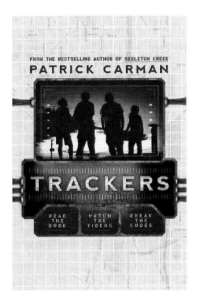

Trackers **by Patrick Carman.**

Cooney, Caroline B. *Code Orange.* Delacorte, 2005. 200 p. Grades 5–up.
Mitty Blake, age 15, has a big problem. While researching his biology assignment on smallpox, he comes across an envelope full of old smallpox scabs from 1902. He inhales them, sneezes, and begins to realize that he himself may have been exposed to a disease that is now believed to be extinct, and, if he has it, he could kill thousands of others. When terrorists capture him during the two-week period before he knows whether the disease will strike or not, he is forced to make some hard decisions. An exciting read!

Cooper, Mark A. *Fledgling: Jason Steed.* Sourcebooks Jabberwocky, 2010. 213 p. Grades 5–8.
"Eleven-year-old British Sea Cadet Jason Steed's easy summer at camp, just off the Jakarta coast, is destroyed when helicopters bring down an enemy that slaughters his friends and threatens the safety of his country." LC

Davies, Stephen. *Hacking Timbuktu.* Clarion, 2010. 272 p. Grades 6–up.
There's a lot of action and adventure in this story of two London teenagers who find a clue on an ancient manuscript that leads them on an exciting and dangerous treasure hunt.

Gilman, David. *Danger Zone* series, published by Delacorte, Grades 7–12.
There is a lot of excitement and nonstop action in these *Da Vinci Code*–like stories about a 15-year-old daredevil named Max Gordon who fights insane evildoers.

The Devil's Breath, 2008
Ice Claw, 2010
Blood Sun, 2011

Grant, Katie. *Hide and Seek.* Peachtree, 2010. 227 p. Grades 5–8.
"In the remote mountains of Arizona where he lives with his mother, stepfather, and two sisters, fourteen-year-old Chase discovers two kidnapped boys and gets caught up in a dangerous adventure when he comes up with a plan to get them to safety." LC

Gutman, Dan. *Mission Unstoppable.* HarperCollins, 2011. 304 p. Grades 5–8.

    Twelve-year-old brother and sister twins Coke and Pepsi McDonald are recruited for a secret government plot to use Young American Geniuses, YAGs, to solve the nation's problems. The first of the *Genius Files* series. The second book in the series is called *Never Say Genius,* 2012.

Harris, M. G. *The Joshua Files* series, published by Walker, Grades 5–8.

    Nonstop action and plenty of adventures guarantee readers a good time. Thirteen-year-old Josh investigates his father's suspicious death and discovers a high-tech secret society that has been hidden for centuries.

    1. *Invisible City,* 2010
    2. *Ice Shock,* 2011

Haven, Paul. *The Seven Keys of Balabad.* Random House, 2009. 276 p. Grades 5–8.

    "Oliver Finch, who lives with his father in Balabad, tries to deal with his boredom when a five-hundred-year-old sacred carpet is stolen and one of his friends disappears, causing Oliver to hunt down members of the Brotherhood of Arachosia and reveal a secret that is centuries old." LC. Nominated for multiple state young reader awards.

Heath, Jack. *Agent 6 of Hearts* series, published by Scholastic, Grades 5–8.

    An incredibly talented teen secret agent has lots of exciting adventures. The first book was written when the author was still in high school.

    The Lab, 2008
    Remote Control, 2010

Herlong, M. H. *The Great Wide Sea.* Viking, 2008. 284 p. Grades 6–10.

    Three brothers face a harrowing experience when their father goes missing on a year-long sailing adventure. Nominated for multiple state young reader awards.

Higgins, Jack, with Justin Richards. *The Chance Twins* series, published by Putnam Juvenile, grades 6–9.

    Nonstop action and excitement ensue when teenage twins Rich and Jade are sent to live with their secret-agent father. Great for spy lovers.

    Sure Fire, 2007
    Death Run, 2008
    Sharp Shot, 2009
    First Strike, 2010

Hobbs, Will. *Go Big or Go Home.* HarperCollins, 2008. 185 p. Grades 5–up.

    "Fourteen-year-old Brady and his cousin Quinn love extreme sports, but nothing could prepare them for the aftermath of Brady's close encounter with a meteorite after it crashes into his Black Hills, South Dakota, bedroom." LC. Nominated for several state young reader awards.

Hobbs, Will. *Take Me to the River,* HarperCollins, 2011. 192 p. Grades 4–8.

    "When North Carolina fourteen-year-old Dylan Sands joins his fifteen-year-old cousin Rio in running the Rio Grande River, they face a tropical storm and a fugitive kidnapper." LC

Honey, Elizabeth. *Remote Man.* Alfred A. Knopf Books for Young Readers, 2002. 260 p. Grades 6–8.

    "Thirteen-year-old Ned and his depressed mother leave Australia for a rest in America, but he is soon on the trail of international smugglers of exotic animals, with help from his Internet friends." LC. Great for spy lovers.

Horowitz, Anthony. *The Alex Rider Adventures,* **published by Philomel, Grades 5–8.**

Fast-paced, page-turning thrillers about Alex Rider, a junior James Bond, complete with fantastic gadgets. Reading these books is like watching an action movie. These are wildly popular with middle school boys.

Stormbreaker, 2001
Point Blank, 2002
Skeleton Key, 2003
Eagle Strike, 2004
Scorpia, 2006
Ark Angel, 2006
Snakehead, 2007
Crocodile Tears, 2009
Scorpia Rising, 2011
Also available: *Stormbreaker: The Graphic Novel,* 2006

Jinks, Catherine. *Evil Genius* **series, published by Harcourt, Grades 7–up.**

Australian Cadel Piggott is definitely a genius, and he is at first unaware that he is being raised to be a genius of evil almost previously unimagined. In his loveless, adoptive environment (he is not much better off than Harry Potter), he is driven to secrecy and subterfuge. Then his counselor enrolls him in the Axis Academy, a college specifically for teaching evil. This is creative and original and hard to put down.

1. *Evil Genius,* 2007
2. *Genius Squad,* 2008
3. *Genius Wars,* 2010

Key, Watt. *Alabama Moon.* Farrar, Straus & Giroux, 2008. 294 p. Grades 7–10.

An adventure and survival story about a 10-year-old kid raised by a paranoid Vietnam vet father who lives in a shelter in the woods. When his dad dies, Moon Blake is taken to a boys' school and leads a grand escape. A compelling, gripping story. *Dirt Road Home,* 2010, is about a secondary character in the first book, Hal Mitchell, who is determined to stay out of trouble so he can get out. The first book was nominated for several state readers' choice awards.

Korman, Gordon. *Griffin Bing* **series, published by Scholastic, Grades 5–7.**

Boys love Gordon Korman books, and there is a good reason for that. Funny, thought-provoking, fast-moving, and interesting, these books about Griffin Bing, "The Man with the Plan," and his talent for getting into trouble, are fine reading.

Swindle, 2008
Zoobreak, 2009
Framed, 2010
Showoff, 2012

Lewis, J. S. *Invasion.* Thomas Nelson, 2011. 336 p. Grades 6–up.

When 16-year-old Colt suddenly loses his parents, he learns that they may have been murdered. Aliens were out to get them and he has to track them down. Fast-paced adventure. The first in the *CHAOS* series.

Framed **by Gordon Korman.**

Logstead, Greg. *Alibi Junior High.* Aladdin, 2009. 244 p. Grades 6–9.

"After thirteen-year-old Cody and his father, an undercover agent, are nearly killed, Cody moves in with his aunt in Connecticut, where he is helped with his adjustment to the trials of attending public school for the first time and investigating a threat in nearby woods by a wounded Iraq War veteran." LC. Great for spy lovers.

London, C. Alexander. *Accidental Adventure* **series, published by Philomel, Grades 5–8.**

Twins Oliver and Celia are stuck. Though they hate adventures, their parents love them, and they get involved in a big one when their mother goes missing. Funny.

We Are Not Eaten by Yaks, 2011
We Dine with Cannibals, 2011

McCaughrean, Geraldine. *The Pirate's Son.* Scholastic, 1998. 194 p. Grades 5–up.

Pirates and adventure mingle in this exciting story of teenage misfits.

McKernan, Victoria. *The Devil's Paintbox.* Alfred A. Knopf Books for Young Readers, 2009. 361 p. Grades 6–9.

Survival and adventure story fans enjoy this tale of orphaned 15-year-old Aiden, who joins a wagon train headed for Oregon with his younger sister.

Mowll, Joshua. *Operation Red Jericho: The Guild Specialists Book 1.* Candlewick, 2005. 288 p. Grades 5–up.

For Joshua Mowll, it was the surprise of a lifetime. There, among the archives inherited from his great-aunt Rebecca MacKenzie, was a 1920s journal recounting the thrilling and dangerous adventures of 15-year-old Rebecca and her younger brother, Doug. Eager to pursue any lead about the mysterious disappearance of their parents, the siblings travel from the bustling streets of Shanghai to the open ocean aboard their uncle's ship to a grisly pirate island fortress. Along the way, the intrepid duo discovers the existence of a secret scientific society, the Honourable Guild of Specialists, which may have answers for them regarding their parents' fates—if the teens can survive long enough to find out! Followed by *Operation Typhoon Shore,* 2006.

Muchamore, Robert. *CHERUB* **series, published by Simon Pulse, Grades 6–9.**

James has had a tough life, but his luck changes dramatically when he is recruited to be part of a top-secret British group of under-17 spies. But before he can join the ranks of the CHERUB agents, he must survive 100 days of grueling basic training. These fast-paced and edgy page-turners were originally published in England.

1. *The Recruit,* 2005
2. *The Dealer,* 2005
3. *Maximum Security,* 2006
4. *The Killing,* 2005
5. *Divine Madness,* 2006
6. *Man vs. Beast,* 2006
7. *The Fall,* 2007
8. *Mad Dogs,* 2007
9. *The Sleepwalker,* 2008
10. *The General,* 2008
11. *Brigands MC,* 2009
12. *Shadow Wave,* 1010

Mulligan, Andy. *Trash*. Random House, 2010. 233 p. Grades 6–10.

"A group of fourteen-year-old boys, who make a living picking garbage from the outskirts of a large city, find something special and mysterious that brings terrifying consequences." LC. Starred review in *School Library Journal*.

Napoli, Donna Jo. *North*. Greenwillow, 2004. 344 p. Grades 5–up.

Alvin is sick to death of his overprotective mother who won't let him do anything. Researching his hero, Matthew Henson, in a class project, Alvin decides to run away from home in Washington, DC, and head north—as far as he can get. Kids love this adventure story and the amazing people Alvin meets on his journey.

Northrop, Michael. *Trapped*. Scholastic, 2011. 240 p. Grades 7–10.

"Seven high school students are stranded at their New England high school during a week-long blizzard that shuts down the power and heat, freezes the pipes, and leaves them wondering if they will survive." LC. Compelling.

Nuzum, K. A. *A Small White Scar*. HarperCollins, 2006. 180 p. Grades 5–up.

Fifteen-year-old Will is sick of living on his family's ranch, still mourning the death of his mother several years ago, and, above all, angry and dismayed that he alone is responsible for his twin brother, Denny, who has Down's Syndrome. Will has saved his money and knows if he can enter the rodeo, he will win first prize and be able to work at another ranch, leaving the life he hates behind him. But first his father says he can't go, then, when he runs away, Denny won't let him go. Moving, powerful, with a lot of rodeo action.

Perkins, Lynne Rae. *As Easy as Falling Off the Face of the Earth*. Greenwillow, 2010. 352 p. Grades 7–11.

Delightful read about 16-year-old Ryan, whose summer program has been canceled at the last minute. He hops off the train in Montana and begins a series of adventures. One of the best reviewed books of 2010.

Pearson, Ridley. *Steel Trapp* series, published by Disney, Grades 5–8.

"On a two-day train trip to enter his invention in the National Science Competition in Washington, D.C., fourteen-year-old Steven 'Steel' Trapp, possessor of a remarkable photographic memory, becomes embroiled in an international plot of kidnapping and bribery that may have links to terrorists." LC. Nominated for state young reader awards.

The Challenge, 2008
The Academy, 2010

Sachar, Louis. *Holes*. Farrar, Straus & Giroux, 1998. 233 p. Grades 5–up.

This is one Newbery Medal Winner that almost everyone likes, especially kids. Stanley Yelnats, unjustly accused of a crime, is sent to Camp Greenlake where the young prisoners spend their days digging holes. But what are they really digging for? Great choice, great book!

**Holes by Louis Sachar.
Courtesy of Farrar Straus
Giroux Books for Young
Readers, an imprint of
the Macmillan Children's
Publishing Group.**

Sachar, Louis. *Small Steps*. Delacorte, 2006. 272 p. Grades 5–up.
Armpit, an African American boy who was digging holes with Stanley Yelnats in *Holes*, gets his own book here. Armpit, who would prefer *not* to be called by his prison name, has a summer job digging holes for landscape gardening, when his friend X-Ray proposes he join him in a get-rich scheme scalping tickets to a concert by a popular young rock star. What happens changes Armpit's life. This is not as good as *Holes*, but is enjoyed by many.

Sedgwick, Marcus. *Revolver*. Roaring Brook, 2010. 160 p. Grades 7–10.
Fourteen-year-old Sig is stranded at a remote cabin in the Arctic wilderness with the body of his father, who died just hours earlier after falling through the ice, when a terrifying man arrives, claiming Sig's father owes him a share of a horde of stolen gold and that he will kill Sig if he does not get his money. A riveting, scary read.

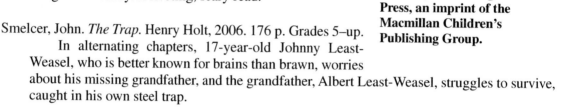

Revolver **by Marcus Sedgwick. Courtesy of Roaring Book Press, an imprint of the Macmillan Children's Publishing Group.**

Smelcer, John. *The Trap*. Henry Holt, 2006. 176 p. Grades 5–up.
In alternating chapters, 17-year-old Johnny Least-Weasel, who is better known for brains than brawn, worries about his missing grandfather, and the grandfather, Albert Least-Weasel, struggles to survive, caught in his own steel trap.

Smith, Roland. *Cryptid Hunters*. Hyperion, 2005. 348 p. Grades 5–8.
"Twins, Grace and Marty, along with a mysterious uncle, are dropped into the middle of the Congolese jungle in search of their missing photojournalist parents." LC. Nominated for several state young reader awards. Sequel is *Tentacles*, published by Scholastic, 2009.

Smith, Roland. *I, Q* **series published by Sleeping Bear, Grades 5–8.**
Quest and his stepsister Angela are thrust into the dangerous world of the American Secret Service and the Israeli Mossad when they learn Angela's real mother was a former secret service agent who was killed by a terrorist group. The first book in the series won the 2009 Oregon Book Award. Book three is expected by early 2012.

    1. *Independence Hall*, 2008
    2. *The White House*, 2010

Somper, Justin. *Vampirates* **series, published by Little, Brown, Grades 5–8.**
In 2512, twins Grace and Connor take their boat out, get in a storm and are shipwrecked. They are rescued—by two different ships, and two different kinds of beings. Exciting and hugely popular.

    1. *Demon of the Ocean*, 2005
    2. *Tide of Terror*, 2006
    3. *Blood Captain*, 2007
    4. *Black Heart*, 2009
    5. *Empire of Night*, 2010
    6. *Immortal War*, 2011

Stewart, Trenton Lee. *The Mysterious Benedict Society* **series, illustrated by Diana Sudkya, published by Little, Brown, Grades 5–8.**

"After passing a series of mind-bending tests, four children are selected for a secret mission that requires them to go undercover at the Learning Institute for the Very Enlightened, where the only rule is that there are no rules." LC. Lots of fun and adventure.

1. *The Mysterious Benedict Society,* 2007
2. *The Mysterious Benedict Society and the Perilous Journey,* 2008
3. *The Mysterious Benedict Society and the Prisoner's Dilemma,* 2009

Stratton, Allan. *Borderline.* HarperTeen, 2010. 298 p. Grades 7–10.

"Despite the strained relationship between them, teenaged Sami Sabiri risks his life to uncover the truth when his father is implicated in a terrorist plot." LC

Wooding, Chris. *Malice* **series, illustrated by Dan Chernett, published by Scholastic, Grades 6–up.**

Teenagers start disappearing into a nightmare realm of a comic book. Exciting, with lots of graphics.

1. *Malice,* 2009
2. *Havoc,* 2010

Young, E. L. *STORM* **series, published by Dial, Grades 5–8.**

A group of young geniuses forms a group called STORM, whose mission is to wipe out global misery. Great for spy lovers.

The Infinity Code, 2008
The Ghost Machine, 2008
The Black Sphere, 2008
The Viper Club, 2008

Malice **by Chris Wooding.**

Chapter 2

Animal Stories

There don't seem to be as many animal books written for children as there were in the past. When you eliminate the animal fantasy books (see chapter 8 for these, including *The Warriors* series and the Redwall books) and the historical fiction books about animals (*War Horse* by Michael Morpurgo and *Elephant Run* by Roland Smith and others are found in chapter 4), there are even fewer to choose from. Here you will find the best of what's new in animal stories and a few that have stood the test of time.

YOUNGER GUYS

***Animal Tales* series, by various authors, published by Bloomsbury, Grades 2–4.**
"Fresh, fun, distinctive adventure stories for young readers starring adorable mice, loveable pups, and other delightful furry or feathered animals. With a book coming out each season, boys and girls will have a new tale to look forward to every few months." Publisher's Description

Angus Macmouse Brings Down the House, by Linda Teitel, 2010
Monkey See, Monkey Zoo, by Erin Soderberg, 2010
The Pup Who Cried Wolf, by Chris Kurtz, 2010
Dreams of a Dancing Horse, by Dandi Daley Mackall, 2011

Auch, Mary Jane. *A Dog on His Own.* Holiday House, 2008. 153 p. Grades 2–5.
"After a daring escape from the animal shelter, Pearl, Peppy, and K-10—so named because he is one step above all the other canines—explore the outside world while moving from one adventure to another." LC

Behrens, Andy. *The Fast and the Furriest*. Alfred A. Knopf Books for Young Readers, 2010. 224 p. Grades 2–5.

"The overweight and unathletic son of a famous former football star discovers that his equally fat and lazy dog is unexpectedly—and obsessively—interested in competing in dog agility contests." LC. *Booklist* called this "a satisfying underdog story in the tradition of Gordon Korman's and David Lubar's novels."

Birney, Betty. *Humphrey* series, published by Putnam Juvenile, Grades 2–5.

Humphrey is a classroom hamster, but he gets to go home with different kids. Adventure, new experiences, and fun combine to make these good books to read aloud, too.

1. *The World According to Humphrey*, 2004
2. *Friendship According to Humphrey*, 2005
3. *Trouble According to Humphrey*, 2007
4. *Surprises According to Humphrey*, 2008
5. *Adventure According to Humphrey*, 2009
6. *Summer According to Humphrey*, 2010
7. *School Days According to Humphrey*, 2011

Butler, Dori. *The Buddy Files* series, published by Whitman, Grades 1–4.

Buddy the dog solves mysteries while looking for his missing owners. An enjoyable series.

1. *The Case of the Lost Boy*, 2010
2. *The Case of the Mixed-Up Mutts*, 2010
3. *The Case of the Missing Family*, 2010
4. *The Case of the Fire Alarm*, 2011
5. *The Case of the Library Monster*, 2011

Cox, Judy. *Tails of Frederick and Ishbu* series, illustrated by Omar Rayyan, published by Marshall Cavendish, Grades 4–6.

Two rat brothers, classroom pets, get involved in adventure and excitement—and mysteries! Fun.

The Mystery of the Burmese Bandicoot, 2007
The Case of the Purloined Professor, 2009

Doder, Joshua. *Grk* series, published by Delacorte, Grades 3–6.

A British series about Tim and his dog, Grk, full of page-turning adventure and mystery.

1. *A Dog Called Grk*, 2006
2. *Grk and the Pelotti Gang*, 2007
3. *Grk and the Hot Dog Trail*, 2008
4. *Grk: Operation Tortoise*, 2009
5. *Grk Smells a Rat*, 2009

Donovan, Gail. *In Memory of Gorfman T. Frog*. Dutton, 2009. 180 p. Grades 4–6.

"When irrepressible fifth-grader Josh finds a five-legged frog in his backyard pond, it leads to him learning a lot about amphibians, and himself." LC

Erickson, John R. *Hank the Cowdog* **series, illustrated by Gerald L. Holmes, most were published by Maverick originally, but then by Puffin, Grades 3–5.**

Hank is "Head of Ranch Security" and has several sidekicks on the M-Cross ranch in Texas. New copyright dates were secured with the new publisher, which made the original dates hard to ascertain.

1. *The Original Adventures of Hank the Cowdog,* 1985
2. *The Further Adventures of Hank the Cowdog,* 1983, 1999
3. *It's a Dog's Life,* 1983, 1999
4. *Murder in the Middle Pasture,* 1989, 1999
5. *Faded Love,* 1989, 1999
6. *Let Sleeping Dogs Lie,* 1999
7. *The Curse of the Incredible Priceless Corncob,* 2011
8. *The Case of the One-Eyed Killer Stud Horse,* 1990, 1999
9. *The Case of the Halloween Ghost,* 1989
10. *Every Dog Has His Day,* 1988
11. *Lost in the Dark Unchanted Forest,* 1988
12. *The Case of the Fiddle Playing Fox,* 1999
13. *The Wounded Buzzard of Christmas Eve,* 1989, 1999
14. *Hank the Cowdog and Monkey Business,* 1990, 1999
15. *The Case of the Missing Cat,* 1990, 1999
16. *Lost in the Blinded Blizzard,* 1999
17. *The Case of the Car-Barkaholic Dog,* 1991, 1999
18. *The Case of the Hooking Bull,* 2000
19. *The Case of the Midnight Rustler,* 1999
20. *The Phantom in the Mirror,* 1999
21. *The Case of the Vampire Cat,* 1999
22. *The Case of the Double Bumblebee Sting,* 1999
23. *Moonlight Madness,* 1994, 1999
24. *The Case of the Black-Hooded Hangmans,* 1995, 1999
25. *The Case of the Swirling Killer Tornado,* 1995
26. *The Case of the Kidnapped Collie,* 1999
27. *The Case of the Night-Stalking Bone Monster,* 1996
28. *The Mopwater Files,* 1999
29. *The Case of the Vampire Vacuum Sweeper,* 2000
30. *The Case of the Haystack Kitties,* 1998, 1999
31. *The Case of the Vanishing Fishhook,* 1999
32. *The Garbage Monster from Outer Space,* 1999
33. *The Case of the Measled Cowboy,* 1999
34. *Slim's Good-Bye,* 2000
35. *The Case of the Saddle House Robbery,* 2000
36. *The Case of the Raging Rottweiler,* 2000
37. *The Case of the Deadly Ha-Ha Game,* 2001
38. *The Fling,* 2001
39. *The Secret Laundry Monster Files,* 2002
40. *The Case of the Missing Bird Dog,* 2002
41. *The Case of the Shipwrecked Tree,* 2003
42. *The Case of the Burrowing Robot,* 2003
43. *The Case of the Twisted Kitty,* 2004
44. *The Dungeon of Doom,* 2004
45. *The Case of the Falling Sky,* 2005
46. *The Case of the Tricky Trap,* 2005
47. *The Case of the Tender Cheeping Chickies,* 2006
48. *The Case of the Monkey Burglar,* 2006
49. *The Case of the Booby-Trapped Pickup,* 2007
50. *The Case of the Most Ancient Bone,* 2008
51. *The Case of the Blazing Sky,* 2008
52. *The Quest for the Great White Quail,* 2008
53. *Drover's Secret Life,* 2009
54. *The Case of the Dinosaur Birds,* 2009
55. *The Case of the Secret Weapon,* 2010
56. *The Case of the Coyote Invasion,* 2010
57. *The Disappearance of Drover,* 2011
58. *The Case of the Mysterious Voice,* 2011

George, Jean. *My Side of the Mountain.* Dutton, 1959. 178 p. Grades 4–8.

"A young boy relates his adventures during the year he spends living alone in the Catskill Mountains, including his struggle for survival, his dependence on nature, his animal friends, and his ultimate realization that he needs human companionship." LC. This is still hugely popular and won a Newbery Honor.

Howe, Peter. *Waggit* **series, illustrated by Omar Rayyan, published by HarperCollins, Grades 4–7.**

"When Waggit is abandoned by his owner as a puppy, he meets a pack of wild dogs who become his friends and teach him to survive in the city park, but when he has a chance to go home with a kind woman who wants to adopt him, he takes it." LC

Waggit's Tale, 2008
Waggit Again, 2009
Waggit Forever, 2010

Author Spotlight: Patrick Jennings

Patrick Jennings was never read to as a child and didn't have books in his home, but that didn't stop him from reading. He went to the library and brought home as many books as he could carry. He did not finish every book, but he read until he found ones that he liked—which most often were funny books and books about animals. His favorite authors were Roald Dahl and Beverly Cleary, who still influence him today, along with William Steig, Edward Gorey, Mark Twain, and E. B. White. Currently he reads a lot of adult books, both fiction and nonfiction, including lots of books about animals. Many of these books affect his writing. For example, Jane Jacobs's book *The Death and Life of Great American Cities* informed *The Beastly Arms* and Mark Harris's *The Southpaw* greatly influenced *Out Standing in My Field.* And he believes that no children's book writer can help but be influenced by the tales of the Brothers Grimm, Lewis Carroll, Frank Baum, and, of course, William Shakespeare.

Patrick Jennings Recommends

M. T. Anderson's *Whales on Stilts*

William Steig's *Dominic*

Jack London's *White Fang*

Beverly Cleary's *Henry and Ribsy*

Norton Juster's *The Phantom Tollbooth*

Adam Rex's *The True Meaning of Smekday*

Roald Dahl's *Charlie and the Chocolate Factory*

Rene Goscinny's *Nicholas*

Lemony Snicket's *A Series of Unfortunate Events*

Jennings, Patrick. *Guinea Dog.* Egmont, 2010. 192 p. Grades 3–5.

His parents deny fifth-grader Rufus's request for a dog, instead buying him a guinea pig he absolutely does not want. But the guinea pig barks, fetches things, and whines—just like a dog. Funny, and great for kids moving on to chapter books.

Jennings, Patrick. *We Can't All Be Rattlesnakes.* HarperCollins, 2009. 121 p. Grades 4–6.

After being captured and imprisoned by an undisciplined human boy, "Crusher" the gopher snake learns a lot of new things. An excellent read, nominated for multiple state young reader awards.

Jukes, Marvis. *Smoke.* Farrar, Straus & Giroux, 2009. 164 p. Grades 4–6.

Kids who like cowboys, cats, and good stories enjoy this one about 12-year-old Colton, whose life isn't the one he wants any more when his parents divorce and he moves with his mother.

Felix Takes the Stage **by Kathryn Lasky.**

Kehret, Peg. *Ghost Dog Secrets.* Dutton, 2010. 192 p. Grades 4–6.

Sixth grader Rusty decides he has to help an abused dog—but you can get into big trouble that way. A fast-paced story.

King-Smith, Dick. *Babe the Gallant Pig.* Random House, 1995. 130 p. Grades 3–5.

"A piglet comes to Farmer Hogget's farm, where he is adopted by an old sheepdog and accomplishes amazing things." LC. A delightful story.

Lasky, Kathryn. *The Deadlies* series, illustrated by Stephen Gilpin, published by Scholastic, Grades 2–5.

"Having been discovered, a family of poisonous but friendly brown recluse spiders must flee their cozy home in a symphony hall and go searching for a new place to live." LC

Felix Takes the Stage, 2010
Spiders on the Case, 2011

Layton, Neal. *The Mammoth Academy.* Henry Holt, 2008. 154 p. Grades 2–4.

"Woolly mammoth siblings Oscar and Arabella enjoy being at Mammoth Academy, but Oscar is accused of stealing oranges and when he follows some mysterious tracks to find the real thief, he discovers humans living nearby." LC. Sequel is *The Mammoth Academy in Trouble,* 2009.

The Mammoth Academy by Neal Layton. Courtesy of Henry Holt Books for Young Readers, an imprint of the Macmillan Children's Publishing Group.

Leach, Sara. *Jake Reynolds: Chicken or Eagle?* Orca, 2009. 112 p. Grades 3–6.

Jake is scared of encountering a wolf—a realistic fear as one has been spotted in the area—and also of running away from it. His worst fears come to pass, and he learns he is not the wimp he thought he was. Good read.

Napoli, Donna Jo. *Mogo, the Third Warthog.* Illustrated by Lita Judge. Hyperion, 2008. 197 p. Grades 3–5.

An exciting story about Mogo, a young warthog that is forced out on his own and must struggle to survive on the savanna. Nominated for multiple state young reader awards.

O'Connor, Barbara. *The Fantastic Secret of Owen Jester.* Farrar, Straus & Giroux/Frances Foster Books, 2010. 176 p. Grades 4–6.

"After Owen captures an enormous bullfrog, names it Tooley Graham, then has to release it, he and two friends try to use a small submarine that fell from a passing train to search for Tooley in the Carter, Georgia, pond it came from, while avoiding nosy neighbor Viola." LC. *School Library Journal* Best Books for Children, 2010.

Rawls, Wilson. *Where the Red Fern Grows.* Delacorte, 1996. 212 p. Grades 4–8.

This remains a beloved classic about a boy in the Ozarks and his dogs.

Spires, Ashley. *Binky the Space Cat* series, published by Kids Can, Grades 1–4.

Binky, a house cat who believes the family home is actually a space station, trains and prepares to travel into outer space, where his humans go everyday and need his protection.

1. *Binky the Space Cat,* 2009
2. *Binky to the Rescue,* 2010
3. *Binky to the Rescue,* 2011

Tolan, Stephanie S. *Wishworks, Inc.* Scholastic, 2009. 152 p. Grades 2–4.

"When he is granted his wish for a dog from Wishworks, Inc., third-grader Max is disappointed to find that his new pet is nothing like the dog in his imagination." LC

Voigt, Cynthia. *Young Fredle.* Illustrated by Louise Yates. Alfred A. Knopf Books for Young Readers, 2011. 224 p. Grades 3–5.

"Fredle, a young mouse cast out of his home, faces dangers and predators outside, makes some important discoveries and allies, and learns the meaning of freedom as he struggles to return home." LC. A companion book to *Angus and Sadie* (2005), by the same author.

Wolf-Morgenlander, Karl. *Ragtag.* Clarion, 2009. 227 p. Grades 3–7.

An animal fantasy about a young swallow named Ragtag who leads a fight to save the birds of Boston against the invading raptors. Fun and exciting.

OLDER GUYS

Boelts, Maribeth. *The PS Brothers.* Harcourt, 2010. 138 p. Grades 5–7.

"Sixth-graders Russell and Shawn, poor and picked on, work together scooping dog droppings to earn money for a Rottweiler puppy to protect them from bullies, but when they learn the puppies' owner is running an illegal dog-fighting ring, they are torn about how to respond." LC. Excellent for reluctant readers.

Corriveau, Art. *How I, Nicky Flynn, Finally Get a Life (and a Dog).* Amulet, 2010. 272 p. Grades 5–8.

"Nicky Flynn's life gets all turned around when his parents divorce and he is forced to start a new life in a new town and school; but when his mother brings home

Reggie, a former seeing-eye dog, from a shelter, Nicky begins to put his life back into perspective." LC

Dixon, Peter. *Hunting the Dragon.* Hyperion, 2010. 233 p. Grades 8–up.

When surfer Billy joins the crew of a ship that is illegally killing dolphins while catching tuna, he is abandoned at sea—but saved by a dolphin.

Fergus, Maureen. *Ortega.* Kids Can, 2010. 224 p. Grades 5–8.

Ortega, a gorilla who was taken by scientists as a baby and taught to talk, read, and write, is enrolled in school where he worries about making friends and being accepted, but confronts a bigger challenge when he is faced with losing everything he has ever known.

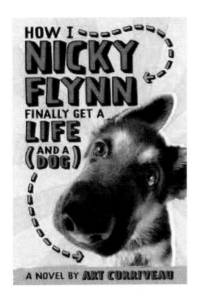

Lasky, Kathryn. *The Wolves of the Beyond* series, published by Scholastic, Grades 5–8.

A wolf pup is abandoned by his pack and has to figure out a way to survive.

1. *Lone Wolf,* 2010
2. *Shadow Wolf,* 2010
3. *Watch Wolf,* 2011

How I, Nicky Flynn, Finally Get a Life (and a Dog) by Art Corriveau. **Used with permission of Amulet Books, an imprint of Abrams.**

Oppel, Kenneth. *Half Brother.* Scholastic, 2010. 375 p. Grades 6–9.

In 1973, when a renowned Canadian behavioral psychologist pursues his latest research project—an experiment to determine whether chimpanzees can acquire advanced language skills—he brings home a baby chimp named Zan and asks his 13-year-old son to treat Zan like a little brother. Oppel always delivers a good read.

Wells, Ken. *Rascal: A Dog and His Boy.* Alfred A. Knopf Books for Young Readers, 2010. 208 p. Grades 5–8.

"Rascal is happy to leave Voclain's farm to live with his boy, Meely, and pair spend their time exploring the Louisiana bayou, but when Meely gets stuck on a rotted bridge it is left to Rascal to find away to save his boy from danger." LC

Chapter 3

Graphic Novels

It is no secret that comics and graphic novels are hugely popular with boys of all ages. It's also a difficult style of book for many librarians and teachers to stay up-to-date with. There are so many series and so many new titles, and many of us don't know how to evaluate (or appreciate) them. All titles included here are well-reviewed and have plenty of guy appeal, so use this chapter to help you make your selections and recommendations.

YOUNGER GUYS

Blanquet, Stephanie. *Toys in the Basement.* Traslated by Kim Thompson. Fantagraphics, 2010. 32 p. Grades 4–7.
    "When two children at a costume party venture into the basement, they find themselves surrounded by abused, broken, and abandoned toys who, because of their costumes, assume the children are toys like themselves and hide them from the enemy—children. The children must protect their secret or be fed to Amelia, a monstrous creature made of broken toy parts." LC

Cammuso, Frank. *Knights of the Lunch Table* series, published by Scholastic/Graphix, Grades 2–5.
    Excellent graphic novel stories of Artie King, new to Camelot Middle School.

1. *The Dodgeball Chronicles,* 2008
2. *The Dragon Players,* 2009
3. *The Battling Bands,* 2011

Craddock, Erik. *Stone Rabbit* series, published by Random, Grades 2–4.
Stone Rabbit is just an ordinary rabbit, but he keeps getting thrown back in time. Graphic novels, lots of fun and very popular!

1. *B.C. Mambo,* 2009
2. *Pirate Palooza,* 2009
3. *Deep Space Disco,* 2009
4. *Superhero Stampede,* 2010
5. *Ninja Slice,* 2010
6. *Night of the Living Dust Bunnies,* 2011

Author Spotlight: Michael Dahl

Michael Dahl, author of the Finnegan Zwake mysteries as well as countless other fiction, nonfiction, and graphic novels, was a voracious reader when he was a boy. He even admits to reading the dictionary, encyclopedias, and atlases for fun. The first book he ever checked out with his own library card was *The Voyages of Doctor Doolittle,* and his childhood favorites were *Children of Odin* by Padraic Colum and D'Aulaires's *Book of Greek Myths.* As an adult his two greatest influences are Edgar Rice Burroughs and Agatha Christie. Burroughs instilled in him the thrill of adventure and the love of exotic locations and other worlds, and he admires Christie as a master of plotting and the queen of the surprise twist.

Michael Dahl Recommends

The Lord of the Rings by J.R.R. Tolkien, the biggest, grandest fantasy of them all. Even better than the movie (which I loved).

The Monstrumologist by Rick Yancey. I read this creepy thriller in one sitting. Monsters and forensics—what a combo!

Flight 1–7, edited by Kazu Kibuishi. Terrific collections of stories by various graphic novel creators.

The *Lunch Lady* books by Jarrett Krosoczka. Funny, crazy sci-fi adventure graphic novels with lots of jokes.

The Day My Butt Went Psycho by Andy Griffiths. Um, I think the title says it all.

Uncle Montague's Tales of Terror by Chris Priestley. These stories are told to the young narrator by his mysterious uncle. They are seriously spooky, and the book has one terrific surprise ending.

Dahl, Michael. *Dragonblood* **series, published by Stone Arch Books, Grades 1–3 (reading level), Grades 3–7 (interest level).**

Large type, brief texts, and a graphic novel look make this series excellent for reluctant readers. Children are discovering they have dragon blood—and eventually dragons will return to earth because of this. This series is not numbered.

Claws in the Snow, 2009
Dawn of the Dragons, 2011
Dead Wing, 2010
Dragon Cowboy, 2010
Dragon Cowboy in the Desert, 2010
Dragon Theft Auto, 2010
Eye of the Monster, 2010
Girl Who Breathed Fire, 2010
It Screams at Night, 2009
Missing Fang, 2010
Stowaway Monster, 2009
Terror Beach, 2009
Wings above the Waves, 2010

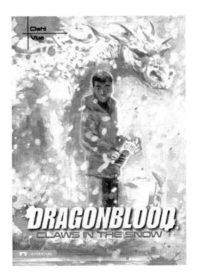

Claws in the Snow **by Michael Dahl.**

Dark Horse Comics: Lucas Books **series, published by ABDO, Grades 4–8.**

Adequate graphic novel retellings of the beloved movies.

Star Wars, Episode I: The Phantom Menace: Volume 1, 2009
Star Wars, Episode I: The Phantom Menace: Volume 2, 2009
Star Wars, Episode I: The Phantom Menace: Volume 3, 2009
Star Wars, Episode I: The Phantom Menace: Volume 4, 2009
Star Wars, Episode I: The Phantom Menace: Volume 5, 2009
Star Wars, Episode I: The Phantom Menace: Volume 6, 2009

Davis, Eleanor. *The Secret Alliance and the Copycat Crook.* Bloomsbury, 2009. 153 p. Grades 4–6.

Eleven-year-old Julian Calendar thought changing schools would mean leaving his "nerdy" persona

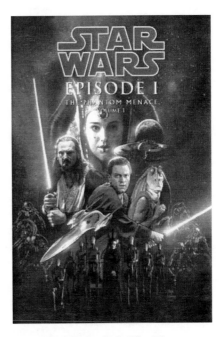

Star Wars, Episode I: The Phantom Menace: Volume 1. **Courtesy of ABDO Publishing Group.**

behind, but instead he forms an alliance with fellow inventors Greta and Ben and works with them to prevent an adult from using one of their gadgets for nefarious purposes. Starred reviews in *Kirkus*, *Publishers Weekly*, and *Booklist*.

Giarrusso, Chris. *G-Man: Learning to Fly*. Image, 2010. 96 p. Grades 3–5.
 Delightful story of a kid who becomes a superhero when he takes over the family's magic blanket.

Godi & Zidrou. *Ducoboo: The Class Struggle*. Translated by Luke Spear. Illustrated by Veronique Grobet. Cinebook, 2010. 46 p. Grades 4–6.
 A quick and funny read that will appeal to *Wimpy Kid*, *Tintin*, and *Asterix* fans.

Graphic Horror Stories series, by various authors, published by Magic Wagon/Graphic Planet, Grades 3–7.
 Very simplified, brief, acceptable abridgements of classic stories that appeal to reluctant readers.

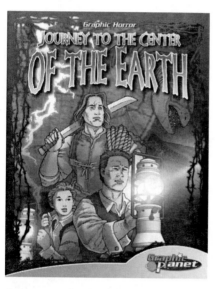

Journey to the Center of the Earth by Joeming Dunn. Courtesy of ABDO Publishing Group.

 The Picture of Dorian Gray, by Daniel Connor, 2009
 The Invisible Man, by Joeming Dunn, 2009
 Journey to the Center of the Earth, by Joeming Dunn, 2009
 The Phantom of the Opera, by Joeming Dunn, 2009
 The Tell-Tale Heart, by Joeming Dunn, 2009

Holm, Jennifer L, and Matthew Holm. *Squish v. 1: Super Amoeba*. Random, 2011. 96 p. Grades 3–5.
 "Squish, inspired by his favorite comic book hero—Super Amoeba—tries to navigate his way through school and save his friends—and the world—from the evils that lurk in the halls." LC

Hunter, Erin, creator. Dan Jolley is the writer. *Warriors Manga* series, published by Harper-Collins, Grades 4–up.
 Manga versions of the popular fantasy series. As with the novels, there are several related series.

Warriors

1. *The Lost Warrior*, 2007
2. *Warrior's Refuge*, 2007
3. *Warrior's Return*, 2008
4. *The Rise of Scourge*, 2008

Tigerstar and Sasha

1. *Into the Woods*, 2008
2. *Escape from the Forest*, 2008
3. *Return to the Clans*, 2009

Ravenpaw's Path

1. *Shattered Peace,* 2009
2. *A Clan in Need,* 2010
3. *The Heart of a Warrior,* 2010

Kibuishi, Kazu. *Amulet* series, published by Scholastic/Graphix, Grades 4–7.
"After moving to their ancestral home, Emily and Navin's mother is kidnapped by a tentacled creature in the basement that leads the children on a deadly chase into the magical world below their home." LC. Action-packed and exciting series that was nominated for several state reader's choice awards.

1. *The Stonekeeper,* 2008
2. *The Stonekeeper's Curse,* 2009
3. *The Cloud Searchers,* 2010
4. *The Last Council,* 2011

Krosoczka, Jarrett. *Lunch Lady* series, published by Knopf/Borzoi, Grades 2–5.
The lunch lady is actually an undercover spy in this wacky, popular, graphic novel series. Amy Poehler is to play her in the movie!

1. *Lunch Lady and the Cyborg Substitute,* 2009
2. *Lunch Lady and the League of Librarians,* 2009
3. *Lunch Lady and the Author Visit Vendetta,* 2009
4. *Lunch Lady and the Summer Camp Shakedown,* 2010
5. *Lunch Lady and the Bake Sale Bandit,* 2010
6. *Lunch Lady and the Field Trip Fiasco,* 2011

Langridge, Roger. *The Muppet Show Comic Book: Family Reunion.* Illustrated by Amy Mebberson. Boom! Kids, 2010. 112 p. Grades 3–6.
Great fun in this dazzlingly illustrated story of the Muppets getting together to put on some fun shows and solve a little mystery.

Lee, Terry. *The Legend of King Arthur.* Illustrated by Sam Hart. Candlewick, 2011. 144 p. Grades 6–10.
"Retells, in graphic novel format, the legend of Arthur Pendragon who, raised in obscurity, draws a legendary sword from a stone and begins the life he was born to lead, guided by the elusive wizard Merlin." LC

Manning, Matthew K. *Ali Baba and the Forty Thieves.* Illustrated by Ricardo Osnaya. Stone Arch Books, 2010. 72 p. Grades 3–5.
A graphic novel adaptation of one of the best adventures stories of all time. This is part of Stone Arch Books' set called Graphic Revolve which includes many famous stories retold in graphic format.

Marunas, Nathaniel. *Manga Claus.* Artwork by Erik Craddock. Razorbill, 2006. 80 p. Grades 2–6.
When one of Santa's elves wants a new job more suited to his abilities—and doesn't get it—he develops a plan that goes horribly wrong. The result—many deranged ninja teddy bears, all out to attack Santa. But Santa has a secret—he has ancient samurai swords and the skill to use them. There are a couple of gross words and scenes in here, but this is a well-reviewed and enjoyable graphic novel.

Matthews, John. *The Chronicles of Arthur: Sword of Fire and Ice.* Illustrated by Mike Collins. Aladdin, 2009. 123 p. Grades 4–8.

A graphic novel version of the story of the young boy who is to become King Arthur.

O'Brien, Anne Sibley. *The Legend of Hong Kil Dong: The Robin Hood of Korea.* Charlesbridge, 2006. Unpaged. Grades 3–6.

This excellent graphic novel is an adaptation of an old Korean legend about Hong Kil Dong, who is the son of a minister to the king and a maidservant. He will never be allowed to advance because of his humble origins, but Hong Kil Dong is determined to become a leader of his people—and this is the story of how he pulls it off. No gory scenes.

Parker, Jake. *Missile Mouse* series, published by Scholastic/Graphix, Grades 3–6.

"Missile Mouse, a secret agent for the Galactic Security Agency, is launched into a grand adventure when he is sent to rescue a scientist kidnapped by the Rogue Imperium of Planets because of his knowledge of the doomsday machine, Star Crusher." LC

1. *Missile Mouse, the Star Crusher,* 2010
2. *Missile Mouse, Rescue on Tankium3,* 2011

Phelan, Matt. *The Storm in the Barn.* Candlewick, 2009. 203 p. Grades 3–6.

In 1937 Kansas, devastated by the Great Depression and constant dust storms, 11-year-old Jack struggles with earning respect, a mysterious and shadowy figure in the barn, and growing up. An outstanding book nominated for several state young reader awards.

Reynolds, Aaron. *Joey Fly, Private Eye* series, published by Henry Holt, Grades 2–5.

A graphic novel featuring Joey Fly, crime-fighting house fly, living in a city whose inhabitants are all insects.

Creepy Crawly Crime, 2009
Big, Hairy Drama, 2010

Robbins, Trina. *Chicagoland Detective Agency* series, illustrated by Tyler Page, published by Lerner/Graphic Universe, Grades 4–7.

Middle school kids Raf and Megan form a detective agency with a genetically altered talking dog as the brains behind the business in these fun graphic novels.

1. *The Drained Brains Caper,* 2010
2. *The Maltese Mummy,* 2011
3. *Night of the Living Dogs,* 2011

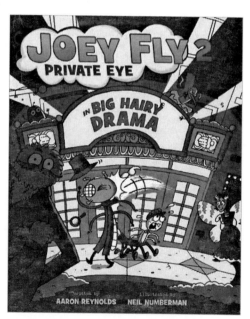

Big, Hairy Drama **by Aaron Reynolds. Courtesy of Henry Holt Books for Young Readers, an imprint of the Macmillan Children's Publishing Group.**

Robinson, Fiona. *The 3–2–3 Detective Agency: The Disappearance of Dave Warthog.* Amulet, 2009. 74 p. Grades 2–5.

Five animal friends, a donkey, a sloth, a penguin, a rat, and a dung beetle, decide to form a detective agency in Whiska City, where they investigate the rash of disappearances linked to a poodle beauty salon.

Rogers, Gregory. *The Boy, the Bear, the Baron, the Bard.* Roaring Brook, 2004. Unpaged. Grades 3–up.

A solitary boy playing ball kicks it accidentally into an abandoned theater. When he goes inside to retrieve it, he suddenly falls through time, coming out on stage in Shakespeare's Globe Theater! Excitement and adventures aplenty follow, as Shakespeare himself, obviously angry at the intrusion, tries to catch the boy. This is a wordless book done in a comic book style, and readers will need a little bit of prior knowledge to understand all that is going on here. But it is a great deal of fun. The sequel is *Midsummer Knight*, 2007.

Sakai, Yohei. *Dinosaur King.* Volume 1 translated from Japanese by Katherine Schilling. Viz Media, 2010, 189 pages, Grades 3–6.

This is based on a Sega arcade card game, and has a lot of action and not a lot of story. It has definite appeal for reluctant readers and fans of the card game and anime. To be followed by volume 2.

Shaw, Murray, and M. J. Cosson. *On the Case with Holmes and Watson* **series, illustrated by Sophie Rohrbach, published by Lerner/Graphic Universe, Grades 4–6.**

Good adaptations of the original Sherlock Holmes stories. A fine introduction to the famous detective.

> *Sherlock Holmes and a Scandal in Bohemia*, 2010
> *Sherlock Holmes and the Adventure of the Blue Gem*, 2010
> *Sherlock Holmes and the Adventure of the Dancing Men*, 2010
> *Sherlock Holmes and the Adventure of the Speckled Band*, 2010
> *Sherlock Holmes and the Adventure of the Sussex Vampire*, 2010

Shiga, Jason. *Meanwhile.* Abrams/Amulet Books, 2010. 20 p. Grades 4–9.

To quote *Booklist*, "In this graphic novel mind boggler, Shiga blows the choose-your-own-adventure concept out of the water." Right on! The book claims to have 3,856 possible stories, all in 80 pages. Boys of all ages go nuts for it.

Smith, Jeff. *Bone* **series, published by Scholastic/Graphix, which took them over from another publisher, Grades 4–up.**

The three Bone cousins leave Boneville and head out for adventures in other lands. These hugely popular graphic novels are great fun.

1. *Out from Boneville*, 1995, 2005
2. *The Great Cow Race*, 1996, 2005
3. *Eyes of the Storm*, 1996, 2006
4. *The Dragonslayer*, 1997, 2007
5. *Rock Jaw, Master of the Eastern Border*, 1998, 2007
6. *Old Man's Cave*, 1999, 2007
7. *Ghost Circles*, 2000, 2008
8. *Treasure Hunters*, 2001, 2008
9. *Crown of Horns*, 2002, 2009
10. *Tall Tales*, 2010

> *Rose*, illustrated by Charles Vess (is a prequel to the series), 2009
> *Quest for the Spark*, written by Tom Sniegoski and illustrated by Jeff Smith, (This is the beginning of a new trilogy set in the world of Bone. It is more of an illustrated novel rather than a graphic novel), 2011

Sonneborn, Scott. *Tom Thumb: A Grimm Graphic Novel.* Illustrated by Nelson Evergreen. Stone Arch Books, 2011. 40 p. Grades 2–4.

A fun graphic novel take on the classic story of Tom Thumb.

Spector, Baron. *Dodging Danger on the Dartmouth.* Illustrated by Dustin Evans. Magic Wagon/ Graphic Planet, 2010. 32 p. Grades 3–5.

"Tank and Joey are transported back to the night of the Boston Tea Party after spotting a ghost while on a field trip at the site of the historical event." LC

Stevenson, Robert Louis. Retold by Wim Coleman and Pat Perrin. *Treasure Island* (Graphic Revolve). Illustrated by Greg Rebis. Stone Arch Books, 2006. 69 p. Grades 3–7.

A graphic retelling of a great classic that is simple but still an appealing story.

Swan, Bill. *Man to Man.* Lorian (distributed by Orca), 2010. 144 p. Grades 4–7.

"Michael Reilly, the youngest and shortest player on his lacrosse team, is usually left on the sidelines, but when tensions with a rival team reach a critical stage, Michael discovers a chance to shine." LC

Townsend, Michael. *Kit Feeny: On the Move.* Alfred A. Knopf Books for Young Readers, 2009. Grades 2–5.

Kit Feeny is moving to the city and needs to find a replacement for his best friend, Arnold. Somewhat similar to the *Babymouse* series, but featuring a bear-shaped creature. Fast paced and fun. Sequel is *The Ugly Necklace,* 2009

Weigel, Jeff. *Thunder from the Sea: The Adventures of Jack Hoyton and the HMS Defender.* Putnam Juvenile, 2010. 48 p. Grades 3–5.

In 1805, Jack Hoyton, a 12-year-old boy, enlists in the British Navy as a crewman and finds a life of hard work, terrible beatings, danger, friendship, and adventure. There's a lot of painless factual information here about ships and history.

Wolverine: First Class series, published by Spotlight/Marvel Age, Grades 3–6.

Fans of Wolverine will grab these acceptable graphic novel adaptations of the story of a super mutant.

> *The Buddy System,* 2009
> *The Last Knights of Wundagore, Part 1,* 2009
> *The Last Knights of Wundagore, Part 2,* 2009
> *Little Girls,* 2009
> *Surprise!* 2009

Wood, Don. *Into the Volcano.* Scholastic/Blue Sky Press, 2008. 175 p. Grades 4–7.

Two brothers are swept into a page-turning adventure when they start exploring a dormant volcano that really isn't dormant anymore. Nominated for multiple state young reader awards.

OLDER GUYS

Avi. *City of Light, City of Dark: A Comic-Book Novel.* Illustrated by Brian Floca. Orchard, 1993. 192 p. Grades 4–8.

In modern-day NYC, a terrible disaster will ensue unless a particular transit token can be found and returned to its proper place on December 21. Two kids, a boy and a girl, get involved in the fast-moving, exciting race to save the city. Compelling, a real page-turner, and a book boys and girls love.

Brown, Bruce. *Howard Lovecraft and the Frozen Kingdom.* Illustrated by Renzo Podesta. Arcana, 2010. 96 p. Grades 5–8.

"Six-year-old Howard Lovecraft reads a book belonging to his father, who is now insane, and discovers the legendary Necronomicon, which he uses to enter a frozen kingdom full of horror and danger." LC

Dixon, Chuck. *Civil War Adventure.* Illustrated by Gary Kwapisz. History Graphics, 2010. 144 p. Grades 6–10.

An excellent and curriculum-friendly look at the Civil War; includes several different stories based on actual events.

Dunning, John Harris. *Salem Brownstone: All Along the Watchtowers.* Illustrated by Nikhil Singh. Candlewick, 2010. Grades 8–up.

"Upon his father's death, Salem inherits a mansion as well as an unfinished battle with creatures from another world, which requires him to seek the help of his guardian familiar and the colorful performers of Dr. Kinoshita's Circus of Unearthly Delights." LC. An eerie horror story. Starred review in *Booklist.*

Erb, Greg, and Jason Oremland. *The Return of King Doug.* Illustrated by Wook-Jin Clark. Oni, 2009. 184 p. Grades 5–8.

"Douglas Peterson, having turned his back on the Kingdom of Valdonia when he was eight years old, must return to the wonderland as an adult and fulfill his destiny of becoming a hero." LC

Hale, Shannon, and Dean Hale. *Calamity Jack.* Bloomsbury, 2010. 144 p. Grades 5–up.

A sequel to the equally outstanding *Rapunzel's Revenge* (2008). A fast, funny interpretation of Jack and the Beanstalk. A real winner.

Hinds, Gareth. *The Odyssey.* Candlewick, 2010. 248 p. Grades 7–up.

Outstandingly reviewed graphic novel of one of the best stories of all time.

Kim, Susan, and Laurence Klavan. *Brain Camp.* Illustrated by Faith Erin Hicks. First Second, 2010. 160 p. Grades 7–10.

"Problem children Jenna and Lucas find themselves invited to Camp Fielding, where they are surrounded by other misfits whose parents hope will be changed into prodigies. When strange things begin happening around them, Jenna and Lucas team up to investigate, but what they discover is beyond anything they could have imagined." LC. A scary story.

Kim, Susan, and Laurence Klavan. *City of Spies.* Illustrated by Pascal Dizin. First Second, 2010. 172 p. Grades 4–7.

"In New York City's Germantown during World War II, Evelyn spends less time with the superheroes in the comics she draws after she makes friends with Tony, her Aunt Lia's building superintendent's son. The two set out to find adventures of their own, but are surprised when they uncover a Nazi spy plot right in their own neighborhood." LC. Starred reviews in *Booklist* and *Publishers Weekly.* Great for spy lovers.

Lagos, Alexander, and Joseph Lagos. *The Sons of Liberty*. Illustrated by Steve Walker. Random House, 2010. 236 p. Grades 5–up.

"Graham and Brody, two slaves on the run prior to the American Revolution, gain extraordinary powers and, on the advice of Benjamin Franklin, try to go unnoticed, but their other mentor, Benjamin Lay, has different plans for them that involve masks and the African martial art of Dambe." LC

Mack, Stan, and Susan Champlin. *Road to Revolution*. Bloomsbury, 2009. Grades 5–9.

Two children aid the rebels in Boston in 1775. Entertaining and interesting.

Marvel Age: Iron Man series, published by ABDO, Grades 3–8.

Essentially simplified comic books in hardbound bindings, these do not offer a lot of quality but have a huge amount of reader appeal. They will not sit on your shelves. Different authors and illustrators.

Destructive Reentry, 2009
Ghost of a Chance, 2009
Pirated! 2009
The Simple Life, 2009

Ghost of a Chance. **Courtesy of ABDO Publishing Group.**

Marvel Illustrated: The Man in the Iron Mask series, published by Abdo/Spotlight, Grades 3–8.

An extremely simplified graphic novel version of the classic book, with lots of appeal to reluctant readers. Told in six volumes.

1. *Three Musketeers,* 2009
2. *High Treason,* 2009
3. *Iron Mask,* 2009
4. *The Man in the Iron Mask,* 2009
5. *The Death of a Titan,* 2009
6. *Musketeers No More,* 2009

Marvel Illustrated: Treasure Island series, published by Abdo /Spotlight, Grades 3–8.

Acceptable graphic novel version of the classic story, told in six volumes.

1. *Treasure Island,* 2009
2. *Treasure Island, Part 2,* 2009
3. *Mutiny on the* Hispaniola, 2009
4. *Embassy-and Attack,* 2009
5. *In the Enemy's Camp,* 2009
6. *Pirate's End,* 2009

McAdoo, David. *Red Moon*. Cossack Comics, 2010. Grades 7–10.

An action-packed story of a dog running away from its family that appeals to fans of the Warriors and the Redwall series. *Booklist* gave it a starred review.

Mechner, Jordan. *Solomon's Thieves*. Illustrated by LeUyen Pham and Alex Puvilland. First Second, 2010. 140 p. Grades 6–10.

"Martin, a Templar Knight, returns from the Crusades to find his love married to someone else, and soon discovers that others are out to destroy the Templar Order and steal their treasure. He bands together with other Templars to keep the Templar treasure safe from the corrupt officials of the Catholic Church." LC

Mucci, Tim (adaptation). *The Odyssey* (All-Action Classics, Book 3). Sterling, 2010. 123 p. Grades 6–up.

It may be fairly short, but it manages to include all of the major action of the great classic. Greatly appealing to reluctant readers.

Neri, G. *Yummy: The Last Days of a Southside Shorty*. Illustrated by Randy DuBurke. Lee & Low Books, 2010. 94 p. Grades 8–12.

"A brief biography, in graphic novel format, of Robert 'Yummy' Sandifer, an eleven-year old African American gang member from Chicago who went on the run after shooting a young girl and was later found dead, shot by members of his own gang." LC. Fictionalized version of a true story.

Nykko. *The Elsewhere Chronicles* series, published by Lerner/Graphic Universe, Grades 4–7.

"Max, Rebecca, Noah, and Theo discover an old movie projector that opens a passage to a fantastic world where the friends must rely on one another to stay safe and find their way back home." LC. Originally published in France.

1. *The Shadow Door,* 2009
2. *The Shadow Spies,* 2009
3. *Master of Shadows,* 2009
4. *The Calling,* 2010

Ottavianai, Jim. *T-Minus: The Race to the Moon*. Illustrated by Zander Cannon and Kevin Cannon. Aladdin, 2009. 124 p. Grades 6–8.

An exciting chronicle detailing the space race between the United States and the Soviet Union (with some clearly noted deviation from the facts).

Petersen, David. *Mouse Guard* series, published by Archaia Studios, Grades 5–8.

Even Redwall fans may enjoy these graphic novels about warrior mice who act as though they were Knights of the Round Table.

Mouse Guard: Fall 1152, 2007
Mouse Guard: Winter 1152, 2009
Mouse Guard: Legends of the Guard Volume 1, 2010
Mouse Guard: Legends of the Guard Volume 2, 2010
Mouse Guard: Legends of the Guard Volume 3, 2010

Raicht, Mike, and Brian Smith. *The Stuff of Legend* series. Illustrated by Charles Paul Wilson III, published by Villard, Grades 5–up.

When a group of toys loses their boy, they become a team of rescuers, entering a world inside a closet where they meet the horrible Boogeyman and go to war with the boy's discarded toys. Battles and violence make this more appropriate for older kids.

The Dark: Book One, 2010
The Jungle, Book Two, 2011

Renier, Aaron. *The Unsinkable Walker Bean*. First Second, 2010. 208 p. Grades 5–8.

The story of Atlantis seems like only a myth, but Walker's beloved grandfather believes it—and knows more about it than the stories reveal. When Grandpa becomes very sick thanks to what seems to be a curse, Walker knows he must find a cure and try to find the secrets of

Atlantis, which are terrifying. Action-packed, exciting, scary, and a sequel is coming! Starred reviews in *Booklist, School Library Journal,* and *Publishers Weekly.*

Riordan, Rick, and Robert Venditti. *The Lightning Thief.* Illustrated by Attila Futaki. Hyperion, 2010. 128 p. Grades 6–9.
Excellent graphic novel adaptation of the hugely popular best seller.

Sakai, Stan. *Usagi Yojimbo* **series, volumes 1–7 published by Fantagraphics, volumes 8 and up published by Dark Horse, Grades 7–up.**
Exciting, long-running, and excellent adventures featuring anthropomorphic samurai and episodes from Japanese history. (I was unable to find original publication dates for several volumes in the series—they have been reissued with new dates. But the series started in 1987 and continues at the rate of roughly one book a year.)

Book 1: The Ronin, 1987
Book 2: Samurai, 1989
Book 3: Wanderer's Road, 1989
Book 4: Dragon Bellow Conspiracy, 1998
Book 5: Lone Goat and Kid, 1992
Book 6: Circles, 1996
Book 7: Gen's Story, 1996
Book 8: Shades of Death, 2010
Book 9: Daisho, 2010
Book 10: The Brink of Life and Death, 2010
Book 11: Seasons, 1999
Book 12: Grasscutter, 1999
Book 13: Grey Shadows, 2000
Book 14: Demon Mask, 2000
Book 15: Grasscutter II: Journey to Atsuta Shrine, 2002
Book 16: The Shrouded Moon, 2003
Book 17: Duel at Kitanoji, 2003
Book 18: Travels with Jotaro, 2004
Book 19: Fathers and Sons, 2005
Book 20: Glimpses of Death, 2006
Book 21: The Mother of Mountains, 2007
Book 22: Tomoe's Story, 2008
Book 23: Bridge of Tears, 2009
Book 24: Return of the Black Soul, 2010
Book 25: Fox Hunt, 2011

Sata, Richard. *Cat Burglar Black.* First Second, Grades 7–10.
"K. Westree arrives at Bellsong Academy, where she hopes to leave her past as a cat-burglar behind, but she quickly learns that the school contains a hidden treasure left by its founder, and as she resumes her old habits, she starts to question whether she really wants a normal life." LC. *Booklist* named this one of the top 10 crime fiction books for youth.

Scaletta, Kurtis. *Mamba Point.* Alfred A. Knopf Books for Young Readers, 2010. 288 p. Grades 5–8.
After moving with his family to Liberia, 12-year-old Linus discovers that he has a mystical connection with the black mamba, one of the deadliest snakes in Africa, which he is told will give him some of the snake's characteristics.

Schweizer, Chris. *Crogan Adventures* **series, published by Oni, Grades 7–12.**
A graphic novel series about different members (in different generations) of the Crogan family. Funny, with a lot of action.

Crogan's Vengeance, 2008
Crogan's March, 2010

Serling, Rod. *Twilight Zone* **series, adapted by Mark Kneece, published by Walker Books, Grades 5–up.**
These excellent graphic novel adaptations of episodes in the original series are lots of fun. They can be read in any order as they are not related to each other.

The After Hours, 2008
Big Tall Wish, 2009
Death's Head Revisited, 2009
The Midnight Sun, 2009
The Monsters are Due on Maple Street, 2008
The Odyssey of Flight 33, 2008
Walking Distance, 2008
Will the Real Martian Please Stand Up, 2009

Shakespeare, William, and Fiona McDonald. *The Merchant of Venice.* Illustrated by Penko Gelev. Barron's, 2010. Grades 6–9.
Full-color artwork is featured in this graphic novel adaptation of the play. Will work well with the curriculum, and got good reviews in *Booklist* and *School Library Journal.*

TenNapel, Doug. *Bad Island.* Scholastic/Graphix, 2011. 224 p. Grades 6–10.
When Reese is forced to go on a boating trip with his family, the last thing he expects is to be shipwrecked on an island—especially one teeming with weird plants and animals. But what starts out as simply a bad vacation turns into a terrible one, as the castaways must find a way to escape while dodging the island's dangerous inhabitants.

TenNapel, Doug. *Ghostopolis.* Scholastic /Graphix, 2010. 288 p. Grades 7–up.
Reviewers raved over this action-packed story of a terminally ill teenager who is accidentally zapped into the afterlife.

Thung, Diana. *Captain Long Ears.* SLG, 2010. 168 p. Grades 5–7.
"To deal with the death of his father, eight-year-old Michael imagines that he and his toy gorilla, Jam, are space ninja Captain Long Ears and Captain Jam on a mission to find Captain Big Nose, otherwise known as Michael's father. When the space ninja report to headquarters, aka the amusement park, and try to help a baby elephant in trouble, Michael finds the closure he needs." LC

Twain, Mark, and others. *The Adventures of Tom Sawyer.* Illustrated by Severine Le Fevebvre. Papercutz, 2009. Unpaged. Grades 5–9.
"A graphic adaptation of the story of Tom Sawyer, a spirited boy growing up in a Mississippi River town in the nineteenth century who has many adventures, including witnessing a murder, running away to an island and pretending to be a pirate, watching his own funeral, and falling in love." LC. Includes almost all of the events in the original.

Watase, Yuu. *Arata: The Legend.* Volume 1 translated from Japanese. Viz Media, 2010. 201 p. Grades 7–up.
"Forced to pose as a girl, Arata, the last in the matriarchal Hime clan, is about undergo a ceremony making him princess when he is framed for murdering the current princess and

Quest for the Silver Tiger by YoYo.

forced to flee. Then, a desperate wish to be elsewhere causes him to switch places with Arata Hinohara in modern-day Japan, leaving Arata to deal with a bully and life in a new high school while Hinohara finds himself in the past and running for his life." LC

Yang, Gene Luen. *American Born Chinese.* First Second, 2006. 240 pages. Grades 7–up.

This Printz award-winner brings three stories together with humor and insight all the while exploring racism, stereotypes, and self-acceptance.

Yang, Gene Luen. *Animal Crackers.* SLG, 2010. 216 p. Grades 8–12.

Printz award-winner Yang here gives us two thought-provoking early graphic stories.

YoYo. *Vermonia* series, published by Candlewick, Grades 5–up.

"Four twelve-year-old skateboarding friends fulfill an ancient prophecy as they discover their true warrior spirits in an epic battle to save the planet of Vermonia. The reader is invited to learn more about the characters by playing an online game after finding hidden clues in the illustrations." LC

1. *Quest for the Silver Tiger,* 2009
2. *Call of the Winged Panther,* 2010
3. *Release of the Red Phoenix,* 2010
4. *The Rukan Prophecy,* 2010
5. *The Warrior's Trial,* 2011

Chapter 4

Historical Fiction

Historical fiction can often be a tough sell to kids, especially to boys. However, the books here are full of action, adventure, and riveting historical time periods. Many make excellent read alouds for social studies classes and are appealing to boys and girls alike. If you are trying to attract reluctant readers, books about war are often an easy sell. Middle school boys especially find World War II and the Vietnam War intriguing.

YOUNGER GUYS

Armstrong, Alan. *Raleigh's Page*. Random House, 2007. 336 p. Grades 4–7.
   Adventures and opportunities abound when Andrew becomes a page to Sir Walter Raleigh and travels to America.

Avi. *Hard Gold: The Colorado Gold Rush of 1859: A Tale of the Old West*. Hyperion, 2008. 230 p. Grades 4–7.
   Early Whitcomb, age 14, heads west when his family is in serious danger of losing their Iowa farm. Adventure and life-changing events follow.

Avi. *Iron Thunder: The Battle Between the Monitor & the Merrimac: A Civil War Novel*. Hyperion, 2009. 203 p. Grades 4–7.
   "Thirteen-year-old Tom Carroll takes his place as head of the family after his father dies fighting for the Union; but his job at the local ironworks, where he helps build an iron ship

for the Union army, and his loyalty come into question when he is approached by Confederate spies to sell secrets about the ship to the South." LC. Nominated for multiple state young reader awards.

Barrow, Randi. *Saving Zasha*. Scholastic, 2011. 240 p. Grades 4–7.
"In 1945 Russia, those who own German shepherds are considered traitors, but thirteen-year-old Mikhail and his family are determined to keep the dog a dying man brought them, while his classmate Katia strives to learn his secret." LC

Calkhoven, Laurie. *Boys of Wartime* series, published by Dutton, Grades 4–7.
Each book focuses on a different war, starting with Daniel in Boston in 1776. Mingles fiction and factual events in a way that makes history gripping.

> *Daniel and the Siege of Boston, 1776,* 2010
> *Will at the Battle of Gettysburg, 1863,* 2011

Crowley, James. *Starfish*. Hyperion, 2010. 352 p. Grades 4–8.
A nine-year-old Blackfoot Nation boy and his big sister run away from their Indian boarding school to survive the winter in a cabin in the wilds of Montana, helped by what they learned from their grandmother and from an African American fugitive. A good survival story set in the early 20th century.

Curtis, Christopher Paul. *Bud, Not Buddy*. Delacorte, 1999. 245 p. Grades 4–7.
"Ten-year-old Bud, a motherless boy living in Flint, Michigan, during the Great Depression, escapes a bad foster home and sets out in search of the man he believes to be his father—the renowned bandleader, H.E. Calloway of Grand Rapids." LC. A 2000 Newbery Medal award-winner.

Davis, Tony. *Roland Wright* series, illustrated by Gregory Rogers, published by Delacorte, Grades 2–4.
Roland Wright may be the son of a blacksmith, but he has big dreams. It's 1409 and he wants to be a knight! Fun, with cartoony art.

> *Future Knight,* 2009
> *Brand New Page,* 2010
> *At the Joust,* 2011

De Felice, Cynthia. *Weasel*. Macmillan, 1991. 119 p. Grades 4–7.
Alone in the frontier wilderness in the winter of 1839 while his father is recovering from an injury, 11-year-old Nathan runs afoul of the renegade killer known as Weasel and makes a surprising discovery about the concept of revenge.

Dunagan, Ted M. *Secret of the Satilfa*. NewSouth/Junebug, 2010. 202 p. Grades 4–7.
"In rural Alabama in the fall of 1948, Ted and Poudlum have their post-Thanksgiving fishing trip to the Cypress Hole on the Satilfa Creek interrupted by fugitive bank robbers and, after managing to escape, return to search for the money rumored to have been buried by the criminals." LC. This is a sequel to *A Yellow Watermelon,* 2007 (see the following entry).

Dunagan, Ted M. *A Yellow Watermelon*. NewSouth/Junebug, 2007. 239 p. Grades 4–7.
"In 1948 Alabama, twelve-year-old cotton pickers Ted Dillon, a white boy, and Poudlum, an African-American, hatch a plan to aid an escaped African-American convict and save Poudlum's family from those who would steal their livelihood." LC

Durango, Julia. *The Walls of Cartagena*. Simon, 2008. 152 p. Grades 4–7.

 An involving story about a slave in Columbia during the 17th century who gets involved in helping out in a leper colony and in protecting a Jewish physician who has fled the Inquisition.

Ferrari, Michael. *Born to Fly*. Delacorte, 2009. 213 p. Grades 4–7.

 "Bird McGill, an eleven-year-old tomboy obsessed with flying in 1942, withholds judgment while her classmates maintain that new Japanese American student Kenji Fujita is a spy, but she realizes Kenji is just as American as she is when they find evidence of real spy activity during their research for a class project." LC

Giblin, James Cross. *The Boy Who Saved Cleveland: Based on a True Story*. Illustrated by Michael Dooling. Henry Holt, 2006. 64 p. Grades 2–4.

 In 1798, there were exactly three homes in Cleveland, Ohio, a brand new settlement on Lake Erie. And one 10-year-old boy managed to save the lives of everyone who lived in those tiny log cabins. This is the story of how he did it, and it is a grand introduction to frontier history.

Going, K. L. *The Liberation of Gabriel King*. Putnam, 2006. 151 p. Grades 4–8.

 In Georgia, it's 1976, and Gabe is lucky indeed to have a fine best friend—Frita, a girl in an activist African American family. But African Americans are far from completely integrated into small town Southern society, and Frita's brushes with racism scare Gabe—and Frita. Frita, however, is one tough cookie, and she and Gabe each write a list of the things they are afraid of. Gabe's list contains 38 items. Frita's has only 10, and she sets the goal of liberating each other from their fears during the summer between the fourth and fifth grades. Nominated for multiple state young reader awards,

Helgerson, Joseph. *Crows & Cards*. Houghton Mifflin, 2009. 344 p. Grades 4–8.

 "Zebulon Crabtree, who was sent by his parents to apprentice with a tanner back in 1849, eventually follows his own instincts and hangs out with a riverboat gambler and a slave who becomes his friend, and when he gets caught up with the Brotherhood, he tries to find a way out." LC

Hemphill, Michael, and Sam Riddleburger. *Stonewall Hinkleman and the Battle of Bull Run*. Dial, 2009. 168 p. Grades 4–6.

 "While participating in a reenactment of the Battle of Bullrun, twelve-year-old Stonewall Hinkleman is transported back to the actual Civil War battle by means of a magic bugle." LC

Jungman, Ann. *Resistance*. Illustrated by Alan Marks. Stone Arch Books, 2006. 83 p. Grades 2–5.

 Dutch Jan is ashamed that his father works for—and thus collaborates with—the Nazis. It is World War II, and the Dutch people are suffering horribly as the war nears its end. With the help of a girl in his class, Jan figures out a way that he can help the Dutch people by working with the underground resistance fighters. This one moves fast and is easy to read.

Resistance **by Ann Jungman.**

Kidd, Ronald. *The Year of the Bomb.* Simon & Schuster, 2009. 202 p. Grades 4–7.

"In 1955 California, as 'Invasion of the Body Snatchers' is filmed in their hometown, thirteen-year-old Arnie discovers a real enemy when he and three friends go against a young government agent determined to find communists at a nearby university or on the movie set." LC

Korman, Gordon. *Titanic* trilogy, published by Scholastic, Grades 4–7.

"The lives of four young passengers aboard the maiden voyage of the RMS "Titanic" become linked, and while Paddy stows away, Sophie and her mother are delivered to the ship by the police, Juliana watches as her father's wealth barely conceals his madness, and Alphie harbors a great secret." LC

1. *Unsinkable,* 2011
2. *Collision Course,* 2011
3. *S.O.S.,* 2011

Lester, Julius. *The Old African.* Illustrated by Jerry Pinkney. Dial, 2005. 79 p. Grades 4–up.

No one on the plantation has ever heard the old African speak, but he can communicate. He has magical, healing powers, and he can explore the minds of the man who is his master and the other people who live near him. The old African was captured long ago and brought to America, and the horrors of his journey are vividly described here. Based on a legend, this is a powerful, beautiful book.

Meyer, Susan Lynn. *Black Radishes.* Delacorte, 2010. 240 p. Grades 4–7.

Eleven-year-old Jewish Gustave hides with his family in occupied France. With a new friend whose family works with the French resistance, he develops a plan to rescue other people in danger of being captured by the Nazis.

Mitchell, Elizabeth. *Journey to the Bottomless Pit: The Story of Stephen Bishop and Mammoth Cave.* Viking, 2004. 99 p. Grades 4–8.

In 1838, Stephen Bishop was only 17 years old when he started leading guided tours through Mammoth Cave, which we now know to be the largest cave system in the world, in Kentucky. He had no choice in his job, for he was a slave and his owner wanted him to do this job. His owner picked the right man for it. Stephen was not only a fine guide, but an amazing explorer who discovered all sorts of new parts of the cave. Some of his tours took 12 hours! This is the fictionalized story of a real man who led a fascinating life. Kids will love it and it makes a good read aloud.

Morris, Gerald. *The Knight's Tales* series, published by Houghton Mifflin, Grades 3–6.

Stories about King Arthur's court for younger readers than fans of *The Squire's Tale* series.

1. *The Adventures of Sir Lancelot the Great,* 2008
2. *The Adventures of Sir Givret the Short,* 2008
3. *The Adventures of Sir Gawain the True,* 2011

Napoli, Donna Jo. *The King of Mulberry Street.* Random House, 2005. 245 p. Grades 4–up.

Journey to the Bottomless Pit: The Story of Stephen Bishop and Mammoth Cave **by Elizabeth Mitchell. Used by permission of Penguin Group (USA) Inc. All rights reserved.**

When Dom arrives alone in America, a stowaway on a cargo ship, he is nine years old. His mother has paid for him to come to America and given him loving orders to survive. He knows he is an illegitimate child, but he is sure he was separated from his mother by accident, and, above all, he wants to go back home to Naples. But now he has a new home, complete with new dangers and no money and no place to live—the Five Points District in New York City in 1892. And he must follow her orders, and survive. A gripping, compelling story.

Park, Linda Sue. *Archer's Quest.* Clarion, 2006. 176 p. Grades 4–8.

Alone in his home on a gloomy February Monday, Kevin broods over his boring homework, especially social studies: "Names and dates and places from ages ago. Boring, boringer, boringest." Suddenly, he is almost hit by an arrow—and sees an extraordinary visitor from ancient Korea, whom, he discovers, is Chu-mong, a great leader, and amazing archer. But how does a man from the past get back to where he should be? And how can Kevin, whose parents are Korean immigrants, begin to appreciate his own heritage?

Paulsen, Gary. *The Legend of Bass Reeves: Being the True and Fictional Account of the Most Valiant Marshal in the West.* Wendy Lamb Books, 2006. 137 p. Grades 4–8.

Gary Paulsen tells us in the preface to the book that he has wanted to write about Bass Reeves ever since he first heard about him. This man, he says, is a man we can all admire—and he also tells us why many of the Wild West heroes are *not* men we can admire. But Bass Reeves, born a slave, has a truly compelling life story that will keep readers turning the pages eagerly.

Philbrick, Rodman. *The Adventures of Homer P. Figg.* Scholastic, 2009. 224 p. Grades 4–7.

"Homer P. Figg escapes from his wretched foster home in Pine Swamp, Maine, and sets out to find his beloved older brother, Harold, who has been illegally sold into the Union Army." LC. Nominated for many state young reader awards and winner of a Newbery Honor.

Pryor, Bonnie. *The Iron Dragon: The Courageous Story of Lee Chin.* Enslow, 2010. 160 p. Grades 4–6.

A fine historical novel about 12-year-old Lee, who comes to America with his father to work on the transcontinental railroad, and faces prejudice and horrible working conditions as he struggles to free his sister from slavery.

Pryor, Bonnie. *Simon's Escape: A Story of the Holocaust.* Enslow, 2010. 160 p. Grades 4–7.

A compelling story about a Jewish kid who survives World War II although his family does not.

Scandiffio, Laura. *Crusades.* Illustrated by John Mantha. Annick, 2010. 72 p. Grades 4–6.

Hans, age 12, blogs about his adventures in the 1212 Children's Crusade. It's a gimmick, but it works, and makes for a fine history lesson.

Tarshis, Lauren. *I Survived* series, illustrated by Scott Dawson, published by Scholastic, Grades 2–5.

Aimed at reluctant readers, these fast-paced books describe fictitious kids who survived actual historical disasters.

1. *The Sinking of the Titanic,* 2010
2. *The Shark Attacks of 1916,* 2010
3. *Hurricane Katrina,* 2011
4. *The Bombing of Pearl Harbor,* 2011

Thompson, Kate. *Highway Robbery.* Greenwillow, 2009. 118 p. Grades 3–5.

The Bombing of Pearl Harbor **by Lauren Tarshis.**

"On a cold day in eighteenth-century England, a poor young boy agrees to watch a stranger's horse for a golden guinea and quickly finds himself in a difficult situation when the king's guard appears and wants to use him as bait in their pursuit of a notorious highwayman." LC

Thompson, Kate. *Most Wanted.* Illustrated by Jonny Duddle. Greenwillow, 2010. 128 p. Grades 3–5.

In a fast-paced story set in ancient Rome, a boy is asked to protect a horse—and readers of *Highway Robbery* will delight in the surprise ending which ties it to that book.

Townson, H. *The Secret Room.* Stone Arch Books, 2006. 75 p. Grades 3–6.

New kid Adam Belman is bored to death in his new school until he has a major adventure and realizes that he has traveled through time—and he is in the middle of an air raid in World War II. Exciting, easy to read, and fast-moving.

Woodruff, Elvira. *George Washington's Socks.* Scholastic, 1991, 2010. 166 p. Grades 4–6.

"In the midst of a backyard campout, five children find themselves transported back into the time of George Washington, where they begin to live out American history firsthand and learn the sober realities of war." LC. Sequel is *George Washington's Spy,* 2010.

The Secret Room **by H. Townson.**

George Washington's Spy **by Elvira Woodruff.**

Wynne-Jones, Tim. *Rex Zero* series, published by Farrar, Straus & Giroux, Grades 4–7.

Funny stories about a kid in Ottawa, Canada, coping with moves and trying to fit in in the early 1960s.

Rex Zero and the End of the World, 2007
Rex Zero, King of Nothing, 2008
Rex Zero, the Great Pretender, 2010

Yep, Laurence. *The Star Maker.* HarperCollins, 2010. 101 p. Grades 3–6.

"With the help of his popular Uncle Chester, a young Chinese American boy tries hard to fulfill a promise to have firecrackers for everyone on the Chinese New Year in 1954." LC

Zimmer, Tracie Vaughn. *The Floating Circus.* Bloomsbury, 2008. 199 p. Grades 4–7.

"In 1850s Pittsburgh, thirteen-year-old Owen leaves his younger brother and sneaks aboard a circus housed in a riverboat, where he befriends a freed slave, learns to work with elephants, and finally comes to terms with the choices he has made in his difficult life." LC. Nominated for multiple state young reader awards.

OLDER GUYS

Rex Zero, King of Nothing by Tim Wynne-Jones. Courtesy of Farrar Straus Giroux Books for Young Readers, an imprint of the Macmillan Children's Publishing Group.

Anderson, Laurie Halse. *Forge*. Atheneum, 2010. 292 p. Grades 6–up.

This riveting sequel to *Chains* (2010), which focuses on a girl slave, continues the story of Curzon, who was rescued from prison by the girl he begins to love, Isabel, and joins the continental revolutionary army at Valley Forge.

Avi. *Crispin* series, different publishers, Grades 5–8.

Crispin's exciting adventures began in the Newbery Medal winning *Crispin: The Cross of Lead*. The story begins in 1377 when Crispin, an illiterate teenager, is orphaned and exciting things begin happening immediately.

Crispin: The Cross of Lead, published by Hyperion, 2002
Crispin: At the End of the World, published by Hyperion, 2006
Crispin: The End of Time, published by Balzer and Bray, 2010

Barratt, Mark. *Joe Rat*. Eerdmans, 2009. 307 p. Grades 5–8.

"In the dark sewers of Victorian London, a boy known as Joe Rat scrounges for valuables which he gives to 'Mother,' a criminal mastermind who considers him a favorite, but a chance meeting with a runaway girl and 'the Madman' transforms all their lives." LC. Sequel is *The Wild Man*, 2010.

Bartoletti, Susan Campbell. *The Boy Who Dared*. Scholastic, 2008. 202 p. Grades 7–up.

Helmuth Huebner, age 17, lives in solitary confinement in a miserable cell on death row in Berlin, Germany, in October 1942. What did he do? He published pamphlets against Hitler and the Nazis. He got caught. This is a fictionalized version of a true story.

Blackwood, Gary. *The Shakespeare Stealer*. Dutton, 2000. 216 p. Grades 5–8.

"Sent by a rival company to nick William Shakespeare's 'Hamlet,' an orphan called Widge is welcomed warmly by the Globe group and finds himself an actor and writer with them out on the road when the London theaters are closed at the threat of plague." LC. This is an exciting read, and has two sequels, *Shakespeare's Scribe*, 2002, and *Shakespeare's Spy,* 2003. All three are available published in one volume.

Bloor, Edward. *London Calling*. Knopf, 2006. 289 p. Grades 5–up.

Martin hates his seventh grade class, his Catholic school, and most of his existence. When his grandmother dies, she leaves him an old radio—and Martin finds that when he listens to it, he is in the London Blitz in 1940, talking to a British boy. This is a compelling, moving read, with more than a touch of mysticism.

Brown, Don. *The Train Jumper*. Roaring Brook, 2007. 128 p. Grades 5–9.

Worried about his brother, who has been drinking heavily and moved to Colorado, Collie decides to ride the

The Train Jumper by Don Brown. Courtesy of Roaring Book Press, an imprint of the Macmillan Children's Publishing Group.

rails, find him, and bring him back home. Along the way he has encounters with both helpful and hateful people and becomes good friends with an African American boy. There's excitement and adventure aplenty here.

Bruchac, Joseph. *Code Talker: A Novel About the Navajo Marines of World War Two.* Dial, 2006. Grades 6–up.

"Bruchac's absorbing historical novel tells the story of a boy who became one of the brave Navajo code talkers, whose messages helped the U.S. achieve victory in World War II." LC. ALA Notable Children's Books.

Carbone, Elisa Lynn. *Blood on the River: James Town 1607.* Viking, 2006. 237 p. Grades 5–8.

Collier has no choice in the matter. At age 11, he leaves the orphanage in London and is sent to the new James Town colony as the servant of a fair but tough master, Captain John Smith. The voyage is horrible, and the new home is far from perfect. There is little to eat and relations with the natives are difficult, to understate the case. But Samuel forges a new life, a new self-respect, and a deep appreciation of this native life. Based closely on historical incidents.

Choldenko, Gennifer. *Al Capone Does My Shirts.* Dial, 2004. 228 p. Grades 5–8.

An entertaining story about a kid whose dad is a guard on Alcatraz Island while Al Capone is imprisoned there. Moving, powerful, highly acclaimed. The first book has a slow start, but once you get into it, it moves quickly. Sequel is *Al Capone Shines My Shoes,* 2009.

Chotjewitz, David. *Daniel Half-Human and the Good Nazi.* Translated by Doris Orgel. Atheneum, 2005. 304 p. Grades 5–up.

In this story of 1930s Germany, a boy who initially enjoys the advantages of an affluent upbringing is forced into a life of deception after discovering that his mother is Jewish. The suspenseful plot revolves around the complicated relationship between Daniel and his friend Armin, who try to remain close even as the rise of Nazism takes them in different directions. Eventually both must make choices that change their own and each other's lives.

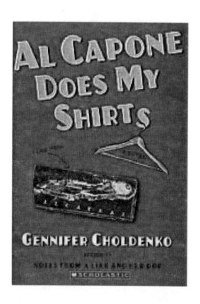

Al Capone Does My Shirts by Gennifer Choldenko.

Conly, Jane. *Murder Afloat.* Hyperion, 2010. 176 p. Grades 5–8.

Fourteen-year-old Benjamin Orville, a German immigrant in the 1880s, encounters prejudice and terror when he is forced to become a crew member of an oyster schooner.

Couloumbis, Audrey. *War Games: A Novel Based on a True Story.* Random, 2009. 233 p. Grades 5–8.

"What were once just boys' games become matters of life and death as Petros and his older brother Zola each wonder if, like their resistance-fighter cousin, they too can make a difference in a Nazi-occupied Greece." LC

Curtis, Christopher Paul. *Elijah of Buxton.* Scholastic, 2007. 341 p. Grades 5–up.

Elijah, the son of escaped slaves, lives in a community of such people in Buxton, Canada. It's 1860 and he is a happy, normal kid with ordinary concerns until he gets involved with trying to buy the family of a fellow resident. The last 100 pages are really exciting, but this could use a little more action in the first 250. It is a good story, though. It received a Newbery Honor in 2008.

Durbin, William. *The Winter War.* Random House, 2008. 227 p. Grades 5–9.
Marko volunteers for the army when the Russians invade Finland in November 1939. Weakened by a left leg crippled by polio, he is put to hard work and little rest, supposedly as a messenger, but really doing anything that needs being done. He makes one good friend who has a surprise for him, and suffers the horrors of one of the coldest wars on record.

Fleischman, Sid. *The Entertainer and the Dybbuk.* Greenwillow, 2007. 180 p. Grades 5–up.
A mediocre American ventriloquist performing in Europe a couple of years after the end of the second world war finds his life changed when he encounters a dybbuk, the ghost of a Jewish boy killed by a Nazi—a boy who is bent on getting revenge. Funny as well as horrifying.

Flood, Nancy Bo. *Warriors in the Crossfire.* Front Street, 2009. 142 p. Grades 5–9.
The 13-year-old son of a local village chief in Saipan, controlled by the Japanese since 1922, experiences the horrors of war and the American invasion during World War II. Starred review in *Booklist.*

Ford, Michael. *Spartan Quest* series, published by Walker Books, Grades 5–8.
"When slaves rebel in ancient Sparta, twelve-year-old Lysander, guarded by an heirloom amulet, the Fire of Ares, is caught between the Spartan ruling class, with whom he has been training as a warrior since his noble heritage was revealed, and those among whom he was recently laboring as a slave." LC

1. *The Fire of Ares,* 2008
2. *Birth of a Warrior,* 2008
3. *Legacy of Blood,* 2009

Fussell, Sandy. *Samurai Kids* series, published by Candlewick, Grades 5–8.
"Even though he has only one leg, Niya Moto is studying to be a samurai, and his five fellow-students are similarly burdened, but sensei Ki-Yaga, an ancient but legendary warrior, teaches them not only physical skills but mental and spiritual ones as well, so that they are well-equipped to face their most formidable opponents at the annual Samurai Games." LC

1. *White Crane,* 2010
2. *Owl Ninja,* 2011
3. *Shaolin Tiger,* 2011

Owl Ninja **by Sandy Fussell.**

Gleitzman, Morris. *Once.* Henry Holt, 2010. 176 p. Grades 7–10.
"After living in a Catholic orphanage for nearly four years, a naive Jewish boy runs away and embarks on a journey across Nazi-occupied Poland to find his parents." LC. Two starred reviews.

Hawkins, Aaron R. *The Year Money Grew on Trees.* Houghton Mifflin, 2010. 304 p. Grades 5–8.
"In early 1980s New Mexico, thirteen-year-old Jackson Jones recruits his cousins and sisters to help tend an elderly neighbor's neglected apple orchard for the chance to make big money and, perhaps, to own the orchard." LC

Hemphill, Helen. *The Adventurous Deeds of Deadwood Jones.* Front Street, 2008. 228 p. Grades 5–up.

Born on the day of the Emancipation Proclamation, Prometheus Jones, age 13, is determined to find his father, who was sold away from his family before Prometheus was born. Exciting and thought-provoking.

Hobbs, Will. *Jason's Gold.* Morrow Junior Books, 1999. 221 p. Grades 6–8.

Jason follows his brother to Alaska and into the Yukon Territory in search of gold in 1897. Hobbs brings the time period to life and gives us a breathtaking survival story.

Holt, Kimberly Willis. *When Zachary Beaver Came to Town.* Henry Holt, 1999. Grades 6–8.

"During the summer of 1971 in a small Texas town, thirteen-year-old Toby and his best friend Cal meet the star of a sideshow act, 600-pound Zachary, the fattest boy in the world." LC

Hughes, Dean. *Missing in Action.* Atheneum, 2010. 240 p. Grades 6–9.

"While his father is missing in action in the Pacific during World War II, twelve-year-old Jay moves with his mother to small-town Utah, where he sees prejudice from both sides, as a part-Navajo himself and through an unlikely friendship with Japanese American Ken from the nearby internment camp." LC

Hughes, Dean. *Soldier Boys.* Simon Pulse, 2001. 230 p. Grades 6–8.

"Two boys, one German and one American, are eager to join their respective armies during World War II, and their paths cross at the Battle of the Bulge." LC. This has great appeal to boys wanting to read about war.

Kerr. P. B. *One Small Step.* McElderry, 2008. 309 p. Grades 7–9.

In the late 1960s, 13-year-old Scott gets an amazing opportunity—to man a top secret space flight to the moon!

Lerangis, Peter. *Smiler's Bones.* Scholastic, 2005. 147 p. Grades 5–up.

In 1897, explorer Robert Peary takes Minik, an Inuit child, with his father and four others to be part of an exhibit in the Museum of Natural History. Within a short time, four die and one returns to Greenland, leaving Minik, now known as Mene Wallace, to grow up alone in New York, an alien culture. As he grows, he learns even more of the horrors that have been perpetrated on his father and his people—and realizes that he himself will always be an outsider wherever he goes. This powerful story works well with *North* by Donna Jo Napoli and *Onward,* the biography of Matthew Henson who traveled with Peary, by Delores Johnson.

Levine, Gail Carson. *Dave at Night.* HarperCollins, 1999. 281 p. Grades 5–8.

"When orphaned Dave is sent to the Hebrew Home for Boys where he is treated cruelly, he sneaks out at night and is welcomed into the music- and culture-filled world of the Harlem Renaissance." LC

Levine, Kristin. *The Best Bad Luck I Ever Had.* Putnam, 2009. 266 p. Grades 6–8.

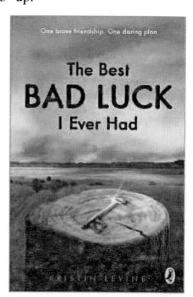

The Best Bad Luck I Ever Had **by Kristin Levine. Used by permission of Penguin Group (USA) Inc. All rights reserved.**

"Harry 'Dit' Sims and his newest friend Emma Walker work together to come up with a plan that could save the town barber, an African-American, who is on put on trial and faces a horrible end." LC

Lisle, Janet Taylor. *Black Duck.* Philomel, 2006. 252 p. Grades 5–up.

Ruben and Jeddy, walking along the shore, come across the body, shot dead, of a flashily dressed man. Newport, Rhode Island, where they live in 1929, is in the thick of rum running, with smugglers bringing in illegal booze from Canada. Who is the dead man? And, intriguingly, why does his body disappear before the police come to look at it? A modern eighth grader interviews the only man, now elderly, who may know more than the official records reveal. Riveting; a heck of a good read.

Lloyd, Alison. *Year of the Tiger.* Holiday House, 2010. 208 p. Grades 5–8.

"In ancient China, two boys forge an unlikely alliance in an effort to become expert archers and, ultimately, to save their city from invading barbarians." LC

Luper, Eric. *Bug Boy.* Farrar, Straus & Giroux, 2009. 248 p. Grades 6–up.

In 1934, 15-year-old Jack's first experiences as an apprentice jockey including dealing with gangsters, bookies, and the reappearance of the father who abandoned him. An exciting read.

Magoon, Kekla. *The Rock and the River.* Aladdin, 2009. 295 p. Grades 6–10.

"In 1968 Chicago, fourteen-year-old Sam Childs is caught in a conflict between his father's nonviolent approach to seeking civil rights for African-Americans and his older brother, who has joined the Black Panther Party." LC. Nominated for multiple state young reader awards. An ALA Notable Children's Book.

Mazer, Harry. *Boy at War: A Novel of Pearl Harbor.* Aladdin, 2002. 104 p. Grades 5–8.

A 14-year-old boy, newly arrived in Hawaii in 1941, witnesses the attack on Pearl Harbor. In a starred review, *Publishers Weekly* said, "Mazer successfully fuses a strong portrayal of Adam's transformation with both a vivid account of the attack and subtle suggestions of the complexities of Japanese-American relations as played out in particular lives." Sequels are *A Boy No More*, 2004, and *Heroes at War*, 2005. Teachers say the boys just love this series.

Bloodline by Katy Moran.

Moran, Katy. *Bloodline* series, published by Candlewick, Grades 7–up.

"While traveling through early seventh-century Britain trying to stop an impending war, Essa, who bears the blood of native British tribes and of the invading Anglish, discovers that his mother is alive and he, himself, is a prince of the northern kingdom, but he has loyalties and loved ones in the south to whom he is compelled to return." LC

1. *Bloodline,* 2009
2. *Bloodline Rising,* 2011

Morpurgo, Michael. *Private Peaceful.* Scholastic, 2003. 202 p. Grades 7–up.

The heartbreaking story of two Irish brothers who fight in World War I and face unimaginable choices. A real gem of a book. Starred reviews in *Booklist* and *Horn Book*.

Morpurgo, Michael. *War Horse.* Scholastic, 2007. 165 pages. Grades 5–8.

"Joey the horse recalls his experiences growing up on an English farm, his struggle for survival as a cavalry horse during World War I, and his reunion with his beloved master." LC

Morris, Gerald. *The Squire's Tales* series, published by Houghton Mifflin, Grades 5–8.

A series of fine reads about King Arthur's court during the Middle Ages. Funny, with appeal to both reluctant and proficient readers.

1. *The Squire's Tale,* 1998
2. *The Squire, His Knight, and His Lady,* 1999
3. *The Savage Damsel and the Dwarf,* 2000
4. *Parsifal's Page,* 2001
5. *The Ballad of Sir Dinadan,* 2003
6. *The Princess, the Crone, and the Dung Cart Knight,* 2004
7. *The Lioness and Her Knight,* 2005
8. *The Quest of the Fair Unknown,* 2006
9. *The Squire's Quest,* 2009
10. *The Legend of the King,* 2010

Myers, Anna. *The Grave Robber's Secret.* Walker, 2011. 196 p. Grades 5–9.

"In Philadelphia in the 1800s, twelve-year-old Robbie is forced to help his father rob graves, then when he suspects his dad of murder, Robbie makes a life-changing decision." LC

Myers, Walter Dean. *Fallen Angels.* Scholastic, 1998. 309 p. Grades 8–11.

"Seventeen-year-old Richie Perry, just out of his Harlem high school, enlists in the Army in the summer of 1967 and spends a devastating year on active duty in Vietnam." LC. This book does not shy away from the atrocities of the Vietnam War. Very popular with middle school (and high school) boys.

Myers, Walter Dean. *Sunrise over Fallujah.* Scholastic, 2008. 290 p. Grades 8–11.

"Robin Perry, from Harlem, is sent to Iraq in 2003 as a member of the Civilian Affairs Battalion, and his time there profoundly changes him." LC. This book's main character is the nephew of the protagonist in *Fallen Angels.*

Naidoo, Beverley. *Burn My Heart.* Amistad, 2009. 209 p. Grades 6–9.

"Matthew and Mungo, boys with a different skin color and culture, have a friendship that is tested during the Mau Mau bid for national independence." LC

O'Brien, Johnny. *Day of the Assassins: A Jack Christie Novel.* Templar Books, 2009. 213 p. Grades 5–9.

"Fifteen-year-old Jack is sent to 1914 Europe as a pawn in the battle between his long-lost father, who has built a time machine, and a secret network of scientists who want to prevent him from trying to use it to change history for the better. Includes historical notes." LC

Park, Linda Sue. *A Long Walk to Water.* Clarion, 2010. 128 p. Grades 6–9.

"Eleven-year-old Salva becomes separated from his family when the Sudanese civil war reaches his village in 1985, and must walk with other Dinka tribe members through southern Sudan, Ethiopia, and Kenya in search of safe haven. Based on the life of Salva Dut, who, after emigrating to America in 1996, began a project to dig water wells in Sudan." LC. Starred review in *Booklist.*

Paulsen, Gary. *Woods Runner.* Random House, 2010. 176 p. Grades 6–9.

"From his 1776 Pennsylvania homestead, thirteen-year-old Samuel, who is a highly-skilled woodsman, sets out toward New York City to rescue his parents from the band of British soldiers and Native Americans who kidnapped them after slaughtering most of their community. Includes historical notes." LC. A fast-paced, good read.

Peck, Richard. *On the Wings of Heroes.* Dial, 2007. 148 p. Grades 5–up.

"A boy in Illinois remembers the homefront years of World War II, especially his two heroes—his brother in the Air Force and his father—who fought in the previous war." LC. Nominated for many state young reader awards.

Preus, Margi. *Heart of a Samurai.* Amulet, 2010. 306 p. Grades 5–9.

The author retells an amazing true story about a Japanese teenager who was shipwrecked with his fishing companions, rescued by an American whaler, and taken into an American home—in 1842. Boys probably would not pick this up on their own, but it would make a fine read aloud that would interest both boys and girls. Action-packed adventure! Starred reviews in *Kirkus*, *Booklist*, and *Publishers Weekly*. Also received a Newbery Honor.

Salisbury, Graham. *Eyes of the Emperor.* Random House, 2005. 229 p. Grades 7–10.

"In this riveting, often painful novel, a 16-year-old Japanese American boy from Hawaii enlists in the army before Pearl Harbor and faces many race-based humiliations." LC. An ALA Notable Children's Book.

Schmidt, Gary D. *Okay for Now.* Clarion, 2011. 360 p. Grades 5–9.

This companion to *The Wednesday Wars* stands alone and is a compulsively readable story about a kid in a severely dysfunctional family and his struggle to make a new life for himself in a new town.

Schmidt, Gary D. *The Wednesday Wars.* Clarion, 2007. 264 p. Grades 5–8.

"During the 1967 school year, on Wednesday afternoons when all his classmates go to either Catechism or Hebrew school, seventh-grader Holling Hoodhood stays in Mrs. Baker's classroom where they read the plays of William Shakespeare and Holling learns much of value about the world he lives in." LC. Received a Newbery Honor.

Schwabach, Karen. *The Storm Before Atlanta.* Random House, 2010. 320 p. Grades 5–8.

When he manages to finagle a position as a drummer boy with a New York regiment in the Union army, Jeremy finds out what war is really like.

Sherrard, Valerie. *The Glory Wind.* Fitzhenry and Whiteside, 2011. 192 p. Grades 6–9.

"When the citizens of a small, rural, 1940s town learn that Gracie and her mother have a shady past, Luke must decide whether he will stand up for his new friend, Gracie, or save his own reputation." LC

Author Spotlight: Roland Smith

A common thread that runs through Roland Smith's books is action—which is what makes his books so appealing to boys. His characters constantly face adversity and encounter adventures whether they are riding elephants in Burma or hiding in plain sight in the federal witness protection program. Smith, a huge reader as a boy, rode his bike to the library every Saturday to load up his basket with books. His parents were avid readers and his curiosity about what made them get so engrossed in books was a factor that made him become a reader as well. Growing up in the 1950s there was no such thing as young adult literature, so he read all of the classics such as *Treasure Island*, *Dracula*, *Kidnapped*, and *Phantom of the Opera*, and then moved on to adult novels such as the James Bond books by Ian Fleming and Nero Wolfe mysteries by Rex Stout. It wasn't until he was in his 30s that he read his first young adult novel—*Hatchet* by Gary Paulsen—and discovered that there were great books being written for young people.

Roland Smith Recommends

Gary Paulsen

Margaret Peterson Haddix

Gordon Korman

Will Hobbs

Anthony Horowitz

The 39 Clues series and all the authors who write them

Smith, Roland. *Elephant Run*. Hyperion, 2007. 336 p. Grades 6–8.
   Nick is sent to live with his father in Burma during World War II, but faces unexpected danger and adventure when his father is taken prisoner by the Japanese, and he and a Burmese girl plan a daring rescue attempt. The details about wild elephants are particularly fascinating.

Spillebeen, Geert. *Age 14*. Houghton Mifflin, 2009. 216 p. Grades 6–up.
   "Twelve-year-old Patrick Condon assumes his brother John's identity and runs away to join the army in order to get away from his boring life in Ireland; however, as World War I erupts, the boy experiences much more than he expected." LC. For the proficient reader; based on a true story.

Spradlin, Michael P. *The Youngest Templar* series, published by Putnam Juvenile, Grades 5–9.
   A teenage boy, raised in a monastery, is asked to become a squire for a knight on the Third Crusade to Jerusalem. Action and adventure follow!

1. *Keeper of the Grail,* 2008
2. *Trail of Fate,* 2009
3. *Orphan of Destiny,* 2010

Whitney, Kim. *The Other Half of My Life: A Novel Based on the True Story of the MS St. Louis.* Alfred A. Knopf Books for Young Readers, 2009. 248 p. Grades 6–10.
"Fifteen-year-old Thomas sets sail on a German ship bound for Cuba in 1939 along with more than nine hundred German Jews expecting to be granted safe haven on the island, but he discovers that although the passengers have landing permits, they may not be allowed to enter the country." LC

Wilson, John. *Death on the River.* Orca, 2009. 195 p. Grades 8–10.
Eighteen-year-old Jake Clay, captured by the Confederates and taken to the horrors of Andersonville prison, has to deal with the living hell there.

Wulffson, Don L. *Soldier X.* Viking, 2001. 226 p. Grades 6–10.
In 1944 a 16-year-old German boy is wounded on the Eastern Front and changes uniforms with a dead Russian soldier. He feigns amnesia and flees from the horrors of the war. This book does not shy away from the brutality of World War II. Boys love it.

Yep, Laurence. *Golden Mountain Chronicles,* published by HarperCollins, Grades 5–8.
These excellent books chronicle the Chinese experience in America, including immigration. All involve members of the Young family. The first date below is part of the title; the second is the publication date for the book.

Dragonwings: 1903, 1975 (Newbery Honor)
Child of the Owl: 1965, 1977
Sea Glass: 1970, 1979
The Serpent's Children: 1849, 1984
Mountain Light: 1885, 1985
Dragon's Gate: 1876, 1993 (Newbery Honor)
The Traitor: 1885, 2003
Dragon Road: 1939, 2008

Chapter —5

Humor

Boys love humor and for some reason it can be hard to find in literature, especially in young adult books. Fortunately the Wimpy Kid phenomenon has ushered in a new wave of fun, cartoony books for boys, of which many good ones are listed here. The younger guys section contains a wealth of funny reading; the older guys section is more sparse. Would-be authors take note—there's a gap here that needs to be filled. Readers, take a look at chapter 2, Realistic Fiction, to find realistic books laced with humor including titles by Jordan Sonnenblick, Andrew Clements, and Carl Hiaasen.

YOUNGER GUYS

Amato, Mary. *The Riot Brothers* **series, illustrated by Ethan Long, published by Holiday House, Grades 2–5.**
Funny, entertaining, and great for kids who like gross stuff. Captain Underpants fans love this!

1. *Snarf Attack, Underfoodle, and the Secret of Life: The Riot Brothers Tell All,* 2004
2. *Drooling and Dangerous: The Riot Brothers Return!* 2006
3. *Stinky and Successful: The Riot Brothers Never Stop,* 2007
4. *Take the Mummy and Run: The Riot Brothers are on a Roll,* 2009

Andrews, Jan. *Rude Stories.* Illustrated by Francis Blake. Tundra Books, 2010. 87 p. Grades 2–4.
Roald Dahl fans will appreciate these funny retellings of traditional tales.

Author Spotlight: Tom Angleberger

The Strange Case of Origami Yoda and *Darth Paper Strikes Back* by Tom Angleberger have been a huge hit with intermediate boys. Angleberger himself read everything he could get his hands on when he was young. He was the kind of kid that took a book on vacation and got so absorbed that he never looked out the window. He had a special love for the Ramona books by Beverly Cleary because he believes that Ramona, like himself, has Asperger's syndrome. Currently his greatest influence is humor writer Daniel Pinkwater, but he also admires Lloyd Alexander and John Christopher.

Tom Angleberger Recommends

John Christopher's *Tripod* series, beginning with *The White Mountains*. Action-packed science fiction! Aliens have enslaved mankind, but three boys have escaped. Can they possibly stop the aliens and their giant, deadly Tripods? These books are unforgettable.

Lizard Music by Daniel Pinkwater. I still remember being so overcome with laughter that I threw myself headfirst at a sofa. But it's more than just laughs—it's mind-blowing. Also Pinkwater's *Snarkout Boys*, *Last Guru*, *Neddiad*, and my favorite, *Alan Mendelson, the Boy From Mars*.

Where the Mountain Meets the Moon by Grace Lin

A Tale Dark and Grimm by Adam Gidwitz

Lloyd Alexander's *Prydain* series, beginning with *The Book of Three*

Bonnie Burton's *Star Wars Craft Book*

Any origami book!

And the book that changed my life forever: *Juggling for the Complete Klutz* by John Cassidy. I learned to juggle by reading this book and eventually became a professional juggler!

Angleberger, Tom. *The Strange Case of Origami Yoda*. Amulet, 2010. 141 p. Grades 3–6.
"Sixth-grader Tommy and his friends describe their interactions with a paper finger puppet of Yoda, worn by their weird classmate Dwight, as they try to figure out whether or not the puppet can really predict the future. Includes instructions for making Origami Yoda." LC. Funny, and spot on. Boys absolutely love it. The sequel is *Darth Paper Strikes Back*, 2011.

Applegate, Katherine. *Roscoe Riley Rules* series, illustrated by Brian Biggs, published by HarperCollins, grades 2–4.
Every title begins and ends with the time-out chair—Roscoe gets into trouble in every book. Good, funny titles for kids transitioning from easy readers to chapter books.

1. *Never Glue Your Friends to Chairs,* 2008
2. *Never Swipe a Bully's Bear,* 2008
3. *Don't Swap Your Sweater for a Dog,* 2008
4. *Never Swim in Applesauce,* 2008
5. *Don't Tap-Dance on Your Teacher,* 2009
6. *Never Race a Runaway Pumpkin,* 2009
7. *Never Walk in Shoes That Talk,* 2009

Arnold, Tedd. *Fly Guy* **series, published by Scholastic, Grades K-3.**

A beautiful friendship begins when Buzz the boy proves that a fly can be one smart pet. These slim, reader-friendly tales have a robust humor and wacky cartoon art, including an eye-popping cover. Most people do not realize that a fly can make a really good—and helpful—pet. Boys love this super silly hero in easy reader books.

Hi! Fly Guy, 2005
Super Fly Guy, 2006
Shoo, Fly Guy, 2006
There was an Old Lady who Swallowed Fly Guy, 2007
Fly High, Fly Guy! 2008
Hooray for Fly Guy! 2008
I Spy, Fly Guy, 2009
Fly Guy Meets Fly Girl, 2010
Buzz Boy and Fly Guy, 2010
Fly Guy vs. the Flyswatter! 2011
Ride, Fly Guy, Ride, 2012

The Strange Case of Origami Yoda **by Tom Angleberger. Used with permission of Amulet Books, an imprint of Abrams.**

Asch, Frank, and Devin Asch. *The Daily Comet: Boy Saves Earth from Giant Octopus.* Kids Can, 2010. 32 p. Grades 2–4.

"Young skeptic Hayward Palmer, who has a logical explanation for everything, is forced to open his mind when he accompanies his father to work at the sensationalistic newspaper 'The Daily Comet' and encounters an enormous fact he cannot explain." LC

Bean, Raymond. *Sweet Farts* **series, published by Amazon Encore, Grades 3–5.**

Keith Emerson, age 10, invents a product that takes the smell out of intestinal gas. But what is he going to invent next? Very silly and funny.

Sweet Farts, 2008
Rippin' It in Old School, 2010

Beaty, Andrea. *Attack of the Fluffy Bunnies.* Amulet, 2010. 192 p. Grades 3–6.

"At Camp Whatsitooya, twins Joules and Kevin and new friend Nelson face off against large, rabbit-like creatures from the Mallow Galaxy who thrive on sugar, but are not above hypnotizing and eating human campers." LC

Boniface, William. *The Extraordinary Adventures of Ordinary Boy* **series, illustrated by Stephen Gilpin, published by HarperCollins, Grades 4–7.**

Ordinary Boy has no superpowers, unlike most of the superheroes in the city where he lives, Superopolis. But he has his own special abilities. Very funny. Nominated for multiple state young reader awards.

1. *The Hero Revealed,* 2006
2. *The Return of Meteor Boy?* 2007
3. *The Great Powers Outage,* 2008

Boyce, Frank Cottrell. *Cosmic.* Walden Pond, 2010. Grades 4–7.

"Twelve-year-old Liam, who looks like he is thirty and is tired of being treated like he is older than he actually is, decides he is going to pose as the adult chaperone on the first space-ship to take civilians into space, but when he ends up in outer space with a group of kids and no adult supervision, he must think fast to make things right." LC. A very funny book!

Boyce, Frank Cottrell. *Framed.* HarperCollins, 2006. 306 p. Grades 4–up.

Dylan, living in a small, gray Welsh town, finds a life-changing experience when the National Gallery in London starts storing its priceless masterpieces in an old mine at the top of the mountain. Funny, by the author of *Millions,* 2005.

Cotler, Steve. *Cheesie Mack is Not a Genius or Anything.* Illustrated by Adam McCauley. Random House, 2011. 213 p. Grades 3–6.

A fun book about a kid who graduates from fifth grade and looks forward to summer camp with his best friend. Then his dad loses his job and there is no money for camp. First in a new series.

Curtis, Christopher Paul. *Mr. Chickee's Funny Money.* Random House, 2005. Grades 3–6.

Steven Carter's friend, blind, elderly Mr. Chickee, gives him some money—a bill worth a quadrillion dollars. The person depicted on the bill is James Brown, the soul singer. Is it a fake? Is it real? Steven, who with his friend Russell and Russell's gigantic dog, Zoopy, has formed the Flint's Future Detectives club, suspects it *is* real—and the reaction of a govern-ment official convinces him that indeed it is. This is slapstick and very silly, and it's obviously the beginning of a series. The second is *Mr. Chickee's Messy Mission,* 2007.

Daneshvari, Gitty. *School of Fear* series, illustrated by Carrie Gifford, published by Little Brown, Grades 4–6.

"Twelve-year-olds Madeleine, Theo, and Lulu, and thirteen-year-old Garrison, are sent to a remote Massachusetts school to overcome their phobias, but tragedy strikes and the quar-tet must work together—with no adult assistance—to face their fears." LC

School of Fear, 2009
Class is Not Dismissed! 2010
The Final Exam, 2011

Fleischman, Paul. *The Dunderheads.* Illustrated by David Roberts. Candlewick, 2009. Unpaged. Grades 3–5.

This is a picture book for older readers, and it is a perfect read aloud to make kids laugh. A group of misfits get together to retrieve something their scary teacher confiscated—and their creativity is astounding!

Fleming, Candace. *The Fabled Fourth Graders of Aesop Elementary School.* Schwartz and Wade, 2007. 186 p. Grades 3–5.

"An unlikely teacher takes over the disorderly fourth-grade class of Aesop Elementary School with surprising results." LC. Followed by *The Fabled Fifth Graders of Aesop Elemen-tary School,* 2010. Nominated for several state young reader awards.

Fraser, Ian. *Ogg and Bob* **series, published by Marshall Cavendish, Grades 2–4.**

Two not particularly bright cave boys acquire a pet mammoth. Funny, silly; good for reluctant readers.

Meet Mammoth, 2010
Life with Mammoth, 2010

Gantos, Jack. *Joey Pigza* **series, published by Farrar, Straus & Giroux, Grades 4–6.**

An absolutely top-notch series of books about a well-meaning kid who clearly has some form of ADHD. Funny and touching. Great for reading aloud.

Joey Pigza Swallowed the Key, 1998
Joey Pigza Loses Control, 2000
What Would Joey Do?, 2002
I am Not Joey Pigza, 2007

Greenburg, Dan. *Secrets of Dripping Fang* **series, published by Harcourt, Grades 3–5.**

Lemony Snicket fans like these gross, fun stories of twins Wally and Cheyenne, who think things have to get better when they are freed from Cincinnati's Jolly Days Orphanage.

1. *The Onts,* 2005
2. *Treachery and Betrayal at Jolly Days,* 2006
3. *The Vampire's Curse,* 2006
4. *Fall of the House of Mandible,* 2006
5. *The Shluffmuffin Boy Is History,* 2005
6. *Attack of the Giant Octopus,* 2007
7. *Please Don't Eat the Children,* 2007
8. *When Bad Snakes Eat Good Children,* 2007

Gutman, Dan. *The Homework Machine.* Simon & Schuster, 2006. 146 p. Grades 4–7.

When three of the four kids assigned to a group at school realize that the fourth has invented a completely effective machine to do his homework, they want in on the action. Two are mediocre students, the third is an excellent student who usually works hard, and Brenton, the creative inventor, is the best student in the class. But mysterious happenings begin to plague their supposedly carefree life, and other kids and even the first-year teacher begin to wonder what is going on. Funny, with some good life lessons painlessly taught. Sequel is *Return of the Homework Machine,* 2009.

Gutman, Dan. *My Weird School* **series, published by HarperTrophy, Grades 2–4.**

Dan Gutman himself says it: This silly series for emerging readers is about a school in which all of the teachers are mentally ill. At Ella Mentry School, all the grownups are quite weird in their own weird way. The main characters are A. J. (a boy who doesn't like school) and his arch-enemy, Andrea Young (who loves school and everything else A. J. hates).

Miss Daisy Is Crazy!, 2004
Mr. Klutz Is Nuts!, 2004
Mrs. Roopy Is Loopy!, 2004
Ms. Hannah Is Bananas!, 2004
Miss Small Is Off the Wall!, 2005
Mr. Hynde Is Out of His Mind!, 2005

Mrs. Cooney Is Loony!, 2005
Ms. LaGrange Is Strange!, 2005
Miss Lazar Is Bizarre!, 2005
Mr. Docker Is Off His Rocker!, 2006
Mrs. Kormel Is Not Normal!, 2006
Ms. Todd Is Odd!, 2006

Mrs. Patty Is Batty!, 2006
Miss Holly Is Too Jolly!, 2006
Mr. Macky Is Wacky!, 2007
Ms. Coco Is Loco!, 2007
Miss Suki is Kooky!, 2007

Miss Yonkers Is Bonkers!, 2007
Dr. Carbles Is Losing His Marbles!, 2007
Mr. Louie Is Screwy!, 2007
Ms. Krup Cracks Me Up!, 2008

Gutman, Dan. *My Weird School Daze* series, published by HarperCollins, Grades 3–5.

A. J., Andrea, and the gang are "graduating" to third grade, where they will have a new teacher and new outrageous adventures at Ella Mentry School.

1. *Mrs. Dole Is Out of Control!*, 2008
2. *Mr. Sunny Is Funny!*, 2008
3. *Mr. Granite Is from Another Planet!*, 2008
4. *Coach Hyatt Is a Riot!*, 2009
5. *Officer Spence Makes No Sense!*, 2009
6. *Mrs. Jafee Is Daffy!*, 2009
7. *Dr. Brad Has Gone Mad!*, 2009
8. *Miss Laney Is Zany!*, 2010
9. *Mrs. Lizzy Is Dizzy!*, 2010
10. *Miss Mary Is Scary!*, 2010
11. *Mr. Tony Is Full of Baloney!*, 2010
12. *Mrs. Leakey Is Freaky!*, 2011

Hale, Bruce. *Underwhere* series, published by HarperCollins, Grades 3–6.

"When Zeke, his twin sister Stephanie, their neighbor Hector, and Hector's cat Fitz slide into the world of Underwhere, Zeke is hailed as a prince who will, according to an ancient prophecy, free the Undies from the evil Underlord's rule by finding and destroying his throne." LC

1. *Prince of Underwhere*, 2008
2. *Pirates of Underwhere*, 2009
3. *Flyboy of Underwhere*, 2009
4. *Fat Cat of Underwhere*, 2009

Holt, K. A. *Brains for Lunch: A Zombie Novel in Haiku?!* Roaring Brook, 2010. 96 p. Grades 4–8.

"Loeb, a zombie in middle school who has a crush on a regular human girl, tries to transcend stereotypes by competing in a haiku competition to make a good impression." LC

Horowitz, Anthony. *Groosham Grange.* Philomel, 2008. 196 p. Grades 4–8.

There is humor and horror in this story of a 13-year-old who goes to a strange and bewildering new school after being expelled from his old one. Sequel is *Return to Groosham Grange: The Unholy Grail*, 2009.

***Brains for Lunch: A Zombie Novel in Haiku?!* by K.A. Holt. Courtesy of Roaring Book Press, an imprint of the Macmillan Children's Publishing Group.**

Hurd, Thacher. *Bongo Fishing*. Henry Holt, 2011. 240 p. Grades 3–6.

    "Berkeley, California, middle-schooler Jason Jameson has a close encounter of the fun kind when Sam, a bluish alien from the Pleiades, arrives in a 1960 Dodge Dart spaceship and invites Jason to go fishing." LC

Kinney, Jeff. *Diary of a Wimpy Kid* series, published by Amulet, Grades 4–8.

    Greg, who hasn't had his growth spurt yet and suffers mightily because of that, keeps a journal of his seventh grade year as not the coolest (by far) kid in the school. Every page has at least one illustration—it's a novel in cartoons, and I was laughing out loud frequently. The whole series is phenomenally popular and a surefire winner.

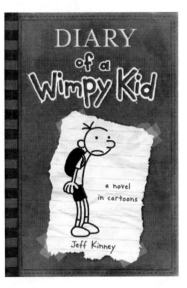

    Diary of a Wimpy Kid, 2007
    Rodrick Rules, 2008
    The Last Straw, 2009
    Dog Days, 2009
    The Ugly Truth, 2010
    Cabin Fever, 2011

Diary of a Wimpy Kid **by Jeff Kinney. Used with permission of Amulet Books, an imprint of Abrams.**

Knudson, Mike. *Raymond and Graham* series, illustrated by Stacy Curtis, published by Viking, Grades 3–5.

    "Best friends Raymond and Graham have looked forward to being the oldest and toughest boys at East Millcreek Elementary School; but everything goes wrong, including the scary teacher." LC

    Raymond and Graham Rule the School, 2008
    Raymond and Graham, Dancing Dudes, 2010
    Raymond and Graham, Bases Loaded, 2010
    Raymond and Graham, Cool Campers, 2011

Korman, Gordon. *The Chicken Doesn't Skate*. Scholastic, 1996. 197 p. Grades 4–7.

    "Wild things happen at the South Middle School when Milo's science project, Henrietta the chicken, becomes the hockey team's mascot and their only chance for a winning season." LC

Korman, Gordon. *Losing Joe's Place*. Scholastic, 1990. 233 p. Grades 4–7.

    "Jason and his two friends move into Jason's brother's apartment and manage to wreak havoc in it during one funny and memorable summer." LC

Korman, Gordon. *Maxx Comedy: The Funniest Kid in America*. Hyperion, 2006. 153 p. Grades 4–6.

    "Eleven-year-old Max Carmody has wanted to be a stand-up comedian since he was five, so when a contest is held to find the "world's funniest kid," he goes through all kinds of craziness to win." LC

Korman, Gordon. *No More Dead Dogs.* Hyperion, 2000. 180 p. Grades 4–8.

"Eighth-grade football hero Wallace Wallace is sentenced to detention attending rehearsals of the school play where, in spite of himself, he becomes wrapped up in the production and begins to suggest changes that improve not only the play but his life as well." LC

Kowitt, H. N. *The Loser List.* Scholastic, 2011. 224 p. Grades 4–7.

Comic-obsessed seventh grader Danny Shine develops major problems when he starts hanging with the bad kids. Funny, and great for both reluctant readers and comic book fans.

Krulik, Nancy. *George Brown, Class Clown* series, published by Grosset and Dunlap, Grades 2–4.

"When fourth-grader George starts at a new school, he vows to become a model student instead of the class clown he has always been, but just as his plan is going really well, he is overtaken by a magic burp that turns him back into a mischief-maker." LC

1. *Super Burp!* 2010
2. *Trouble Magnet,* 2010
3. *The World's Worst Wedgie,* 2010
4. *What's Black and White and Stinks All Over?* 2011
5. *Wet and Wild,* 2011

Lewis, Josh. *Super Chicken Nugget Boy and the Furious Fry.* Hyperion, 2010. 141 p. Grades 2–4.

"Super Chicken Nugget Boy, normally a student at Bert Lahr Elementary School, must step in to save the day when a giant, mutated French fry threatens to destroy the school." LC

Lindo, Elvira. *Manolito Four-Eyes* series, translated by Caroline Travalia, published by Marshall Cavendish, Grades 4–6.

Funny series, with cartoon illustrations, about a contemporary kid in Madrid, Spain, who doesn't really fit in.

Manolito Four-Eyes, 2008
Manolito Four-Eyes: The 2nd Volume of the Great Encyclopedia of My Life, 2009
Manolito Four-Eyes: The 3rd Volume of the Great Encyclopedia of my Life, 2010

Look, Lenore. *Alvin Ho* series, published by Schwartz and Wade, Grades 1–4.

Very funny books about an Asian American boy with a lot of hang-ups. We can all identify. Delightful! Nominated for several state young reader awards, and on several best books of the year lists.

Alvin Ho: Allergic to Girls, School, and Other Scary Things, 2008
Alvin Ho: Allergic to Camping, Hiking, and Other Natural Disasters, 2009
Alvin Ho: Allergic to Birthday Parties, Science Projects, and Other Man-Made Catastrophes, 2010

Lowry, Lois. *Sam* books, published by Houghton Mifflin, Grades 3–6.

Sam, Anastasia Krupnik's younger brother, tells us the story of his life from his point of view. These are extremely funny books and excellent read alouds.

All About Sam, 1988
Attaboy, Sam, 1992
See You Around Sam, 1996
Zooman Sam, 1999

Author Spotlight: David Lubar

David Lubar's humorous books include *Sleeping Freshmen Never Lie*, *Punished*, and the *Weenies* series. As a child, he devoured the books that his mother (a librarian) supplied for him. The biographies, fiction, math, and science books were an essential part of his childhood. Today his writing is influenced by the masters of plotted short fiction, especially Ray Bradbury, Stephen King, and Rod Serling.

David Lubar Recommends

Bruce Coville

Dan Gutman

Roland Smith

Gordon Korman

Lubar, David. *Nathan Abercombie, Accidental Zombie* **series, published by Starscape. Grades 3–6.**

As a result of a failed science experiment, fifth grader Nathan turns into a zombie.

1. *My Rotten Life,* 2009
2. *Dead Guy Spy,* 2010
3. *Goop Soup,* 2010
4. *The Big Stink,* 2010
5. *Enter the Zombie,* 2011

Lubar, David. *Punished!* Darby Creek, 2005. 96 p. Grades 3–6.

Fooling around in the library with his best friend, Logan is stopped by a weird old guy who thinks Logan ought to be punished—and, boy, is he ever. Logan is made to speak in puns. What is the cure? Well, he has to take pictures of seven oxymorons, then find seven anagrams and seven palindromes. By the end of this fun story, kids will remember exactly what those are!

Lubar, David. *Weenies* **series, published by Starscape, Grades 3–7.**

Collections of gross, icky short stories that reluctant readers absolutely love! They do not need to be read in order.

In the Land of the Lawn Weenies: And Other Warped and Creepy Tales, 2003
Invasion of the Road Weenies: And Other Warped and Creepy Tales, 2006
The Curse of the Campfire Weenies: And Other Warped and Creepy Tales, 2007
The Battle of the Red Hot Weenies: And Other Warped and Creepy Tales, 2009
Attack of the Vampire Weenies: And Other Warped and Creepy Tales, 2011
Beware the Ninja Weenies: And Other Warped and Creepy Tales, 2012

Lyons, Jayne. *100% Wolf.* Illustrated by Victor Rivas. Atheneum, 2009. 245 p. Grades 3–6.
  Ten-year-old Freddie is eager to transform into a werewolf—but when the big day comes, he transforms into a werepoodle. Silly and fun. Sequel is *100% Hero*, 2010.

MacDonald, Amy. *Too Much Flapdoodle!* Illustrated by Cat Bowman Smith. Farrar, Straus & Giroux, 2008. 182 p. Grades 3–8.
  Parker, a hypochondriac city slicker, has to spend the summer visiting his great-aunt and great-uncle on their farm, and is appalled that he can't get a cell phone signal, and they aren't wired for the net. Funny, fun, and an excellent read aloud.

McCloskey, Robert. *Homer Price.* Viking, 1943. 149 p. Grades 2–5.
  This classic and funny story of the events in the life of a kid still holds up brilliantly.

McDonald, Megan. *Stink* series, illustrated by Peter H. Reynolds, published by Candlewick, Grades 2–3.
  Stink is Judy Moody's younger brother, and these books are just as funny.

  Stink: The Incredible Shrinking Kid, 2005
  Stink and the Incredible Super-Galactic Jawbreaker, 2006
  Stink and the World's Worst Super-Stinky Sneakers, 2007
  Stink and the Great Guinea Pig Express, 2008
  Stink-O-Pedia Super Stink-Y Stuff from A to Zzzzz, 2009
  Stink: Solar System Superhero, 2010
  Stink and the Ultimate Thumb-Wrestling Smackdown, 2011
  Judy Moody and Stink: The Holly Joliday, 2007
  Judy Moody and Stink: The Mad Mad Mad Mad Treasure Hunt, 2009

Moss, Marissa. *Max Disaster* series, published by Candlewick, Grades 2–4.
  "Max writes down his thoughts and ideas in the form of comics and contraptions while dealing with pimply older brothers, school, and the fights his parents get into." LC

  1. *Alien Eraser to the Rescue,* 2009
  2. *Alien Eraser Unravels the Mystery of the Pyramids,* 2009
  3. *Alien Eraser Reveals the Secrets of Evolution,* 2009

***Alien Eraser to the Rescue* by Marissa Moss.**

Myers, Laurie. *Surviving Brick Johnson.* Illustrated by Dan Yaccarino. Clarion, 2001. Grades 4–6.
  "Fifth-grader Alex discovers that the classmate he fears as bully is nothing of the sort—in fact, he becomes a friend. With an open format and quirky, humorous illustrations, it's a perfect choice for reluctant readers." LC. A fine read aloud.

Nelson, Peter, and Rohitash Rao. *Herbert's Wormhole: A Novel in Cartoons.* HarperCollins, 2009. 295 p. Grades 3–6.
  Captain Underpants fans enjoy this fun novel, with a lot of graphic elements, about two sixth-graders who have to save the planet from really weird aliens.

Nesbo, Jo. *Doctor Proctor's Fart Powder.* Illustrated by Mike Lowery. Aladdin, 2010. 265 p. Grades 4–7.

Nilly, a tiny boy with a lot of pizzazz, moves into a new neighborhood in Oslo, Norway, and there meets a neighbor girl and an inventor who has come up with some incredibly creative ideas which Nilly improves on. The most exciting is his fart powder, which does not spell and has no harmful aftereffects—but can even propel someone into the air. The author is the most successful Norwegian author ever and this is his first children's book. If you dare to try it, it would undoubtedly make a fine read aloud. Sequel is *The Bubble in the Bathtub*, 2011.

Oliver, Lin. *Who Shrunk Daniel Funk?* series, illustrated by Stephen Gilpin, published by Simon & Schuster, Grades 3–6.

Daniel discovers he has a tiny twin brother, who was born inside Daniel's ear and raised by their granny. Slapstick comedy.

1. *Attack of the Growling Eyeballs,* 2008
2. *Escape of the Mini-Mummy,* 2008
3. *Revenge of the Itty Bitty Brothers,* 2009
4. *Secret of the Super-Small Superstar,* 2010

Paulsen, Gary. *Harris and Me.* Harcourt, 1993. 168 p. Grades 4–up.

I have a male friend who says that this is the magic bullet that will turn reluctant boys into readers. The 11-year-old hero spends the summer on a farm and gets into numerous scrapes with his distant cousin Harris, the funniest of which involves peeing on an electric fence—a scene guaranteed to crack up anyone who reads it.

Paulsen, Gary. *Lawn Boy.* Random House, 2007. 88 p. Grades 4–8.

A 12-year-old kid accidentally falls into the lawn mowing business when his grandmother gives him an old riding lawn mower. Then the business starts to take off—like crazy! A funny (and short) book about how capitalism works. Sequel is *Lawn Boy Returns*, 2011.

Paulsen, Gary. *Mudshark.* Random House, 2009. 86 p. Grades 3–6.

Very funny, very short book about a 12-year-old super problem solver who is enlisted by the school principal to help solve the problem of the missing erasers. Nominated for multiple state young reader awards.

Peck, Richard. *A Long Way from Chicago.* Dial, 1998. 148 p. Grades 4–8.

This fine book was followed by *A Year Down Yonder* (2000). During the Depression, two Chicago kids go to stay with their grandmother—a real character—in rural Illinois. The girl returns in the second for more hilarious adventures. I was on the Newbery Committee that picked this one, so what can I say? Fun books and fine read alouds. *A Season of Gifts* (2009) is set in the 1950s but is a companion to the other two.

Peirce, Lincoln. *Big Nate* series, published by HarperCollins, Grades 4–6.

Wimpy Kid fans will like these funny stories about a sixth grader who hates school and is constantly getting into trouble.

Big Nate: In a Class by Himself, 2010
Big Nate Strikes Again, 2010
Big Nate: From the Top, 2010
Big Nate, the Boy with the Biggest Head in the World, 2010
Big Nate Out Loud, 2011
Big Nate Boredom Buster: Super Scribbles, Cool Comix, and Lots of Laughs, 2011

Pilkey, Dav. *The Adventures of Ook and Gluk* series, published by Blue Sky, Grades 3–6.
Two prehistoric boys living in Caveland, Ohio, half-a-million years ago journey to the future to prevent a crime. Hysterically funny to boys of a certain age!

The Adventures of Ook and Gluk, Kung-Fu Cavemen from the Future, 2010
The Adventures of Ook and Gluk, Kung-Fu Cavemen from the Future, the Second Graphic Novel . . . , 2011

Pilkey, Dav. *Captain Underpants* series, published by Scholastic, Grades 1–4.
The boys adore these. These are filled with bathroom humor (obviously!).

The Adventures of Captain Underpants, 1997
Captain Underpants and the Attack of the Talking Toilets, 1999
Captain Underpants and the Invasion of the Incredibly Naughty Cafeteria Ladies from Outer Space . . . , 1999
Captain Underpants and the Perilous Plot of Professor Poopypants, 2000
Captain Underpants and the Wrath of the Wicked Wedgie Woman, 2001
Captain Underpants and the Big, Bad Battle of the Bionic Booger Boy, Part 1: The Night of the Nasty Nostril Nuggets, 2003
Captain Underpants and the Big, Bad Battle of the Bionic Booger Boy, Part 2: The Revenge of the Ridiculous Robo-Boogers, 2003
Captain Underpants and the Preposterous Plight of the Purple Potty People, 2006

The Adventures Of Ook And Gluk, Kung-Fu Cavemen From The Future **by Dav Pilkey.**

Power, Timothy. *The Boy Who Howled.* Bloomsbury, 2010. 256 p. Grades 4–6.
"A boy who has been raised by wolves from a young age unexpectedly finds himself back in human society, trying to figure out how to fit in." LC

Scieszka, Jon. *SPHDZ* series, published by Simon & Schuster, Grades 3–5.
Scieszka's zany humor delights kids, and he delivers it well in this story of a new kid in the fifth grade who learns that some of his classmates are actually aliens who need his help to save the world.

Spaceheadz, Book One, 2010
Spaceheadz, Book Two, 2010
Spaceheadz, Book Three, 2011

Scieszka, Jon. *The Time Warp Trio* series, published by Viking, Grades 3–6.
The time-traveling Brooklyn trio of Joe, Sam, and Fred venture into the past and future. Fast-moving and silly, this whole series is a guaranteed boy-pleaser.

Knights of the Kitchen Table, 1991
The Not-So-Jolly Roger, 1991
The Good, the Bad, and the Goofy, 1992

Your Mother was a Neanderthal, 1993
2095, 1995
Tut Tut, 1996
Summer Reading is Killing Me, 1998
It's All Greek to Me, 1999
See You Later, Gladiator, 2000
Sam Samurai, 2001
Viking It and Liking It, 2002
Me Oh Maya, 2003
Hey Kid, Want to Buy a Bridge? 2003
Da Wild, Da Crazy, Da Vinci, 2004
Marco? Polo, 2006.
Seven Blunders of the World, 2006
Oh, Say, I Can't See, 2007
Wushu Were Here, 2007

Seltzer, Adam. *Andrew North Blows Up the World.* Delacorte, 2009. 119 p. Grades 3–5.

Lots of fun in this story of a third grader who wants to become a spy, just like his dad and older brother—except they're not, and readers are in on it.

Seuling, Barbara. *Oh, No, It's Robert!* Illustrated by Paul Brewer. Cricket Books, 1999. 118 p. Grades 2–4.

Robert Dorfman hates math (and isn't very good at it, which annoys his father, a math teacher), loves guinea pigs, and is determined to win a prize for being a good student. It isn't easy when he keeps messing up and taking bad advice, such as his brother's suggestion that he give a talk on the toilet as the greatest invention of all time. Fun.

Shreve, Steve. *The Adventures of Benny.* Marshall Cavendish, 2009. 160 p. Grades 2–5.

Just the thing for Captain Underpants and Wimpy Kid fans. This fun, heavily illustrated book includes plenty of gross stuff.

Stauffacher, Sue. *Donuthead.* Alfred A. Knopf Books for Young Readers, 2003. 144 pages Grades 4–6.

In the hilarious first-person voice of the unfortunately named Franklin Delano Donuthead, this novel chronicles an improbable friendship between two philosophically mismatched 11-year-olds that is actually just what they both need. The sequel is *Donutheart,* 2006.

Thaler, Mike. *The Black Lagoon Adventures* series, illustrated by Jared Lee, published by Scholastic, Grades 3–4 and younger.

These are pretty simple and funny for kids. They seem to have reissued the books regularly and they go in and out of print. Some have been redone as picture books. Even Thaler does not list them all on his website. I include the publication dates I could find of the latest reissues, but many were written quite some time ago.

1. *The Class Trip from the Black Lagoon,* 2004
2. *The Talent Show from the Black Lagoon,* 2005
3. *The Class Election from the Black Lagoon,* 2004
4. *The Science Fair from the Black Lagoon,* 2005
5. *The Halloween Party from the Black Lagoon,* 2006
6. *The Field Day from the Black Lagoon,* 2008

7. *The School Carnival from the Black Lagoon,* 2005
8. *The Valentine's Day from the Black Lagoon,* 2006
9. *The Christmas Party from the Black Lagoon,* 2006
10. *The Little League Team from the Black Lagoon,* 2009
11. *The Snow Day from the Black Lagoon,* 2008
12. *The April Fool's Day from the Black Lagoon,* 2011
13. *The Back-to-School Fright from the Black Lagoon,* 2011
14. *The New Year's Eve Sleepover from the Black Lagoon,* 2011
15. *The Spring Dance from the Black Lagoon,* 2011

Trine, Greg. *Melvin Beederman, Superhero* series, published by Henry Holt, Grades 2–5.
Melvin Beederman graduates from the Superhero Academy and heads for Los Angeles, where he teams up with school play actress Candace Brinkwater in order to catch the evil McNasty Brothers.

1. *Curse of the Bologna Sandwich,* 2006
2. *The Revenge of the McNasty Brothers,* 2006
3. *The Grateful Fred,* 2006
4. *Terror in Tights,* 2007
5. *The Fake Cape Caper,* 2007
6. *Attack of the Valley Girls,* 2008
7. *Brotherhood of the Traveling Underpants,* 2009
8. *Invasion from Planet Dork,* 2010

Trueit, Trudi. *Secrets of a Lab Rat* series, illustrated by Jim Paillot, published by Aladdin, Grades 3–5.
Scab is always getting into trouble and likes gross, yucky things. Funny and entertaining.

1. *No Girls Allowed (Dogs Okay),* 2010
2. *Mom, There's a Dinosaur in Beeson's Lake,* 2010
3. *Scab for Treasurer?* 2011

Venuti, Kristin Clark. *Leaving the Bellweathers.* Egmont, 2009. 250 p. Grades 4–6
A very funny story about a wacky family and the butler whose own service and that of his ancestors totals 200 years. *School Library Journal* called this "a blend of Roald Dahl and Lemony Snicket." Sequel is *The Butler Gets a Break: A Bellweather Tale,* 2010.

Vernon, Ursula. *Dragonbreath* series, published by Dial, grades 2–5.
Bullied dragon Danny hasn't figured out how to breathe fire yet and that's just one of his problems. Comics and text intersperse here; lots of fun.

1. *Dragonbreath,* 2009
2. *Attack of the Ninja Frogs,* 2010
3. *Curse of the Were-Weiner,* 2010
4. *Lair of the Bat Monster,* 2011
5. *No Such Thing as Ghosts,* 2011

Dragonbreath by Ursula Vernon. Used by permission of Penguin Group (USA) Inc. All rights reserved.

Weeks, Sarah. *Oggie Cooder* **series, illustrated by Doug Holgate, published by Scholastic, Grades 3–5.**

Oggie is more than a bit of a dork, but finds that some of his unusual abilities can also make him into a popular kid. Nominated for several state young reader awards.

Oggie Cooder, 2008
Oggie Cooder, Party Animal, 2009

Whitehouse, Howard. *Bogbrush the Barbarian.* Illustrated by Bill Slavin. Kids Can, 2010. 184 p. Grades 4–6.

"Bogbrush the barbarian, strong in body but not in mind, is determined to seek his fortune and sets off on his noble steed from the Temple of the Great Belch in the frozen north, to a city in the far south, and fortunately meets some smarter adventurers to join along the way." LC

Wight, Eric. *Frankie Pickle* **series, published by Simon & Schuster, Grades 2–4.**

Fourth grader Frankie Piccolini has an alter ego, Frankie Pickle, who gets into trouble and solves problems. With cartoon illustrations on every page, these fun books will appeal to Captain Underpants fans.

1. *Frankie Pickle and the Closet of Doom,* 2009
2. *Frankie Pickle and the Pine Run 3000,* 2010
3. *Frankie Pickle and the Mathematical Menace,* 2011

Fizzy Whiz Kid **by Maiya Williams. Used with permission of Amulet Books, an imprint of Abrams.**

Williams, Maiya. *The Fizzy Whiz Kid.* Amulet, 2010. 273 p. Grades 4–6.

An entertaining read about a kid who shoots to stardom when he makes a commercial for Fizzy Whiz Soda—which turns out to have an astonishingly high sugar content, which is not good news for his career.

Yee, Lisa. *Warp Speed.* Scholastic, 2011. 320 p. Grades 4–7.

Seventh grade loser Marley is a bullied geek in this excellent, funny book about middle school.

OLDER GUYS

Allen, Crystal. *How Lamar's Bad Prank Won a Bubba-Sized Trophy.* Balzer and Bray, 2011. 288 p. Grades 5–8.

"When thirteen-year-old, bowling-obsessed Lamar Washington finds out that his idol is coming to town, he finds himself involved in some unsavory activities as he tries to change his image to impress people." LC

Anderson, M. T. *Pals in Peril* **series, illustrated by Kurt Cyrus, published by Beach Lane, Grades 5–9.**

Utterly silly and ridiculous stories about improbable mysteries. Very funny! These stories were packaged as a series in 2010.

Whales on Stilts, 2005
The Clue of the Linoleum Lederhosen, 2006
Jasper Dash and the Flame Pits of Delaware, 2009
Agent Q, or the Smell of Danger, 2010

Barry, Dave, and Ridley Pearson. *Science Fair: A Story of Mystery, Danger, International Suspense, and a Very Nervous Frog.* Disney, 2008. 400 p. Grades 5–8.
    International terrorists have developed a horrible plot—get rich middle school kids to unknowingly make a weapon of mass destruction. Action packed and funny.

Briant, Ed. *Choppy Socky Blues.* Flux, 2010. 264 p. Grades 6–up.
    "In the South of England, fourteen-year-old Jay resumes contact with his father, a movie stuntman and karate instructor, after two years of estrangement, to impress a girl who turns out to be the girlfriend of Jay's former best friend." LC. Very funny. Probably better for proficient readers than struggling ones.

Brown, Jason Robert, and Dan Elish. *13: A Novel.* HarperCollins, 2008. 202 p. Grades 5–7.
    When Evan's parents divorce, he has to leave Manhattan and move to a small town in Indiana. Who of his almost all Christian classmates will come to his Bar Mitzvah? Fun.

Chatterton, Martin. *The Brain Finds a Leg.* Peachtree, 2009. 212 p. Grades 5–9.
    A wildly funny comedy from Australia about two teenage boys who solve a mystery. A real winner.

Collins, Tim. *Notes from a Totally Lame Vampire: Because the Undead have Feelings Too!* Illustrated by Andrew Pinder. Aladdin, 2010. 336 p. Grades 6–9.
    A wimpy 15-year-old vampire is doomed to stay at that awkward age forever, and there is nothing cool about him. A very funny British story.

Jennings, Richard. *Ghost Town.* Houghton Mifflin, 2009. 169 p. Grades 5–8.
    "Thirteen-year-old Spencer Honesty and his imaginary friend, an Indian called Chief Leopard Frog, improbably achieve fame and riches in the abandoned town of Paisley, Kansas, when Spencer begins taking photographs with his deceased father's ancient camera and Chief Leopard Frog has his poems published by a shady businessman in the Cayman Islands." LC

Korman, Gordon. *Born to Rock.* Hyperion, 2005. 261 p. Grades 7–10.
    "High school senior Leo Caraway, a conservative Republican, learns that his biological father is a punk rock legend." LC

Korman, Gordon. *Schooled.* Hyperion, 2007. 208 p. Grades 5–7.
    "Cap lives in isolation with his grandmother, a former hippie; but when she falls from a tree and breaks her hip, Cap is sent to a foster home where he has his first experience in a public school." LC. Nominated for many state young reader awards.

Korman, Gordon. *Son of the Mob.* Hyperion, 2002, 262 p. Grades 7–9.
    A very funny and hugely popular story about the son of a gangster and his girlfriend, the daughter of an FBI agent. Nominated for many state young reader awards. Sequel is *Son of the Mob: Hollywood Hustle,* 2006.

Lieb, Josh. *I Am a Genius of Unspeakable Evil and I Want to Be Your Class President.* Razorbill, 2009. 303 p. Grades 6–8.
    "Twelve-year-old evil genius, Oliver, uses his great brain to become the third richest person in the world, and finds that overthrowing foreign dictators is easier than getting the kids in his middle school to vote him class president." LC

Lubar, David. *Sleeping Freshmen Never Lie.* Dutton, 2005. 279 p. Grades 8–10.
"While navigating his first year of high school and awaiting the birth of his new baby brother, Scott loses old friends and gains some unlikely new ones as he hones his skills as a writer." LC. Lubar infuses this thoughtful book with generous doses of humor and wordplay.

McGowan, Anthony. *Jack Tumor.* Farrar, Straus & Giroux, 2009. 295 p. Grades 7–10.
"Fourteen-year-old Hector, suffering from severe headaches, is diagnosed with a brain tumor which speaks in his head, calling itself Jack Tumor and making an effort to improve Hector's home life, increase his popularity, and win him a girlfriend before the operation that will mean the end of one or both of them." LC

Paulsen, Gary. *Liar, Liar.* Wendy Lamb Books, 2011. 128 p. Grades 5–8.
"Fourteen-year-old Kevin is very good at lying and doing so makes life easier, but when he finds himself in big trouble with his friends, family, and teachers, he must find a way to end his lies forever." LC

Peck, Richard. *The Teacher's Funeral: A Novel in Three Parts.* Dial, 2004. 190 p. Grades 5–8.
When the much-despised elderly one-room schoolhouse teacher unexpected dies (she must have been at least 40!), Russell is horrified to find that his older sister Tansy is going to take over the job. His life, he knows, will be ruined. This is an absolute riot!

Seegert, Scott. *Vordak the Incomprehensible: How to Grow Up and Rule the World.* Egmont, 2010. 208 p. Grades 5–8.
"A top supervillain offers rules and advice to readers on how to develop an evil plan to rule the world." LC. First in an irreverent series that is bound to have kids laughing and wanting more.

Tolan, Stephanie S. *Surviving the Applewhites.* HarperCollins, 2002. 216 p. Grades 5–up.
Jake Semple knows how to scare people and how to look and act tough. No one has really ever let him do anything else. He was kicked out of his school in Rhode Island, sent to North Carolina to live with his grandfather, and kicked out again. Now he has a last chance—home schooling with one of the most eccentric families on the planet, the Applewhites. This is great fun and a heck of a good read. Was a Newbery Honor Book, 2002.

Chapter ⎯⎯⎯⎯⎯ 6

Mystery, Suspense, and Horror Books

Many young boys come to the library asking for scary books. Others love mysteries and want to read every book in various detective series. We've combined mystery, horror, and suspense here because sometimes they are hard to separate and often they appeal to the same kinds of readers. From the *A to Z Mysteries* all the way up to Rick Yancey's *Monstrumologist* series there is a wide range of books here to satisfy boys who like spine-tingling suspense.

YOUNGER GUYS

39 Clues **series, by various authors, published by Scholastic, Grades 3–8.**
Heavily promoted series in which kids, with clues from the books, cards, and website, can win actual monetary prizes as they solve the mystery. Reminiscent of *The Da Vinci Code.*

1. *The Maze of Bones,* by Rick Riordan, 2008
2. *One False Note,* by Gordon Korman, 2009
3. *The Sword Thief,* by Peter Lerangis, 2009
4. *Beyond the Grave,* by Jude Watson, 2009
5. *Black Circle,* by Patrick Carman, 2009
6. *In Too Deep,* by Jude Watson, 2009
7. *The Viper's Nest,* by Peter Lerangis, 2010
8. *The Emperor's Code,* by Gordon Korman, 2010
9. *Storm Warning,* by Linda Sue Park, 2010

10. *Into the Gauntlet,* by Margaret Peterson Haddix, 2010
    Extra: *The Black Book of Buried Secrets,* by Mallory Kass and Rick Riordan, 2010
11. *Vespers Rising,* by Rick Riordan, Peter Lerangis, Gordon Korman, and Jude Watson, 2011

39 Clues: Cahills vs. Vespers series, by various authors, published by Scholastic, Grades 3–8.
The follow-up series to the original *39 Clues* series.

1. *The Medusa Plot,* by Gordon Korman, 2011
2. *A King's Ransom,* by Jude Watson, 2011
3. *The Dead of Night,* by Peter Lerangis, 2012

Arnold, Louise. *Golden & Grey* series, published by McElderry, Grades 3–7.
"When a downhearted ghost becomes the 'invisible friend' of an eleven-year-old boy who is an outcast in his new school, the two help each other find their place in their respective worlds." LC

Golden & Grey: (An Unremarkable Boy and A Rather Remarkable Ghost), 2005
Golden & Grey: The Nightmares That Ghosts Have, 2006
Golden & Grey: A Good Day for Haunting, 2008

Balliett, Blue. Art mysteries series, published by Scholastic, Grades 4–7.
This series does not really have a name, but in the three (so far) books about the same characters, a boy, Calder, and a girl, Petra, solve several art-related mysteries. Nominated for multiple state young reader awards.

Chasing Vermeer, 2005
The Wright 3, 2007
The Calder Game, 2008

Barnett, Mac. *The Brixton Brothers* series, published by Simon & Schuster, Grades 4–7.
A 12-year-old fan of a Hardy Boys–like detective series suddenly finds himself in the middle of real mystery. Fun and funny.

1. *The Case of the Case of Mistaken Identity,* 2009
2. *The Ghostwriter Secret,* 2010
3. *It Happened on a Train,* 2011

Bellairs, John. *Anthony Monday* series, originally published by Dial, Grades 4–7.
John Bellairs wrote the following three series of really scary horror novels dealing with death and the supernatural. All end with no one being hurt! Most are illustrated by Edward Gorey. Bellairs died in 1991, but, as is only too appropriate, new titles have been appearing, thanks to a fan, Brad Strickland, who kept the series going. I love these.

The Treasure of Alpheus Winterborn, 1978
The Dark Secret of Weatherend, 1984
The Lamp from the Warlock's Tomb, 1988
The Mansion in the Mist, 1992

Bellairs, John. *Johnny Dixon* series, originally published by Dial, Grades 4–7.

The Curse of the Blue Figurine, 1983
The Mummy, the Will, and the Crypt, 1983
The Spell of the Sorcerer's Skull, 1984

The Revenge of the Wizard's Ghost, 1985
The Eyes of the Killer Robot, 1986
The Trolley to Yesterday, 1989
The Chessmen of Doom, 1989
The Secret of the Underground Room, 1990
The Drum, the Doll, and the Zombie (with Brad Strickland), 1994
The Hand of the Necromancer, by Brad Strickland, 1996
The Bell, the Book, and the Spellbinder, by Brad Strickland, 1997
The Wrath of the Grinning Ghost, by Brad Strickland, 1999

Bellairs, John. *Lewis Barnevelt* series, originally published by Dial, Grades 4–7.

The House with a Clock in its Walls, 1973
The Figure in the Shadows, 1975
The Letter, the Witch, and the Ring, 1976
The Ghost in the Mirror (with Brad Strickland), 1993
The Vengeance of the Witch-Finde (with Brad Strickland), 1993
The Doom of the Haunted Opera (with Brad Strickland), 1995
The Beast Under the Wizard's Bridge, by Brad Strickland, 2000
The Tower at the End of the World, by Brad Strickland, 2001
The Whistle, the Grave, and the Ghost, by Brad Strickland, 2003
The House Where Nobody Lived, by Brad Strickland, 2006
The Sign of the Sinister Sorcerer, by Brad Strickland, 2008

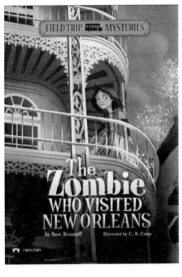

The Zombies Who Visited New Orleans by Steve Brezenoff.

Brezenoff, Steve. *Field Trip Mysteries* series, illustrated by C. B. Canga, published by Stone Arch Books, Grades 3–6.

Sixth grade friends Cat, Sam, Egg, and Gum solve mysteries while on field trips. Short chapters, fun stories. These books are not numbered.

The Burglar Who Bit the Big Apple, 2010
The Crook Who Crossed the Golden Gate Bridge, 2011
The Ghost Who Haunted the Capitol, 2011
The Painting That Wasn't There, 2011
The Teacher Who Forgot Too Much, 2010
The Village That Almost Vanished, 2011
The Zombie Who Visited New Orleans, 2010
The Zoo with the Empty Cage, 2010
The Cave That Shouldn't Have Collapsed, 2011
The Ride That Was Really Haunted, 2011
The Seals That Wouldn't Swim, 2011
The Symphony That Was Silent, 2011

The Curse of the Ancient Mask and Other Case Files by Simon Cheshire. Courtesy of Roaring Book Press, an imprint of the Macmillan Children's Publishing Group.

Cheshire, Simon. *Saxby Smart, Private Detective* series, published by Roaring Brook, Grades 4–6.

Ten-year-old Saxby wants to be one of the all time great detectives, and he makes a fine start of it in this enjoyable series.

The Curse of the Ancient Mask and Other Case Files, 2009
The Treasure of Dead Man's Lane and Other Case Files, 2010
The Pirate's Blood and Other Case Files, 2011

Chick, Bryan. *The Secret Zoo* **series, published by Greenwillow, Grades 4–6.**
"Noah and his friends follow a trail of mysterious clues to uncover a secret behind the walls of the Clarksville City Zoo—a secret that must be protected at all costs." LC

1. *The Secret Zoo,* 2010
2. *Secrets and Shadows,* 2011
3. *Riddles and Danger,* 2011

Dahl, Michael. *Library of Doom* **series, published by Stone Arch Books, Grades 3–8 (reading level is Grades 1–3).**
Scary but very easy to read. High interest, low vocabulary. Neither of these series is numbered.

Attack of the Paper Bats, 2007
The Book That Dripped Blood, 2007
The Cave of the Bookworms, 2008
Escape from the Pop-up Prison, 2008
The Beast Beneath the Stairs, 2007
The Poison Pages, 2007
The Creeping Bookends, 2008
The Eye in the Graveyard, 2007
The Golden Bowl of Death, 2008
The Smashing Scroll, 2007
The Twister Trap, 2008
The Word Eater, 2008

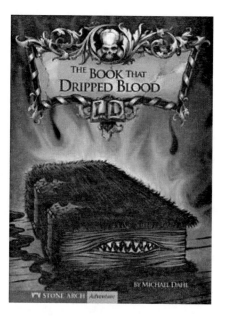

The Book That Dripped Blood by Michael Dahl.

Return to the Library of Doom **series (longer stories)**

Rats on the Page by Michael Dahl.

Blood in the Library, 2011
Dictionary of 1000 Rooms, 2011
Ghost Writer, 2011
Inkfoot, 2011
Killer App, 2011
Rats on the Page, 2011
The Book That Ate My Brother, 2011
The Sea of Lost Books, 2011
The Vampire Chapter, 2011
Zombie in the Library, 2011

Donbavand, Tommy. *Scream Street* **series, published by Candle-wick, Grades 3–6.**
Comedic horror stories about a vampire, a werewolf, and a mummy, good friends and intrepid adventurers.

1. *Fang of the Vampire,* 2009
2. *Blood of the Witch,* 2009
3. *Heart of the Mummy,* 2009

    4. *Flesh of the Zombie,* 2010
    5. *Skull of the Skeleton,* 2010
    6. *Claw of the Werewolf,* 2010

Falcone, L. M. *The Midnight Curse.* Kids Can, 2010. 208 p. Grades 3–6.
    "Eleven-year-old Charlie and his twin sister, Lacey, having traveled to England to claim an inheritance from their late great-uncle, learn they have until midnight to solve the mystery of a family curse that could spell doom for Charlie." LC. Fast-moving and very exciting.

Freeman, Martha. *Chickadee Court Mysteries* series, published by Holiday House, Grades 4–6.
    Two amateur detectives, Alex and his best friend, Yasmeen, age 11, solve crimes in their own neighborhood.

    1. *Who Stole Halloween?* 2008
    2. *Who is Stealing the Twelve Days of Christmas?* 2008
    3. *Who Stole Uncle Sam?* 2008
    4. *Who Stole Grandma's Million-Dollar Pumpkin Pie?* 2009

Hale, Bruce. *Chet Gecko, Private Eye* series, published by Harcourt, Grades 3–5.
    Chet Gecko is not only a lizard (with a helpful ability to shed his tail whenever he needs to), but also a fourth-grade detective at Emerson Hicky Elementary School. Silly.

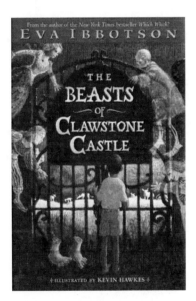

The Chameleon Wore Chartreuse, 2000
The Mystery of Mr. Nice, 2000
Farewell, My Lunchbag, 2001
The Big Nap, 2001
The Hamster of the Baskervilles, 2002
This Gum for Hire, 2002
The Malted Falcon, 2003
Trouble Is My Beeswax, 2003
Give My Regrets to Broadway, 2004
Murder, My Tweet, 2004
Chet Gecko's Detective Handbook (and Cookbook):
    Tips for Private Eyes & Snack Food Lovers, 2005
The Possum Always Rings Twice, 2006
Key Lardo, 2006
Hiss Me Deadly, 2007
From Russia with Lunch, 2009
Dial M for Mongoose, 2009

***The Beasts of Clawstone Castle* by Eva Ibbotson. Used by permission of Penguin Group (USA) Inc. All rights reserved.**

Ibbotson, Eva. *The Beasts of Clawstone Castle.* Illustrated by Kevin Hawkes. Dutton, 2006. 243 p. Grades 4–7.
    Madlyn and Rollo are not happy campers when they have to go spend the summer with their elderly great-aunt and great-uncle in crumbling Clawstone Castle in the north of England. But Clawstone has something really special: a herd of all white cattle. But the place needs money and what better to attract tourists than several of the most interesting ghosts you've ever read about! This author is one of the best around, and this makes a fine read aloud, full of mystery, suspense, and good humor.

Ibbotson, Eva. *Dial-a-Ghost.* Scholastic, 2002. Grades 4–7.

Oliver Smith discovers that he is the heir to a huge estate in northern England—but does not know that he has evil relatives who are his new guardians and want him dead. When a family of ghosts comes mistakenly to haunt the house, exciting things happen constantly.

Ibbotson, Eva. *The Haunting of Granite Falls.* Illustrated by Kevin Hawkes. Dutton, 2004. 216 pages Grades 4–7.

Alex MacBuff, who owns Carra Castle, was brought up by the ghosts that haunt the place. He loves them dearly, but he must sell the castle—and must ask them to leave. They love both Alex and their home, but they are willing to make the sacrifice to help him when a Texas millionaire buys the place, and decides to dismantle it and take it back home and put it up again. Eva Ibbotson has the most creative mind around, and kids will love this one. Few more lovable ghosts exist in children's literature!

Klise, Kate. *43 Old Cemetery Road* series, published by Harcourt, Grades 3–6.

Lots of graphics and humor light up these stories about an author with writer's block, a ghost, and an 11-year-old boy. The first book was nominated for several state young reader awards.

1. *Dying to Meet You,* 2009
2. *Over My Dead Body,* 2009
3. *Till Death Do Us Bark,* 2011

Krieg, Jim. *Griff Carver, Hallway Patrol.* Razorbill, 2010. 240 p. Grades 4–7.

"Legendary Griff Carver joins the Rampart Middle School Hallway Patrol and with the help of his new friends, solves the case of counterfeit hall passes." LC. Starred review in *Booklist.*

Lalicki, Tom. *Houdini and Nate Mystery* series, illustrated by Carlyn Beccia, published by Farrar, Straus & Giroux, Grades 3–6.

When 12-year-old Nate meets the great magician in a hat shop in 1911, he has no idea that the two will become partners in solving mysteries. Fun.

Danger in the Dark, 2006
Shots at Sea, 2007
Frame-Up on the Bowery, 2009

Lancett, Peter. *Dark Man* series, published by Saddleback Educational, Grades 3–6.

The Dark Man fights the demons employed by the evil Shadow Masters. Lots of mood, mystery, and appeal for reluctant readers in this British series. Interest level is higher than the extremely low reading level. Lots of white space; very little text.

Danger in the Dark, 2010
Dying for the Dark, 2010
Killer in the Dark, 2010
The Dark Dreams, 2010
The Dark Glass, 2010
The Dark Machine, 2010
The Dark Side of Magic, 2010
The Dark Waters of Time, 2010
The Day is Dark, 2010
The Shadow in the Dark, 2010

Lincoln, Christopher. *Billy Bones: A Tale from the Secrets Closet.* Little, Brown, 2008. 287 p. Grades 4–7.

"The secrets of High Manners Manor, carefully guarded in a closet by Billy and his skeleton parents, begin to unravel when the orphan Millicent arrives and the two children start uncovering ghosts, apparitions, and scurrilous lies that have been festering in the house for far too long." LC. The sequel is *The Road to Nevermore*, 2009.

Lorey, Dean. *Nightmare Academy* series, published by HarperCollins, Grades 4–7.

Rescued from a very sheltered life, 13-year-old Charlie learns that the monsters of his nightmares are real when he becomes a student at Nightmare Academy and begins training to harness his powers to fight terrible creatures and return them to the Netherworld.

1. *Monster Hunters,* 2007
2. *Monster Madness,* 2008
3. *Monster War,* 2010

Loux, Matthew. *Salt Water Taffy: The Seaside Adventures of Jack and Benny* series, published by Oni, Grades 3–6.

Middle grade adventurers enjoy these stories about two brothers who solve mysteries in their seaside hometown.

The Legend of Old Salty, 2008
A Climb up Mt. Barnabas, 2008
The Truth about Doctor True, 2009
Caldera's Revenge, 2011

Malone, Marianne. *The Sixty-Eight Rooms.* Illustrated by Greg Call. Random House, 2010. 227 p. Grades 4–6.

On a field trip to the Art Institute of Chicago, Jack and Ruthie find a key that leads them to a mystery and adventure as they shrink to tiny size and enter the 68 miniature Thorne Rooms.

Mass, Wendy. *The Candymakers.* Little, Brown, 2010. 153 p. Grades 4–8.

"Four gifted twelve-year-olds, including Logan, the candymaker's son, are set to be contestants in the Confectionary Association's national competition to determine the nation's tastiest sweet, but nobody anticipates that a friendship will form between them." LC. Starred review in *Kirkus*.

McKenzie, Riford. *The Witches of Dredmoore Hollow.* Illustrated by Peter Ferguson. Marshall Cavendish, 2008. 264 p. Grades 4–7.

"Elijah, a nearly 12-year-old boy growing up on a farm in rural New England in 1927, makes the shocking discovery that his mother is a witch when two strangely glamorous aunts arrive, who are suspiciously interested in his first chin whisker, to spirit him away to Moaning Marsh." LC. Lots of action and adventure.

Montgomery, Lewis B. *Milo & Jazz Mysteries* series, published by Kane, Grades 2–4.

Milo and Jazz are two kids who want to be detectives and decide to join forces to solve mysteries. *Booklist* called the first book one of the top 10 crime fiction novels for youth.

1. *The Case of the Stinky Socks,* 2009
2. *The Case of the Poisoned Pig,* 2009
3. *The Case of the Haunted Haunted House,* 2009

4. *The Case of the Amazing Zelda,* 2009
5. *The Case of the July 4 Jinx,* 2010
6. *The Case of the Missing Moose,* 2011

Mould, Chris. *Something Wickedly Weird* series, published by Roaring Brook, Grades 3–6.

Eleven-year-old Stanley Buggle inherits a huge old house from his great-uncle, but learns, on his first visit, that his relative was a pirate and a thief—and that the village the house is in is full of pirates, thieves, and at least one werewolf. Fun.

1. *The Wooden Mile,* 2008
2. *The Icy Hand,* 2008
3. *The Silver Casket,* 2009
4. *The Darkling Cave,* 2009
5. *The Smuggler's Mine,* 2010
6. *The Treasure Keepers,* 2010

The Icy Hand **by Chris Mould. Courtesy of Roaring Book Press, an imprint of the Macmillan Children's Publishing Group.**

Peterson, Will. *Triskellion* series, published by Candlewick, Grades 4–9.

"After their parents' divorce, Rachel and Adam are sent to live with their grandmother in the English village of Triskellion, where they find danger and paranormal activity as they discover hidden secrets that some will kill to keep buried." LC

1. *Triskellion,* 2008
2. *The Burning,* 2009
3. *The Gathering,* 2010

Poblocki, Dan. *The Stone Child.* Random House, 2009. 278 p. Grades 4–7.
"When friends Eddie, Harris, and Maggie discover that the scary adventures in their favorite author's fictional books come true, they must find a way to close the portal that allows evil creatures and witches to enter their hometown of Gatesweed." LC

Ramthun, Bonnie. *The White Gates.* Random House, 2008. 245 p. Grades 4–8.
"When his mother becomes the doctor in Snow Park, Colorado, 12-year-old Tor learns of a curse placed on the town's doctors many years before by an eccentric Ute woman, but suspects that a villain is hiding behind that curse." LC. Nominated for multiple state young reader awards.

Rand, Jonathan. *American Chillers* series, published by Audiocraft, Grades 4–7.

These are self-published, but teachers and librarians all over the country are saying boys absolutely love them. Rand started publishing them in 2002, and they are not in any order.

Alien Androids Assault Arizona, 2004
Creepy Condors of California, 2004
Curse of the Connecticut Coyotes, no publication date found

Dangerous Dolls of Delaware, 2003
Florida Fog Phantoms, 2002
Haunting in New Hampshire, 2007
Invisible Iguanas of Illinois, 2002

Iron Insects Invade Indiana, 2003
Kentucky Komodo Dragons, 2009
Michigan Mega-Monsters, 2001
Minnesota Mall Mannequins, 2002
Mississippi Megladon, 2008
Missouri Madhouse, 2003
Mutant Mammoths of Montana, 2007
Nebraska Nightcrawlers, 2004
New York Ninjas, 2002
North Dakota Night Dragons, 2006
Nuclear Jellyfish of New Jersey, 2007
Ogres of Ohio, 2002
Oklahoma Outbreak, 2008

Oregon Oceanauts, no publication date found
Poisonous Pythons Paralyze Pennsylvania, 2003
South Carolina Sea Creatures, 2005
Terrible Tractors of Texas, 2002
Terrifying Toys of Tennessee, 2007
Vicious Vacuums of Virginia, no publication date found
Virtual Vampires of Vermont, 2004
Washington Wax Museum, 2005
Wicked Velociraptors of West Virginia, 2006
Wisconsin Werewolves, 2003

Roy, Ron. *A to Z Mysteries* **series, published by Random House, Grades 1–4.**

Very simple, enjoyable mysteries about three young friends, Dink, Josh, and Ruth Rose, who solve mysteries in their hometown of Green Lawn, Connecticut. The books can be read in any order.

1. *The Absent Author,* 1998
2. *The Bald Bandit,* 1998
3. *The Canary Caper,* 1998
4. *The Deadly Dungeon,* 1998
5. *The Empty Envelope,* 1998
6. *The Falcon's Feathers,* 1998
7. *The Goose's Gold,* 1999
8. *The Haunted Hotel,* 1999
9. *The Invisible Island,* 1999
10. *The Jaguar's Jewel,* 2000
11. *The Kidnapped King,* 2000
12. *The Lucky Lottery,* 2000
13. *The Missing Mummy,* 2001
14. *The Ninth Nugget,* 2001
15. *The Orange Outlaw,* 2001
16. *The Panda Puzzle,* 2002
17. *The Quicksand Question,* 2002
18. *The Runaway Racehorse,* 2002
19. *The School Skeleton,* 2003
20. *The Talking T. Rex,* 2003
21. *The Unwilling Umpire,* 2004
22. *The Vampire's Vacation,* 2004
23. *The White Wolf,* 2004
24. *The X'ed out X-Ray,* 2005
25. *The Yellow Yacht,* 2005
26. *The Zombie Zone,* 2005
27. *Super Edition 1 Detective Camp,* 2006
28. *Super Edition 2 Mayflower Treasure Hunt,* 2007
29. *Super Edition 3 White House White-Out,* 2008
30. *Super Edition 4 Sleepy Hollow Sleepover,* 2010

San Souci, Robert D. *Dare to Be Scared* **series, illustrated by David Ouimet, published by Cricket Books, Grades 4–8.**

Kids who enjoy being scared—and who doesn't—enjoy these anthologies of spooky and scary stories.

1. *Dare to Be Scared: Thirteen Stories to Chill and Thrill,* 2003
2. *Double-Dare to Be Scared: Another Thirteen Chilling Tales,* 2004
3. *Triple-Dare to Be Scared: Thirteen Further Freaky Tales,* 2007
4. *Dare to Be Scared 4: Thirteen More Tales of Terror,* 2009

San Souci, Robert D. *Haunted Houses.* Henry Holt, 2010. 288 p. Grades 4–8.

A collection of 10 spooky stories about haunted houses. This will not sit on your shelves.

Santopolo, Jill. *Alec Flint, Super Sleuth* series, published by Scholastic, Grades 3–5.

Fourth grader Alec solves mysteries with his friend Gina. Lots of fun.

1. *The Nina, the Pinta, and the Vanishing Treasure,* 2008
2. *The Ransom Note Blues,* 2009

Schwartz, Alvin *Scary Stories to Tell in the Dark* series, published by HarperCollins, Grades 4–9.

These new editions with illustrations by Brett Helquist, published in 2010, are genuine classics, always popular, and still as scary and delicious as they ever were.

Scary Stories to Tell in the Dark, 1991, 2010
More Scary Stories to Tell in the Dark, 1984, 2010
Scary Stories 3, 1991 (does not have a new edition and appears to be out of print)

The Ransom Note Blues by Jill Santopolo.

Sherry, Maureen. *Walls within Walls.* Illustrated by Adam Stower. HarperCollins, 2010. 368 p. Grades 4–7.

"When the Smithfork family moves into a lavish Manhattan apartment building, they discover clues to a decades-old mystery hidden behind the walls of their new home." LC

Sinden, David, Matthew Morgan, and Guy MacDonald. *Awfully Beastly Business* series, illustrated by Jonny Duddle, published by Aladdin, Grades 4–7.

Ulf is a young werewolf who lives on a preserve run by people who wish to prevent cruelty to beasts. Funny and full of adventure.

Werewolf vs. Dragon, 2009
Sea Monsters and Other Delicacies, 2009
Bang Goes the Troll, 2009
The Jungle Vampire, 2009
Battle of the Zombies, 2009

Sobol, Donald. *Encyclopedia Brown* series, published by various publishers, Grades 3–6.

Encyclopedia Brown, boy detective, has been around solving at least 10 cases per book, for just about as long as any librarian living has been working. All of them have been reissued multiple times. They still work and they are still popular. Lots of fun! Apparently the publishers changed the numbering of these books, as indicated by numbers in parentheses in the following list.

1. *Encyclopedia Brown, Boy Detective,* 1963
2. *Encyclopedia Brown Strikes Again (The Case of the Secret Pitch),* 1965
3. *Encyclopedia Brown Finds the Clues,* 1966
4. *Encyclopedia Brown Gets His Man,* 1967
5. *Encyclopedia Brown Solves Them All,* 1968
6. *Encyclopedia Brown Keeps the Peace,* 1969
7. *Encyclopedia Brown Saves the Day,* 1970
8. *Encyclopedia Brown Tracks Them Down,* 1971
9. *Encyclopedia Brown Shows the Way,* 1972
10. *Encyclopedia Brown Takes the Case,* 1973

11. *Encyclopedia Brown Lends a Hand,* 1974, reissued as *Encyclopedia Brown and the Case of the Exploding Plumbing and Other Mysteries*
12. *Encyclopedia Brown and the Case of the Dead Eagles,* 1975
13. *Encyclopedia Brown and the Case of the Midnight Visitor,* 1977
14. *Encyclopedia Brown Carries On,* 1980
15. *Encyclopedia Brown Sets the Pace,* 1981
16. (15 1/2) *Encyclopedia Brown Takes the Cake* (co-written with Glenn Andrews), 1982
17. (16) *Encyclopedia Brown and the Case of the Mysterious Handprints,* 1985
18. (17) *Encyclopedia Brown and the Case of the Treasure Hunt,* 1988
19. (18) *Encyclopedia Brown and the Case of the Disgusting Sneakers,* 1990,
20. (19) *Encyclopedia Brown and the Case of the Two Spies,* 1995
21. (20) *Encyclopedia Brown and the Case of Pablo's Nose,* (1996); (21) *Encyclopedia Brown and the Case of the Sleeping Dog,* 1998
22. *Encyclopedia Brown and the Case of the Slippery Salamander,* 2000
23. *Encyclopedia Brown and the Case of the Jumping Frogs,* 2003
24. *Encyclopedia Brown Cracks the Case,* 2007
25. *Encyclopedia Brown, Super Sleuth,* 2009

Stewart, Paul. *Barnaby Grimes* series, illustrated by Chris Riddell, published by Random House, Grades 4–6.

Historical horror stories featuring a young, fast, and punctual messenger who keeps getting involved with supernatural creatures.

Curse of the Night Wolf, 2008
Return of the Emerald Skull, 2009
Legion of the Dead, 2010
Phantom of Blood Alley, 2010

Stine, R. L. *Ghosts of Fear Street* series, published by Aladdin, Grades 3–6.

The Attack of the Aqua Apes and Nightmare in 3-D: Twice Terrifying Tales, 2009
The Boy Who Ate Fear Street, 2011
Fright Knight and The Ooze: Twice Terrifying Tales, 2010
Hide and Shriek and Who's Been Sleeping in My Grave? Twice Terrifying Tales, 2009
How to Be a Vampire, 2011
Night of the Werecat, 2011
Revenge of the Shadow People, and the Bugman Lives! Twice Terrifying Tales, 2010
Stay Away from the Tree House and Eye of the Fortuneteller: Twice Terrifying Tales, 2009

Stine, R. L. *Goosebumps HorrorLand*, published by Scholastic, Grades 4–7.

The ever-so-popular (at one time) *Goosebumps* author is back with a series of horror novels.

1. *Welcome to HorrorLand: A Survival Guide,* 2009
2. *Revenge of the Living Dummy,* 2008
3. *Creep from the Deep,* 2008
4. *Monster Blood for Breakfast!* 2008
5. *The Scream of the Haunted Mask,* 2008
6. *Dr. Maniac vs. Robby Schwartz,* 2008
7. *Who's Your Mummy?* 2009

8. *My Friends Call Me Monster,* 2009
9. *Say Cheese—and Die Screaming!* 2009
10. *Welcome to Camp Slither,* 2009
11. *Help! We Have Strange Powers!* 2009
12. *Escape From HorrorLand,* 2009
13. *The Streets of Panic Park,* 2009
14. *When the Ghost Dog Howls,* 2010
15. *Little Shop of Hamsters,* 2010
16. *Heads, You Lose,* 2010
17. *Weirdo Halloween: Special Edition,* 2010
18. *The Wizard of Ooze,* 2010
19. *Slappy New Year,* 2010
20. *The Horror at Chiller House,* 2011
21. *Claws!,* 2011
22. *Night of the Giant Everything,* 2011
23. *The Five Masks of Dr. Screem: Special Edition,* 2011

Tashjian, Janet. *My Life as a Book.* Illustrated by Jake Tashjian. Henry Holt, 2010. 224 p. Grades 4–7.

Dubbed a "reluctant reader" by his teacher, 12-year-old Derek spends summer vacation learning important lessons even though he does not complete his summer reading list. There's a mystery and a great deal for Wimpy Kid fans to like here.

Torrey, Michele. *Doyle and Fossey, Science Detectives* series, illustrated by Barbara Johansen Newman, published by Sterling, Grades 2–5.

Humorous stories about a fifth grade boy and a girl who are science detectives. They solve mysteries using the scientific method, and there are experiments at the ends of the books. Good reads.

1. *The Case of the Mossy Lake Monster,* 2002, 2009
2. *The Case of the Gasping Garbage (and Other Super-Scientific Cases),* 2009
3. *The Case of the Graveyard Ghost (and Other Super-Scientific Cases),* 2009
4. *The Case of the Barfy Birthday (and Other Super-Scientific Cases),* 2009
5. *The Case of the Crooked Carnival (and Other Super-Scientific Cases),* 2010
6. *The Case of the Terrible T. Rex (and Other Super-Scientific Cases),* 2010

Van Draanen, Wendelin. *Gecko & Sticky* series, illustrated by Stephen Gilpin, published by Alfred A. Knopf Books for Young Readers, Grades 3–5.

Aspiring 13-year-old-detective Dave Sanchez and his mouthy pet gecko humorously solve mysteries. Good adventures.

1. *Villain's Lair,* 2009
2. *Greatest Power,* 2009
3. *Sinister Substitute,* 2010
4. *Power Potion,* 2010

Van Eekhout, Greg. *Kid vs. Squid.* Bloomsbury, 2010 196 p. Grades 4–6.

In the summer before he enters seventh grade, Thatcher helps out his great-uncle Griswold, who runs a sort of museum of curiosities in a coastal town in California. Things start happening when Thatcher finds that one of the shriveled-up curiosities is actually the head of a witch, who still controls the people of Atlantis—who happen to be all around him. Funny and creepy.

Watson, Geof. *Edison's Gold.* Egmont, 2010. 320 p. Grades 4–7.

"Tom Edison, the 13-year-old great-great-grandson of the famous inventor, finds a clue to his ancestor's legendary secret formula for changing metal into gold, and while he searches desperately for the key to the life-changing discovery, he must also evade billionaire Curtis Keller and his minions, who want the formula to seize control of the world." LC

OLDER GUYS

Abrahams, Peter. *Reality Check.* HarperTeen, 2009. 330 p. Grades 8–up.

"After a knee injury destroys sixteen-year-old Cody's college hopes, he drops out of high school and gets a job in his small Montana town; but when his ex-girlfriend disappears from her Vermont boarding school, Cody travels cross-country to join the search." LC. Nominated for multiple state young reader awards.

Anderson, M. T. *The Game of Sunken Places* **series, published by Scholastic, Grades 5–8.**

"When two boys stay with an eccentric relative at his mansion in rural Vermont, they discover an old-fashioned board game that draws them into a mysterious adventure." LC

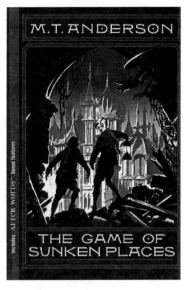

The Game of Sunken Places by **M.T. Anderson.**

The Game of Sunken Places, 2005
The Suburb Beyond the Stars, 2010
The Empire of Gut and Bone, 2011

Balliett, Blue. *The Danger Box.* Scholastic, 2010. 320 p. Grades 5–8.

"In small-town Michigan, 12-year-old Zoomy and his new friend Lorrol investigate the journal found inside a mysterious box and find family secrets and a more valuable treasure, while a dangerous stranger watches and waits." LC. Starred review in *School Library Journal.*

Bell, Cathleen Davit. *Slipping.* Bloomsbury, 2008. 216 p. Grades 6–9.

"Thirteen-year-old Michael and an unlikely group of allies journey to the river of the dead to help Michael's grandfather release his hold on a ghostly life and, in the process, heal wounds that have kept Michael's father distant." LC

Berk, Josh. *The Dark Days of Hamburger Halpin.* Alfred A. Knopf Books for Young Readers, 2010. 250 p. Grades 6–9.

"When Will Halpin transfers from his all-deaf school into a mainstream Pennsylvania high school, he faces discrimination and bullying, but still manages to solve a mystery surrounding the death of a popular football player in his class." LC

Black, Bekka. *iDrakula.* Sourcebooks Fire, 2010. 160 p. Grades 7–up.

Fast-moving version of the famous story, told through emails, text messages, screenshots, and attachments.

Bodeen, S.A. *The Gardener.* Feiwel and Friends, 2010. 234 p. Grades 7–10.

"When high school sophomore Mason finds a beautiful but catatonic girl in the nursing home where his mother works, the discovery leads him to revelations about a series of disturbing human experiments that have a connection to his own life." LC

Brewer, Heather. *Chronicles of Vladimir Tod* series, published by Dutton, Grades 5–9.

Vlad believes he is half-vampire, perhaps the only real vampire still alive in the world, and he is not sure what to do with himself. Lots of fun for vampire fans.

1. *Eighth Grade Bites*, 2008
2. *Ninth Grade Slays*, 2009
3. *Tenth Grade Bleeds*, 2010
4. *Eleventh Grade Burns*, 2010
5. *Twelfth Grade Kills*, 2010

Bruchac, Joseph. *Night Wings.* HarperCollins, 2009. 195 p. Grades 5–8.

"After being taken captive by a band of treasure seekers, thirteen-year-old Paul and his Abenaki grandfather must face a legendary Native American monster at the top of Mount Washington." LC

Carey, Benedict. *The Unknowns.* Amulet, 2009. 262 p. Grades 5–9.

"When people start vanishing from a godforsaken trailer park next to the Folsom Energy Plant, two eleven-year-olds investigate using mathematical clues that were hastily planted by their friend Mrs. Clarke before she disappeared." LC

***Eighth Grade Bites* by Heather Brewer. Used by permission of Penguin Group (USA) Inc. All rights reserved.**

***Skeleton Creek* by Patrick Carman.**

Carman, Patrick. *Skeleton Creek* series, published by Scholastic, Grades 5–8.

What is going on in the haunted woods by Skeleton Creek? Ryan writes down his observations and activities, and Sarah videotapes interesting (scary) things. To get the full story, you have to experience them both—and the author's website makes that possible.

1. *Skeleton Creek,* 2009
2. *The Ghost in the Machine,* 2009
3. *The Crossbones,* 2010
4. *The Raven,* 2011

Cooney, Caroline. *If the Witness Lied.* Delacorte, 2009. 215 p. Grades 6–9.

A thrilling read about four kids whose parents have died tragically and whose aunt sells their story to a reality show. A page-turner with bad guys. Nominated for multiple state young reader awards.

Corrigan, Eireann. *Accomplice.* Scholastic, 2010. 296 p. Grades 7–up.

"High school juniors and best friends Finn and Chloe hatch a daring plot to fake Chloe's disappearance from their rural New Jersey town in order to have something compelling to put on their college applications, but unforeseen events complicate matters." LC

Coville, Bruce. *Oddest of All.* Harcourt, 2008. 185 p. Grades 5–8.
  Nine creepy, frightening, funny stories entertain fans of anything eerie.

Dahl, Michael. *Finnegan Zwake* series, published by Simon & Schuster, Grades 5–9.
  Middle schooler Finnegan Zwake lives with his mystery-writer Uncle Stoppard in Minneapolis, but travels to exotic locales around the world to solve mysteries, especially those associated with the disappearance of his archaeologist parents. Funny and exciting.

When I Was Joe **by Keren David. Courtesy of Farrar Straus Giroux Books for Young Readers, an imprint of the Macmillan Children's Publishing Group.**

  The Horizontal Man, 1999
  The Worm Tunnel, 1999
  The Ruby Raven, 1999
  The Viking Claw, 2001
  The Coral Coffin, 2002

David, Keren. *When I Was Joe.* Frances Lincoln, 2010. 364 p. Grades 6–10.
  "Ty changes his identity after witnessing a murder and being forced to join a witness protection program, but he draws attention to himself when girls become interested in him and he succeeds as a runner in his new high school." LC. Starred review in *Kirkus.*

Delaney, Joseph. *The Last Apprentice* series, published by Greenwillow, Grades 5–up.
  Will Thomas Ward be The Spook's last apprentice? His beloved mother, who seems to know an awful lot about many things, says so. Thomas is the seventh son of a seventh son, and thus eligible to be apprenticed to the feared, lonely man who travels the County seeking out and fighting evil in what seems to be England in around 1700. Thomas meets ghosts and witches and boggarts—and learns to deal with them. These are truly scary, riveting, compellingly good reads.

  Revenge of the Witch, 2005
  Curse of the Bane, 2006
  Night of the Soul Stealer, 2007
  Attack of the Fiend, 2008
  Wrath of the Bloodeye, 2008
  The Spook's Tale, 2009
  Clash of the Demons, 2009
  Coven of Witches, 2010
  Rise of the Huntress, 2010
  Rage of the Fallen, 2011

Dowd, Siobhan. *The London Eye Mystery.* David Fickling, 2008. 323 p. Grades 5–up.
  Ted and Kat's cousin Samil wants to ride the London Eye the first time he visits them in London; he gets into the pod alone with 20 other people, and does not get out. The pod is sealed. The wheel went completely around. What happened to him? Ted, who has some unnamed form of Asperger's, has nine theories. This is a real mystery and a can't-put-it-down read!

Feldman, Jody. *The Seventh Level.* Greenwillow, 2010. 336 p. Grades 5–8.

"Twelve-year-old Travis is invited to become a member of The Legend, Lauer Middle School's most exclusive secret society, but first he must solve seven puzzles." LC

Ferrairolo, Jack D. *The Big Splash.* Amulet, 2008. 280 p. Grades 5–8.

"Matt Stevens, an average middle schooler with a glib tongue and a knack for solving crimes, uncovers a mystery while working with "the organization," a mafia-like syndicate run by seventh-grader Vincent "Mr. Biggs" Biggio, specializing in forged hall passes, test-copying rings, black market candy selling, and taking out hits with water guns." LC

Ford, John C. *The Morgue and Me.* Viking, 2009. 314 p. Grades 7–up.

"Eighteen-year-old Christopher, who plans to be a spy, learns of a murder cover-up through his summer job as a morgue assistant and teams up with Tina, a gorgeous newspaper reporter, to investigate, despite great danger." LC

Author Spotlight: Chris Grabenstein

Chris Grabenstein, author of *Riley Mack and the Other Known Troublemakers* as well as the award-winning *Haunted Mystery* series, loved to read when he was a kid—especially Mad magazine and Mad books. He also loved the short stories of Edgar Allan Poe and O. Henry and all sorts of historical novels, including one called *If the South Had Won the Civil War*. When he was in his 30s, Chris realized that he had something of an incomplete literary education and went back to read all the books he probably should've read when he was younger, devouring *The Three Musketeers*, *The Last Of The Mohicans*, *Treasure Island*, and all the rip-roaring classics. His work today is influenced by Stephen King (for strong characters and narrative voice), James Patterson (for page-turning excitement), and William Shakespeare, who knew you always had to write in enough funny stuff so people would stick around for the heavy stuff.

Chris Grabenstein Recommends

Holes by Louis Sachar. Funny, exciting, and full of heart.

Harry Potter series by J. K. Rowling. A great retelling of the classic orphan story.

The Dangers Days Of Daniel X by James Patterson. It's a comic book come to life; a world filled and fueled by imagination.

The Hunger Games by Suzanne Collins (for seventh and eighth graders). Talk about a movie in your mind. The author builds an unbelievably real and terrifying world.

Gibbs, Stuart. *Belly Up.* Simon & Schuster, 2009, 304 p. Grades 5–8.

When FunJungle's star attraction, Henry the Hippo, dies mysteriously, 12-year-old Teddy decides to investigate. He thinks it was murder. Lots of action and fun here!

Giles, Stephen M. *The Body Thief: The Death (and Further Adventures) of Silas Winterbottom.* Sourcebooks Jabberwocky, 2010. 240 p. Grades 5–7.

"Lured to their sick Uncle Silas's home under the pretense of becoming heirs to his vast fortune, cousins Adele, Isabella, and Milo soon learn that the old man has a diabolical plan to prevent his own death." LC

Grabenstein, Chris. *Haunted Mystery* series, published by Random House, Grades 5–8.

All sorts of terrifying supernatural creatures seem to find Zack Jennings wherever he goes. Scary, guaranteed kid pleasers!

1. *The Crossroads,* 2008
2. *The Hanging Hill,* 2009
3. *The Smoky Corridor,* 2010

Grisham, John. *Theodore Boone: Kid Lawyer.* Dutton, 2010. 263 p. Grades 5–8.

Theodore, middle school son of two attorneys, wants to be a trial lawyer and freely gives his classmates legal advice. Exciting things happen when he unexpectedly becomes involved in a big murder trial. Followed by *Theodore Boone: The Abduction,* 2011.

Hahn, Mary Downing. *Closed for the Season: A Mystery Story.* Clarion, 2009. 183 p. Grades 5–8.

"When thirteen-year-old Logan and his family move into a run-down old house in rural Virginia, he discovers that a woman was murdered there and becomes involved with his neighbor Arthur in a dangerous investigation to try to uncover the killer." LC. Nominated for many state young reader awards.

Henderson, Jason. *Vampire Rising, Book One.* HarperTeen, 2010. 256 p. Grades 6–10

Fourteen-year-old Alex discovers his last name is not just famous: it comes with a heritage. Alex, too, is a vampire hunter, and vampires are out to get him! Very exciting! This is the first in a planned *Alex Van Helsing* series. Starred review in *School Library Journal.*

Hoffman, Mary. *The Falconer's Knot: A Story of Friars, Flirtation and Foul Play.* Bloomsbury, 2007. 297 p. Grades 6–up.

In 1316, Silvano, falsely accused of murder, finds sanctuary in a monastery near Assisi. In the neighboring convent, a beautiful teenager whose brother forced her to become a postulant, sees him and is immediately attracted. As both are involved in mixing pigments for the Basilica of Saint Francis, a series of murders in the monastery creates mystery, suspense, and excitement. This reads more like an adult mystery, but it is darn hard to put down!

Holt, Simon. *The Devouring* series, published by Little, Brown, Grades 6–10.

Although the heroine is female, she has a brother who is possessed by a demon and a male best friend. Juicy, can't-stop-reading horror stories.

1. *The Devouring,* 2008
2. *Soulstice,* 2009
3. *Fearscape,* 2010

Hoobler, Dorothy, and Thomas Hoobler. *Samurai Detective* **series, published by Philomel, Grades 6–up.**

These books, set in 18th-century feudal Japan, are outstandingly reviewed and were nominated for many state young reader awards.

1. *The Ghost in the Tokaido Inn,* 1999
2. *The Demon in the Teahouse,* 2001
3. *In Darkness, Death,* 2004, 2005 (Edgar Allan Poe Award for best YA mystery)
4. *The Sword That Cut the Burning Grass,* 2005
5. *A Samurai Never Fears Death,* 2007
6. *Seven Paths to Death,* 2008

Horowitz, Anthony. *Gatekeepers* **series, published by Scholastic, Grades 5–8.**

Lots of excitement and adventure fill this story of the gatekeepers, teenagers chosen to save the world from the Old Ones.

1. *Raven's Gate,* 2005
2. *Evil Star,* 2006
3. *Nightrise,* 2007
4. *Necropolis,* 2009

Horowitz, Anthony. *Horowitz Horror* **series, published by Philomel, Grades 6–9.**

Three books full of short horror stories by Horowitz. Kids love them!

Horowitz Horror, 2006
More Horowitz Horror, 2007
Bloody Horowitz, 2010

***Raven's Gate* by Anthony Horowitz.**

Jones, Kari. *Storm Tide.* Orca, 2011. 128 p. Grades 5–8.
"A mysterious stranger visits the island where Simon and his sister Ellen live, bringing with him an unexpected storm and a riddle that may lead to treasure." LC

Karlsson, Val. *The Protectors.* Darby Creek, 2010. 112 p. Grades 5–8.
"After the accident that killed Luke's mother, he begins to get messages from the bodies in the funeral home where he lives with his stepfather, who is acting even stranger than usual, and in trying to solve his mother's death, he uncovers a horrifying secret." LC

Kenyon, Sheilynn. *Chronicles of Nick* **series, published by St. Martin's Griffin, Grades 7–up.**

After 14-year-old Nick makes enemies of his friends for refusing to mug an innocent tourist, he takes up with Kyrian of Thrace, a vampire slayer and Dark-Hunter who introduces Nick to a dangerous world where he must find strength within himself to survive battles with demons.

Infinity, 2010
Invincible, 2011

Kirby, Matthew. *The Clockwork Three*. Scholastic, 2010. 391 p. Grades 5–7.

"As mysterious circumstances bring Giuseppe, Frederick, and Hannah together, their lives soon interlock like the turning gears in a clock and they realize that each one holds a key to solving the others' mysteries." LC. Starred review in *Kirkus*.

Lake, Nick. *Blood Ninja* series, published by Simon & Schuster, Grades 7–11.

"After his father is murdered and a ninja saves his life, Taro discovers the connection between ninjas and vampires and finds himself being dragged into a bitter conflict between the rival lords ruling Japan." LC

  1. *Blood Ninja,* 2009
  2. *The Revenge of Lord Oda,* 2010

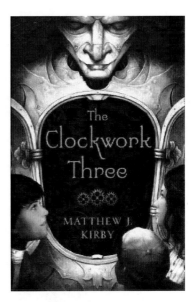

The Clockwork Three by Matthew Kirby.

Landy, Derek. *Skulduggery Pleasant* series, illustrated by Tom Percival, published by HarperCollins, Grades 5–8.

"When twelve-year-old Stephanie inherits her weird uncle's estate, she must join forces with Skulduggery Pleasant, a skeleton mage, to save the world from the Faceless Ones." LC. Though the heroine is female, boys like it. Nominated for several state young reader awards.

  1. *Skulduggery Pleasant,* 2007
  2. *Playing with Fire,* 2008
  3. *The Faceless Ones,* 2009
  4. *Dark Days,* 2011

Lane, Andrew. *Sherlock Holmes: The Legend Begins* series, published by Farrar, Straus & Giroux, Grades 6–9.

Fourteen-year-old Sherlock begins his detective career on vacation at his uncle's estate. This is the first teen series to be granted endorsement by the Arthur Conan Doyle literary estate.

  1. *Death Cloud,* 2011
  2. *Rebel Fire,* 2012

Death Cloud by Andrew Lane. Courtesy of Farrar Straus Giroux Books for Young Readers, an imprint of the Macmillan Children's Publishing Group.

Lang, Diane, and Michael Buchanan. *The Fat Boy Chronicles*. Sleeping Bear, 2010. 224 p. Grades 6–9.

"Jimmy Winterpock, 187 pounds at the age of fourteen, finds the constant taunts over his weight difficult to bear, but his life changes when his friend Paul enlists him in helping solve a local murder case." LC

Leck, James. *The Adventures of Jack Lime*. Kids Can, 2010. 126 p. Grades 5–8.

"Collects three adventures in which teenager Jack Lime, a self-made private investigator, looks into problems for his classmates while dealing with cases involving hostage hamsters, stolen bikes and difficult clients." LC. *Booklist* starred this and chose it as one of the top 10 best crime fiction for youth.

MacDonald, Bailey. *The Secret of the Sealed Room: A Mystery of Young Ben Franklin.* Aladdin, 2010. 208 p. Grades 5–8.
A good mystery about a young indentured servant suspected of murder and the assistance the young Ben Franklin provides in solving the problem.

Morton-Shaw, Christine. *The Hunt for the Seventh.* HarperCollins, 2008. 277 p. Grades 5–9.
"Jim moves with his dad and sister to Minerva Hall where a ghostly voice urging him to 'find the Seventh' draws him into a sort of macabre treasure hunt for clues to an ancient prophecy that threatens them all." LC. Nominated for multiple state young reader awards.

Newsome, Richard. *The Billionaire's Curse* (first book in the *Archer Legacy* series). Walden Pond, 2010. 344 p. Grades 5–8.
When his great-aunt dies, 13-year-old Gerald becomes fabulously wealthy—but has to investigate her death. Lots of action and adventure, similar to the *39 Clues* series. Book two is *The Emerald Casket*, 2011.

Night Fall series, by various authors, published by Darby Creek, Grades 7–up.
High-interest horror stories about unusual teen problems in a small New England town.

Unthinkable, by Shirley Smith, 2010
Skin, by Rick Jasper, 2010
The Protectors, by Val Karlsson, 2010
Thaw, by Rick Jasper, 2010
Messenger from Beyond, by Stephanie Watson, 2010
The Club, by Stephanie Watson, 2010

Parker, Robert B. *Chasing the Bear: A Young Spenser Novel.* Philomel, 2009. 169 p. Grades 7–10
Hardboiled detective Spenser remembers when he was 14 years old and helped rescue his best friend, who was abducted by her abusive father. If this was going to be a series, it did not happen. The author died in 2010.

Parkkola, Seita. *The School of Possibilities.* Sourcebooks Jabberwocky, 2010. 368 p. Grades 5–8.
Sent to a school where "desperate children learn obedience," Storm, age 12, joins a group of rebels who are determined to uncover the secret in the school basement. A scary good read.

Peacock, Shane. *The Boy Sherlock Holmes* series, published by Tundra Books, Grades 6–up.
Growing up in London, the brilliant young Sherlock Holmes is bullied, poor, and miserable. The first title was chosen one of *Booklist*'s Top Ten Mysteries of the Year.

1. *Eye of the Crow,* 2007
2. *Death in the Air,* 2008
3. *The Vanishing Girl,* 2009
4. *The Secret Friend,* 2010
5. *The Dragon Turn,* 2011

Poblocki, Dan. *The Nightmarys.* Random House, 2010. 336 p. Grades 6–10.
"Seventh-grader Timothy July and his new friend Abigail try to break a curse that is causing them and others to be tormented by their greatest fears brought to life." LC. A mystery and horror story.

Potter, Ellen. *The Kneebone Boy.* Feiwel and Friends, 2010. 288 p. Grades 5–8.

"Otto, Lucia, and Max Hardscrabble, whose mother has been missing for many years, have unexpected and illuminating adventures in the village of Snoring-by-the-Sea after their father, who paints portraits of deposed monarchs, goes away on a business trip." LC

Raven, Nicky. *Dracula.* Illustrated by Anne Yvonne Gilbert. Templar Books, 2010. 96 p. Grades 5–8.

"A modern, illustrated retelling of the Bram Stoker classic, in which young Jonathan Harker first meets and then must destroy the vampire, Count Dracula, in order to save those closest to him." LC

Rees, Douglas. *Vampire High* series, published by Delacorte, Grades 7–up.

Cody Elliott gets into Vlad Dracul high school because he can get wet—and vampires can't. The school has to have a water polo team, so there it is. Funny, smart, and fast-moving. First book nominated for several state young reader awards.

    1. *Vampire High,* 2005, 2008
    2. *Vampire High, Sophomore Year,* 2010

Shan, Darren. *Cirque du Freak: The Saga of Darren Shan* series, published by Little, Brown, Grades 6–9.

A boy voluntarily chooses to become a vampire, dies, and is buried—but his best friend is suspicious and vows to hunt him down wherever he is and put a stake through his heart. Dark and scary and very popular.

    1. *Cirque du Freak,* 2001
    2. *The Vampire's Assistant,* 2001
    3. *Tunnels of Blood,* 2002
    4. *Vampire Mountain,* 2002
    5. *Trials of Death,* 2003
    6. *The Vampire Prince,* 2003
    7. *Hunters of the Dusk,* 2003
    8. *Allies of the Night,* 2005
    9. *Killers of the Dawn,* 2005
   10. *The Lake of Souls,* 2005
   11. *Lord of the Shadows,* 2006
   12. *Sons of Destiny,* 2006

Shan, Darren. *The Saga of Larten Crepsley* series, published by Little, Brown, Grades 6–8.

This four-book series covers the life of the master vampire before he connected up with the Cirque du Freak. This author is hugely popular with boys.

    1. *Birth of a Killer,* 2010
    2. *Ocean of Blood,* 2011
    3. *Palace of the Damned,* 2011
    4. *Brothers to the Death,* 2012

Shusterman, Neal. *Full Tilt.* Simon & Schuster, 2005. 224 p. Grades 7–10.

Brothers Blake and Quinn find themselves in a horrific amusement park where each ride embodies their deepest, darkest fears and in order to survive they must live through all seven rides. A great horror story for reluctant readers.

Silvey, Craig. *Jasper Jones.* Alfred A. Knopf Books for Young Readers, 2011. 320 p. Grades 7–up.

"In small-town Australia, teens Jasper and Charlie form an unlikely friendship when one asks the other to help him cover up a murder until they can prove who is responsible." LC

Sleator, William. *Blackbriar.* Marshall Cavendish, 1972, 2009. 215 p. Grades 5–9.

> The classic story about Danny, age 15, who moves with his foster mother to a mysterious house near the sea—an old house with many secrets. Mysterious and suspenseful.

Stine, R. L. *99 Fear Street: The House of Evil*, published by Simon Pulse, Grades 7–up.

1. *The First Horror,* 1994
2. *The Second Horror,* 1994
3. *The Third Horror,* 1994

Stine, R. L., editor. *Fear: 13 Stories of Suspense and Horror.* Dutton, 2010. 320 p. Grades 7–10

> Stine did not actually write these stories—it's a collection—but they are good choices that will delight many a reader.

Fear: 13 Stories of Suspense and Horror **by R.L. Stine. Used by permission of Penguin Group (USA) Inc. All rights reserved.**

Stine, R. L. *Fear Street* and other series novels, published by Simon & Schuster, Grades 6–up.

> He is popular all over again, and many of his books have been reissued with new covers. Below is a selection of some that were in print as of March 2011. There are many series, and publication dates are often new because the books have new covers.

Fear Street

All Night Party, 2005
Bad Dreams, 1994
The Best Friend, 2006
The Boy Next Door, 1996
The Cheater, 1993
The Confession, 2005
The Dare, 1994
Double Date, 1994
The Perfect Date, 1996
Fear Hall: The Beginning, 1997
First Date, 2005
Halloween Party, 2006
Killer's Kiss, 2005
The New Girl, 2006
The Perfect Date, 2005
The Rich Girl, 2005
Secret Admirer, 2005
The Stepsister, 2005
Switched, 2006
Wrong Number, 1990

Fear Street Nights

1. *Moonlight Secrets,* 2005
2. *Midnight Games,* 2005
3. *Darkest Dawn,* 2005

Fear Street Saga trilogy

1. *The Betrayal,* 1993
2. *The Secret,* 2005
3. *The Burning,* 1993

Fear Street Sagas

A New Fear, 1996
House of Whispers, 1996

Fear Street Superchillers

Broken Hearts, 1993
The New Year's Party, 1991
Party Summer, 1991
Silent Night, 1991

Sylvester, Kevin. *Neil Flambé* **series, published by Key Porter, Grades 5–8.**
Fourteen-year-old Neil is not only a chef, but an aspiring detective. Humor, intrigue, and fun in this Canadian series.

1. *Neil Flambé and the Marco Polo Murders,* 2010
2. *Neil Flambé and the Aztec Abduction,* 2010
3. *Neil Flambé and the Crusader's Curse,* 2011

Turner, Max. *Zack Thomson* **series, published by St. Martin's Griffin, Grades 7–up.**
When Zack, institutionalized for years, discovers that he is actually a vampire, the action takes off like a rocket!

1. *Night Runner,* 2009
2. *End of Days,* 2010

Updale, Eleanor. *Johnny Swanson.* Random House, 2011. 384 p. Grades 5–7.
"In 1929 England, eleven-year-old Johnny Swanson helps his widowed mother by starting a newspaper advertising scam, which leads him to a real-life murder mystery that places his mother in mortal danger." LC

Whinnem, Reade Scott. *The Pricker Boy.* Random House, 2009. 277 p. Grades 7–9.
"After finding a mysterious package in the spooky woods where they have grown up, fourteen-year-old Stucks Cumberland and his friends are forced to consider that their childhood bogeyman might be all too real." LC. For horror fans.

Whitcomb, Laura. *The Fetch.* Houghton Mifflin, 2009. 380 p. Grades 6–12.
Calder, a Fetch, or death escort, breaks the rules when he enters the body of Rasputin and tries to escort the souls of Alexis, the Tsarevich, and his sister, Anastasia, to heaven.

Whyman, Matt. *Icecore.* Atheneum, 2007. 307 p. Grades 8–up.

"Seventeen-year-old Englishman Carl Hobbes meant no harm when he hacked into Fort Knox's security system, but at Camp Twilight in the Arctic Circle, known as the Guantanamo Bay of the north, he is tortured to reveal information about a conspiracy of which he was never a part." LC *Goldstrike: A Thriller,* 2010, is the sequel.

Wooding, Chris. *The Haunting of Alaizabel Cray.* Orchard, 2004. 292 p. Grades 5–up.

Seventeen-year-old Thaniel is a wych-hunter, an extremely dangerous profession, in an alternate turn-of-the twentieth-century London. He meets and falls in love with a girl who is possessed by a hostile spirit—and, unbeknownst to her, an important part of a plot to destroy all of London and life as everyone knows it. If you can make it through the first couple of pages, you won't be able to put it down.

Yancey, Rick. *Monstrumologist* series, published by Simon & Schuster, Grades 8–up.

An absolutely terrifying horror series about a boy apprenticed to a monstrumologist—who studies and finds monsters many consider to be only mythological. They are wrong. Really good if you have the stomach for it.

1. *The Monstrumologist,* 2009
2. *The Curse of the Windigo,* 2010
3. *The Isle of Blood,* 2011

Zafon, Carlos Ruiz. *The Prince of Mist.* Little, Brown, 2010. 208 p. Grades 5–8.

When 13-year-old Max realizes that something dead is active in their midst, he, his sister, and their friend have to deal with it—in the middle of World War II. A riveting horror story.

Chapter

7

Realistic Fiction

There are some real winners here in the realistic fiction books. While many boys lean toward fantasy or science fiction or graphic novels, for many readers there is nothing better than a book about real life. Boys will relate to these books that are set in the here and now and deal with real-life problems and situations facing boys everywhere.

YOUNGER GUYS

Atinsky, Steve. *Trophy Kid: Or How I was Adopted by the Rich and Famous.* Delacorte, 2008. 185 p. Grades 4–7.
Croatian war orphan Joe was adopted by two famous movie stars as a toddler, but feels a real pull toward his origins. When he asked to write an autobiography, he comes to terms with who he really is and who he wants to be. Funny, and a good story.

Clements, Andrew. *Extra Credit.* Atheneum, 2009. 183 p. Grades 4–7.
"Three young middle-school-age children, Abby, Amira, and Sadeed, exchange letters back and forth between the prairies of Illinois and the mountains of Afghanistan and begin to bridge a gap across cultural and religious divides." LC. Nominated for many state young readers awards.

Clements, Andrew. *Frindle.* Simon and Schuster, 1996. Grades 3–5.
"When he decides to turn his fifth-grade teacher's love of the dictionary around on her, clever Nick Allen invents a new word and begins a chain of events that quickly moves beyond his control." LC

Clements, Andrew. *Jake Drake, Bully Buster*. Illustrated by Janet Pedersen. Aladdin, 2007. 67 p. Grades 2–4.

Jake Drake, now in fourth grade, tells us he has been a bully magnet all of his life. He possesses all the attributes bullies like. It wasn't until he was in second grade and a new kid, Link Baxter, started picking on him that he figured out what to do to solve the problem. Followed by *Jake Drake, Know-it-All* (2007), *Jack Drake, Teacher's Pet* (2007), and *Jake Drake, Class Clown* (2007).

Clements, Andrew. *Lost and Found*. Illustrated by Mark Elliott. Atheneum, 2008. 162 p. Grades 3–6.

Identical twins move to a new school and find the school has records for only one of them. They take turns being Jay!

Clements, Andrew. *Lunch Money*. Simon & Schuster, 2005. 222 p Grades 4–8.

Twelve-year-old Greg, who has always been good at moneymaking projects, is surprised to find himself teaming up with his lifelong rival, Maura, to create a series of comic books to sell at school.

Clements, Andrew. *No Talking*. Simon & Schuster, 2007. 146 p. Grades 4–6.

The fifth grade boys and girls decide to have a contest—no talking for two whole days! Well, if a teacher asks you a direct question, you can answer with three words—they don't count. Who will win? Can the teachers and the principal stand it?

Clements, Andrew. *A Week in the Woods*. Simon and Schuster, 2002. Grades 4–7. 190 p.

Mark Chelmsey is sick when his wealthy parents move to a small town in New Hampshire, leaving him in the care of their Russian servants. He fit in at his old school, and he did not want to leave. Now he is at a hick school where every year the entire fifth grade leaves to spend a week in the woods, led by a dedicated teacher. How everyone involved changes is the crux of this compelling story.

Couloumbis, Audrey. *Jake*. Random House, 2010. 176 p. Grades 3–6.

"Ten-year-old Jake forms an unexpected bond with his estranged grandfather after his mother's injury puts the pair together in time for the Christmas holiday." LC

Creech, Sharon. *Love That Dog*. HarperCollins, 2001. Grades 4–up.

Jack is a middle school student who hates poetry—until he discovers some by Mr. Walter Dean Myers. A joy. Read it aloud. Kids will relate. *Hate That Cat*, 2008, is a companion to this.

David, Peter. *Mascot to the Rescue!* Illustrated by Colleen Doran. HarperCollins, 2008. 232 p. Grades 4–6.

When Josh discovers that his favorite comic book hero's sidekick, Mascot, is going to die in the next issue, he is terrified—for it seems like everything that happens to Mascot happens to Josh, too.

Fagan, Cary. *The Big Swim*. Groundwood, 2010 128 p. Grades 4–6.

"Ethan, whose goal is to survive summer camp and emerge from the ordeal with at least one positive experience, meets his new cabin mate, Zachary, an unusual boy who does not seem to care about the Big Swim, a camp event in which a select few try to swim across the lake and back." LC

Feldman, Jody. *The Gollywhopper Games*. Greenwillow, 2008. 308 p. Grades 4–8.

"Twelve-year-old Gil Goodson competes against thousands of other children at extraordinary puzzles, stunts, and more in hopes of a fresh start for his family, which has been ostracized since his father was falsely accused of embezzling money from Golly Toy and Game Company." LC

Fleming, Candace. *Lowji Discovers America*. Atheneum, 2005. 151 p. Grades 3–5.
Nine-year-old Lowji moves with his mother and father to Illinois from east India. He is nervous especially about making friends, and he really wants a pet. It takes a while, but all of his dreams come true. This is just an excellent look at what it feels like to be a newcomer, even one from a family that already speaks English.

Fletcher, Ralph. *Spider Boy*. Clarion, 1997. 183 p. Grades 4–8.
"After moving to another state, seventh grader Bobby deals with the change by telling people at school made-up stories and then retreating into his world of pet spiders and books about spiders." LC

French, Susan. *Operation Redwood*. Amulet, 2009. 355 p. Grades 4–7.
"In northern California, Julian Carter-Li and his friends old and new fight to save a grove of redwoods from an investment company that plans to cut them down." LC. Nominated for multiple state young reader awards.

Gervay, Suzanne. *I am Jack*. Tricycle, 2009. 126 p. Grades 3–6.
Eleven-year old Jack has a bully problem, and he doesn't know what to do to solve it. A good story from Australia.

Gifaldi, David. *Listening for Crickets*. Henry Holt, 2008. 181 p. Grades 3–6.
"With parents that fight all the time, ten-year-old Jake finds comfort and escape in the stories he creates for himself and his little sister." LC
Gilson, Jamie. *Thirteen Ways to Sink a Sub*. Marshall Cavendish, 1982, 2009. 103 p. Grades 3–5.
The boys and the girls in a fourth grade classroom have a competition. Who can make the substitute teacher cry first? New edition of a popular title.

Gutman, Dan. *The Talent Show*. Simon & Schuster, 2010. 213 p. Grades 4–7.
After a tornado hits a small town in Kansas, the principal decides to hold a talent show to raise spirits. Gutman is always fun.

Henkes, Kevin. *Bird Lake Moon*. Greenwillow, 2008. 179 p. Grades 4–8.
Twelve-year-old Mitch, devastated by his father leaving the family, acts out some of his anger at the family, also harboring pain, that moves in to the house next to that of his grandparents, where he and his mom are staying. A beautifully written, powerful book.

Hiaasen, Carl. *Chomp*. Alfred A. Knopf Books for Young Readers, 2012. 304 p. Grades 4–8.
Wahoo Cray's dad is an animal wrangler in need of some money. He and Wahoo sign on with *Expedition Survival!*, a reality TV show filming in the Florida Everglades. They bring along a girl named Tuna who has been abused by her father. When the egotistical star of the show is bitten by a bat and goes missing, and Tuna's dad shows up with a gun, surviving becomes serious business.

Hiaasen, Carl. *Flush*. Alfred A. Knopf Books for Young Readers, 2006. 263 p. Grades 4–8.
Noah and his younger sister, Abbey, try to prove that a local casino boat is dumping human waste into the waters off the coast of Florida. Very popular with boys. An ALA Notable Children's Book.

Hiaasen, Carl. *Hoot*. Alfred A. Knopf Books for Young Readers, 2002. 292 p. Grades 4–8.
Roy is used to moving, but he misses his old home in Montana and is not much taken with his new one in Florida. In his new school, a bully torments him regularly. But Roy

notices another boy, seeing him from the school bus, an unusual boy who is about his age, can run very fast, and has no shoes. He does not seem to be in school. Who that boy is and what he is up to form the main story of this funny, informative book about a group of kids determined to prevent the 469th restaurant in a pancake chain from building on a burrowing owl habitat. This is a Newbery Honor Book.

Hiaasen, Carl. *Scat.* Alfred A. Knopf Books for Young Readers, 2009. Knopf, 2009. 373 p. Grades 4–8.

> "Nick and Marta are both suspicious when their biology teacher, the feared Mrs. Bunny Starch, disappears, and try to uncover the truth despite the police and headmaster's insistence that nothing is wrong." LC. Nominated for many state young reader awards.

Hirsch, Odo. *Darius Bell and the Glitter Pool.* Kane-Miller, 2010. 240 p. Grades 4–7.

> In return for the large estate the Bell family was given more than 100 years ago, the family has to give the community a gift every 25 years—and this is the year and they are dead broke. When Darius finds a cave under the property, he hopes what he finds there will solve the problem. An excellent Australian story that *Booklist* highly recommends as a read aloud.

Jones, Marcia. *Ratfink.* Dutton, 2010. 216 p. Grades 3–6.

> "Creative, impulsive Logan vows to turn over a new leaf in fifth grade so his parents will let him have a pet, but when a competitive new girl arrives at school and his forgetful and embarrassing grandfather takes over the basement of Logan's house, doing the right thing becomes harder than it has ever been." LC

Kehoe, Tim. *Vincent Shadow* series, illustrated by Guy Francis, published by Little, Brown, Grades 3–6.

> "Vincent Shadow has always been different from the other kids his age, thanks to his creative mind, which he uses to develop unique toys in his secret attic lab, and when a toy inventor offers Vincent the chance to make his dreams a reality, he realizes his creativity is what makes him special, not just strange." LC

> *The Unusual Mind of Vincent Shadow,* 2009
> *Toy Inventor,* 2011
> *The Whizzer Wishbook,* 2011

Kelly, Katy. *Melonhead* series, published by Delacorte, Grades 3–5.

> "In the Washington, D.C. neighborhood of Capitol Hill, Lucy Rose's friend Adam 'Melonhead' Melon, a budding inventor with a knack for getting into trouble, enters a science contest that challenges students to recycle an older invention into a new invention." LC

> *Melonhead,* 2009
> *Melonhead and the Big Stink,* 2010
> *Melonhead and the Undercover Operation,* 2011

Kerrin, Jessica. *Martin Bridge* series, illustrated by Joseph Kelly, published by Kids Can, Grades 2–4.

> Chapters in the life of Martin are funny, insightful, and dead on. In one book, he discovers the hamster he has been caring for while its owners are on vacation—dead. In another, he has a fight with his best friend, and, in the third, his plans to pay tribute to the wonderful new substitute school bus driver have an unexpected outcome. They are fine read alouds for second and third graders. Martin is a neat kid and a great role model.

Martin Bridge Ready for Takeoff, 2005
Martin Bridge on the Lookout, 2005
Martin Bridge Blazing Ahead, 2006
Martin Bridge Sound the Alarm, 2007
Martin Bridge Out of Orbit, 2007
Martin Bridge in High Gear, 2008
Martin Bridge the Sky's the Limit, 2008
Martin Bridge Onwards and Upwards, 2009

Klein, Abby. *Ready, Freddy!* series, published by Blue Apple, Grades 2–4.
Typical plot: Freddy agrees to ride laps in the bike-a-thon fundraiser for the animal shelter, but he has a horrible problem. He still uses training wheels and that's against the rules. He has to learn how to ride a two-wheeler and ride it fast—or else.

1. *Tooth Trouble,* 2004
2. *The King of Show-and-Tell,* 2004
3. *Homework Hassles,* 2004
4. *Don't Sit on My Lunch!* 2005
5. *Talent Show Scaredy-Pants,* 2005
6. *Help! A Vampire's Coming!* 2005
7. *Yikes! Bikes!* 2006
8. *Halloween Fraidy-Cat,* 2006
9. *Shark Tooth Tale,* 2006
10. *Super Secret Valentine,* 2007
11. *Pumpkin Elf Mystery,* 2007
12. *Stop That Hamster!* 2007
13. *The One Hundredth Day of School,* 2008
14. *Camping Catastrophe!* 2008
15. *Thanksgiving Turkey Trouble,* 2008
16. *Ready, Set, Snow!* 2009
17. *Firehouse Fun!* 2009
18. *The Perfect Present,* 2009
19. *The Penguin Problem,* 2010
20. *Apple Orchard Race,* 2010
21. *Going Batty,* 2010
22. *Science Fair Flop,* 2010

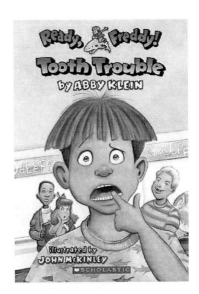

***Tooth Trouble* by Abby Klein.**

23. *A Very Crazy Christmas,* 2011
24. *Shark Attack!* 2011

Kuhlman, Evan. *The Last Invisible Boy.* Illustrated by J. P. Coovert. Atheneum, 2008. 234 p. Grades 4–7.
A Wimpy Kid–style story of a boy who feels he is becoming invisible after his father dies.

Nielsen, Susin. *Word Nerd.* Tundra Books, 2008. 248 p. Grades 4–8.
When Ambrose is forced into home schooling due to a brutal attack by bullies at his new school, he becomes friends with the landlord's son, an ex-con teenager. An excellent story.

Park, Barbara Ann. *Mick Harte Was Here.* Random House, 1996. Grades 4–7.
There are very few more powerful openers than the one in this book, about the grieving family of a boy killed in an accident. It's a sad story with lots of humor narrated by Mick Harte's sister.

Parry, Rosanne. *Heart of a Shepherd*. Random House, 2009. Random House, 2009. 165 p. Grades 4–8.

> Sixth grader Ignatius, separated from his parents and brothers, helps his grandfather run his Oregon ranch and decides who and what kind of a person he wants to be. Nominated for many state young reader awards.

Pitchford, Dean. *The Big One-Oh*. Putnam Juvenile, 2007. 181 p. Grades 4–6.

> "Determined not to be weird all his life like his neighbor, Charley Maplewood decides to throw himself a tenth birthday party, complete with a "house of horrors" theme, but first he will have to make some friends to invite." LC. Nominated for several state young reader awards.

Pitchford, Dean. *Captain Nobody*. Putnam Juvenile, 2009. 197 p. Grades 4–6.

> An excellent book about a kid who decides to keep wearing his superhero costume after Halloween to try to make a difference in the lives of the people in his town and to help his injured brother. Nominated for several state young reader awards.

Preller, James. *Justin Fisher Declares War!* Scholastic, 2010. 135 p. Grades 4–6.

> "When Justin Fisher, long-time class clown, realizes that his classmates are growing tired of his misdeeds, he declares war on their fifth-grade teacher, Mr. Tripp, in hopes of regaining his popularity." LC

Roberts, Ken. *Thumb* series, illustrated by Leanne Franson, published by Groundwood, Grades 2–5.

> Humorous, positive stories about a motherless boy in a remote Canadian town on the Pacific coast. I just love these.

> *Thumb in the Box*, 2002
> *Thumb on a Diamond*, 2006
> *Thumb and the Bad Guys*, 2009

Roy, James. *Max Quigley: Technically Not a Bully*. Houghton Mifflin, 2009. 202 p. Grades 3–7.

> "After playing a prank on one of his 'geeky' classmates, sixth-grader Max Quigley's punishment is to be tutored by him." LC

Salisbury, Graham. *Calvin Coconut* series, illustrated by Jacqueline Rogers, published by Random House, Grades 3–5.

> In the first of the series, nine-year-old Calvin catches the attention of the school bully on the day before he starts fourth grade, and back at home, the unfriendly 15-year-old daughter of his mother's best friend has taken over his room.

> *Trouble Magnet*, 2009
> *Zippy Fix*, 2009
> *Dog Heaven*, 2010
> *Zoo Breath*, 2010
> *Hero of Hawaii*, 2011
> *Kung Fooey*, 2011

Sheth, Kashmira. *Boys without Names*. Balzer and Bray, 2010. 316 p. Grades 4–7.

> "Eleven-year-old Gopal and his family leave their rural Indian village for life with his uncle in Mumbai, but when they arrive his father goes missing and Gopal ends up locked in a sweatshop from which there is no escape." LC

Vail, Rachel. *Justin Case: School, Drool, and Other Daily Disasters.* Illustrated by Matthew Cordell. Feiwel and Friends, 2010. 256 p. Grades 3–5.

"Justin is very nervous about starting third grade and must make the best of things when he does not get the teacher he wanted, his best friend is in another class, and his favorite stuffed animal disappears." LC

Weissman, Elissa Brent. *The Trouble with Mark Hopper.* Dutton, 2009. 229 p. Grades 4–7.

"When two eleven-year-olds with the same name, similar looks, and very different personalities go to the same Maryland middle school, confusion and bad feelings ensue, but things improve after a teacher insists that they become study partners." LC

Winerip, Michael. *Adam Canfield* series, published by Candlewick, Grades 4–7.

Adam and his friend Jennifer serve as co-editors of their middle school newspaper, and have a lot of funny and exciting adventures. Nominated for multiple state young reader awards.

> *Adam Canfield of the Slash,* 2005
> *Adam Canfield: Watch Your Back!* 2007
> *Adam Canfield, the Last Reporter,* 2009

Winkler, Henry, and Lin Oliver. *Hank Zipzer* series, published by Grosset & Dunlap, Grades 2–4.

Fourth grader Hank isn't the best student (the subtitle of the first book is *The Mostly True Confessions of the World's Best Underachiever*), but with the help of a sympathetic and understanding music teacher, he realizes he has some learning differences and is an intelligent and capable kid. Supposedly semiautobiographical. Some funny scenes. The actual writer of the books is Lin Oliver.

1. *Niagara Falls, or Does It?* 2003
2. *I Got a "D" in Salami,* 2003
3. *Day of the Iguana,* 2003
4. *The Zippity Zinger,* 2004
5. *The Night I Flunked My Field Trip,* 2004
6. *Holy Enchilada!* 2004
7. *Help! Somebody Get Me Out of Fourth Grade!* 2004
8. *Summer School! What Genius Thought Up That?* 2005
9. *My Secret Life as a Ping-Pong Wizard,* 2005
10. *My Dog's a Scaredy-Cat,* 2006
11. *The Curtain Went Up, My Pants Fell Down,* 2007
12. *Barfing in the Backseat,* 2007

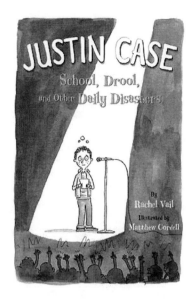

Justin Case: School, Drool, and Other Daily Disasters by Rachel Vail. Courtesy of Feiwel and Friends, an imprint of the Macmillan Children's Publishing Group.

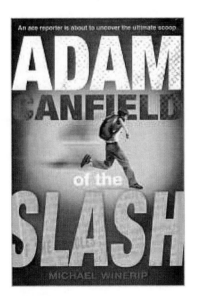

Adam Canfield of the Slash by Michael Winerip.

13. *Who Ordered this Baby? Definitely Not Me,* 2007
14. *The Life of Me,* 2008
15. *Tale of Two Tails,* 2008
16. *Dump Trucks and Dogsleds,* 2009
17. *A Brand New Me,* 2010

Yee, Lisa. *Bobby vs. Girls* series, published by Scholastic, Grades 2–4.

A fourth grader is somewhat unsure that he should have a girl for his best friend, but it happened—until they get into a fight and stop being friends. Very funny.

Bobby vs. Girls (Accidentally), 2009
Bobby the Brave (Sometimes), 2010

OLDER GUYS

Alexie, Sherman. *The Absolutely True Diary of a Part-Time Indian.* Little, Brown, 2007. 230 p. Grades 7–up.

Junior, growing up on the Spokane Indian reservation, wants to be a cartoonist—but knows there is no hope for becoming anything on the "rez." In spite of the fact that it alienates his best friend, he decides against all odds to go to a good school in a town 22 miles away. This is funny, heartwarming, and incredibly moving; and it's a National Book Award winner.

Alonzo, Sandra. *Riding Invisible.* Hyperion, 2010. 236 p. Grades 7–up.

Reminiscent in look to *Diary of a Wimpy Kid,* this is the fictitious journal of 15-year-old Yancy, who runs away from home and his mentally ill brother to work as a ranch-hand and figure out what he really wants to do.

Amato, Mary. *Invisible Lines.* Egmont, 2009. 299 p. Grades 5–8.

"Coming from a poor, single-parent family, seventh-grader Trevor must rely on his intelligence, artistic ability, quick wit, and soccer prowess to win friends at his new Washington, D.C. school, but popular and rich Xander seems determined to cause him trouble." LC

Ayarbe, Heidi. *Freeze Frame.* HarperTeen, 2008. 376 p. Grades 7–up.

"Fifteen-year-old Kyle believes he does not deserve to live after accidentally shooting and killing his best friend." LC

Bancks, Tristan. *Mac Slater* series, published by Simon & Schuster, Grades 5–8.

"Mac, an Australian youth, has one week to prove that he can be a 'coolhunter,' identifying emerging trends and posting images on a Web site, but he is competing against a classmate on whom he has a crush and dealing with resistance from his best friend and his own confusion over what 'cool' means." LC

Mac Slater Hunts the Cool, 2010
Mac Slater vs. the City, 2011

Baskin, Nora. *Anything but Typical.* Simon & Schuster, 2009. 197 p. Grades 5–8.

Jason, a 12-year-old autistic boy, loves to write. When the opportunity arises to meet an online friend he worries that his disability will destroy their friendship. Nominated for many state young reader awards.

Cadnum, Michael. *Flash*. Farrar, Straus & Giroux, 2010. 240 p. Grades 8–11.

"Relates one momentous day in the lives of five young people in the San Francisco Bay Area, including two teen-aged bank robbers, a witness, and a wounded military policeman recently returned from duty in Iraq." LC. *Booklist* recommends it for reluctant readers.

Carbone, Elisa Lynn. *Jump*. Viking, 2010. 288 p. Grades 8–10

Short chapters make for a quick, fast-paced read in this story of two troubled teens who meet at a climbing gym and run away together to climb in Nevada and Yosemite.

Correa, Shan. *Gaff*. Peachtree, 2010. 224 p. Grades 6–8.

"In Hawaii, thirteen-year-old Paul Silva is determined to find a way to get his family out of the illegal cockfighting business." LC

Flash **by Michael Cadnum. Courtesy of Farrar Straus Giroux Books for Young Readers, an imprint of the Macmillan Children's Publishing Group.**

Crutcher, Chris. *The Sledding Hill*. Greenwillow, 2005. 230 p. Grades 7–up.

Eddie Proffit and Billy Bartholomew were best friends, but Billy was killed in a freak accident shortly after Eddie's beloved dad died in *another* freak accident, and now Eddie has stopped talking. But Billy is still out there and he is communicating with Eddie. Eddie joins a reading group led by the school librarian and gets involved in the center of a big censorship issue involving one of Chris Crutcher's books. Unusual and fascinating.

Cummings, Priscilla. *Red Kayak*. Puffin, 2004. 209 p. Grades 5–7.

Living near the water on Maryland's Eastern Shore, 13-year-old Brady and his best friends, J. T. and Digger, become entangled in a tragedy that tests their friendship and their ideas about right and wrong. A gripping read.

De Goldi, Kate. *The 10 p.m. Question*. Candlewick, 2010. 256 p. Grades 7–up.

"Twelve-year-old Frankie Parsons has a quirky family, a wonderful best friend, and a head full of worrying questions that he shares with his mother each night, but when free-spirited Sydney arrives at school with questions of her own, Frankie is forced to face the ultimate ten p.m. question." LC

de la Pena, Matt. *We Were Here*. Delacorte, 2009. 359 p. Grades 7–12.

"After a judge sentences Miguel to spend a year in a group home and write in a journal, he makes plans to escape the youth detention center and go to Mexico, where he can put his past behind him." LC. Nominated for multiple state young reader awards.

Ehrenhaft, Dan. *A Friend is Not a Verb*. HarperTeen, 2010. 240 p. Grades 7–up.

"While sixteen-year-old Hen's family and friends try to make his supposed dreams of becoming a rock star come true, he deals with the reality of being in a band with an ex-girlfriend, a friendship that may become love, and his older sister's mysterious disappearance and reappearance." LC

Gardner, Graham. *Inventing Elliott*. Dial, 2004. 192 p. Grades 5–up.

Elliot, the new guy at school, is noticed by the Guardians, the mysterious, manipulative group who run the school according to their own rules. For the first time, Elliot has power, but it comes at a terrible price.

Gephart, Donna. *How to Survive Middle School*. Delacorte, 2010. 256 p. Grades 5–8.

"When eleven-year-old David Greenberg's best friend makes the start of middle school even worse than he feared it could be, David becomes friends with Penny, who shares his love of television shows and posts one of their skits on YouTube, making them wildly popular—online, at least." LC

Gosselink, John. *The Defense of Thaddeus A Ledbetter*. Amulet, 2010. 231 p. Grades 5–8.

"Twelve-year-old Thaddeus A. Ledbetter, who considers it a duty to share his knowledge and talent with others, refutes each of the charges which have sent him to "In-School Suspension" for the remainder of seventh grade." LC

Hinton, S. E. *The Outsiders*. Viking, 1967. 188 p. Grades 6–up.

The struggle of three brothers to stay together after their parents' death and their quest for identity among the conflicting values of their adolescent society seems as relevant today as when it was written. Timeless and still very popular.

Houtman, Jacqueline. *The Reinvention of Edison Thomas*. Front Street, 2010 189 p. Grades 5–8.

"Eddy Thomas, a boy who is much better with science than people, creates an invention that makes him suddenly popular and leads him to a new understanding of friendship." LC

Howard, Barb. *The Dewpoint Show*. Fitzhenry and Whiteside, 2011. 231 p. Grades 6–9.

"Leonard is fond of observing the world around him, but when he becomes friends with Vivian, the older lady who lives next door, he learns that life is not just something to watch." LC

Hyde, Catherine Ryan. *Diary of a Witness*. Alfred A. Knopf Books for Young Readers, 2009. 201 p. Grades 7–up.

"Ernie, an overweight high school student and long-time target of bullies, relies on his best friend Will to watch his back until Will, overwhelmed by problems at home and guilt over his brother's death, seeks a final solution." LC. Nominated for multiple state young reader awards.

Koertge, Ron. *Strays*. Candlewick, 2007. 167 p. Grades 5–up.

Sixteen-year-old Ted has to go into foster care when his weird parents are killed in an accident. Ted is weird, too; he knows it. His mom was an animal freak, and Ted can talk to animals himself—and understand them. But ever so slowly, his life begins to change, as he bonds with the other two guys in foster care with him and begins to make friends. A fine read.

Korman, Gordon. *The Juvie Three*. Hyperion, 2008. 249 p. Grades 6–10.

"Gecko, Arjay, and Terence, all in trouble with the law, must find a way to keep their halfway house open in order to stay out of juvenile detention." LC

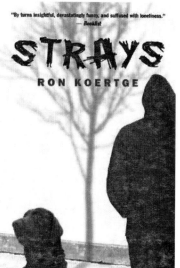

Strays **by Ron Koertge.**

Leavitt, Martine. *Heck Superhero*. Front Street, 2005. Grades 5–up.

"Abandoned by his mother, thirteen-year-old Heck tries to survive on his own as his mind bounces between the superhero character he imagines himself to be and the harsh reality of his life." LC

Lynch, Janet Nichols. *Messed Up*. Holiday House, 2009. 250 p. Grades 6–8.

When his family situation changes dramatically, Latino teen R. D. is on his own, living alone—and trying to prevent the authorities from finding out.

Maldonado, Torey. *Secret Saturdays*. Putnam Juvenile, 2010. 198 p. Grades 5–9.

"Justin, a fatherless twelve-year-old in a dangerous neighborhood in New York, starts to worry about his friend Sean, who has started telling lies and getting into trouble at school, and when he suspects that the change in attitude is connected to mysterious trips Sean takes with his mother, he tries to get involved." LC

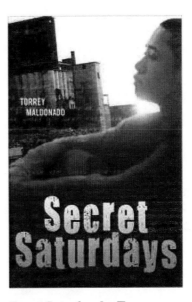

McCormick, Patricia. *Purple Heart*. HarperCollins, 2009. 202 p. Grades 7–up.

"While recuperating in a Baghdad hospital from a traumatic brain injury sustained during the Iraq War, eighteen-year-old soldier Matt Duffy struggles to recall what happened to him and how it relates to his ten-year-old friend, Ali." LC. Nominated for several state young reader awards.

Secret Saturdays by Torey Maldonado. Used by permission of Penguin Group (USA) Inc. All rights reserved.

Millard, Glenda. *A Small Free Kiss in the Dark*. Holiday House, 2010. 180 p. Grades 6–8.

"Skip, an eleven-year-old runaway, becomes friends with Billy, a homeless man, and together they flee a war-torn Australian city with six-year-old Max and camp out at a seaside amusement park, where they are joined by Tia, a fifteen-year-old ballerina, and her baby." LC

Myers, Walter Dean. *The Cruisers*. Scholastic, 2010. 128 p. Grades 5–8.

Four eighth graders in a Harlem school for the gifted and talented do their best to underachieve. A Civil War project splits their class into Union and Confederate sympathizers and causes a great deal of tension. This is planned to be the first in a series of four. *Booklist* gave it a starred review.

Myers, Walter Dean. *Lockdown*. Amistad, 2010. 247 p. Grades 8–up.

"Teenage Reese, serving time at a juvenile detention facility, gets a lesson in making it through hard times from an unlikely friend with a harrowing past." LC

Nolan, Han. *Crazy*. Harcourt, 2010. 352 p. Grades 7–10.

"Fifteen-year-old loner Jason struggles to hide his father's declining mental condition after his mother's death, but when his father disappears he must confide in the other members of a therapy group he has been forced to join at school." LC

Orca Currents series, by various authors, published by Orca, Grades 5–8 (most have about a 4th-grade reading level).

Quoting the publisher: Orca Currents are short high-interest novels with contemporary themes, written expressly for middle-school students reading below grade level. Some well-reviewed ones with boy-friendly topics include:

121 Express, by Monique Polak, 2008
Bank Job, by James Heneghan, 2009
Benched, by Christy Watson, 2011
Beyond Repair, by Lois Peterson, 2011
Bio-Pirate, by Michele Martin Bossley, 2008
The Big Dip, by Melanie Jackson, 2009
Branded, by Eric Walters, 2010
Camp Wild, by Pam Withers, 2005
Cellular, by Ellen Schwartz, 2010
Cracked, by Michelle Martin Bossley, 2007
Crossbow, by Dayle Campbell Gaetz, 2007
Daredevil Club, by Pam Withers, 2006
Dog Walker, by Kareen Spafford-Fitz, 2006
Explore, by Christy Goerzen, 2009
Fast Slide, by Melanie Jackson, 2010
Finding Elmo, by Monique Polak, 2007
Fraud Squad, by Michele Martin Bossley, 2009
Hypnotized, by Don Trembath, 2007

In a Flash, by Eric Walters, 2008
Junkyard Dog, by Monique Polak, 2009
Laggan Lard Butts, by Eric Walters, 2006
Marked, by Norah McClintock, 2008
Nine Doors, by Vicki Grant, 2009
Pigboy, by Vicki Grant, 2006
Rebel's Tag, by K. L. Denman, 2007
Reckless, by Lesley Choyce, 2010
See No Evil, by Diane Young, 2006
Sewer Rats, by Sigmund Brouwer, 2006
Skate Freak, by Lesley Choyce, 2008
The Snowball Effect, by Deb Loughead, 2010
Special Edward, by Eric Walters, 2009
Splat! by Eric Walters, 2008
Storm Tide, by Kari Jones, 2011
Swiped, by Michele Martin Bosley, 2006
Watch Me, by Norah McClintock, 2009
Wired, by Sigmund Brouwer, 2005

Orca Soundings series, by various authors, published by Orca, Grades 7–12 (most have about a 4th-grade reading level).

Quoting the publisher: "Orca Soundings are short high-interest novels with contemporary themes, written expressly for teens reading below grade level." *Booklist* magazine described this series as excellent. Some well-reviewed books with boy-friendly topics include:

B Negative, by Vicki Grant, 2011
Back, by Norah McClintock, 2009
Bang, by Norah McClintock, 2007
Battle of the Bands, by K. L. Denman, 2006
Big Guy, by Robin Stevenson, 2008
Blue Moon, by Marilyn Halvorson, 2004
Bull Rider, by Marilyn Halvorson, 2003
Cellular, by Ellen Schwartz, 2010
Chill, by Colin Frizzell, 2006
The Darwin Expedition, by Diane Tullson, 2007
Down, by Norah McClintock, 2007
Exit Point, by Laura Langston, 2006
Fastback Beach, by Shirlee Matheson, 2003
Grind, by Eric Walters, 2004
The Hemingway Tradition, by Kristin Butcher, 2002
Hit Squad, by James Heneghan, 2003

Home Invasion, by Monique Polak, 2005
I.D., by Vicki Grant, 2007
Impact, by James C. Dekker, 2009
In the Woods, by Robin Stevenson, 2009
Jacked, by Carrie Mac, 2009
Juice, by Eric Walters, 2005
Last Ride, by Laura Langston, 2011
Learning to Fly, by Paul Yee, 2008
Lockdown, by Diane Tullson, 2008
Middle Row, by Sylvia Olsen, 2008
No More Pranks, by Monique Polak, 2004
No Problem, by Dayle Campbell Gaetz, 2003
Outback, by Robin Stevenson, 2011
Overdrive, by Eric Walters, 2004
Pain and Wastings, by Carrie Mac, 2008
Picture This, by Norah McClintock, 2009
Plastic, by Sarah Harvey, 2010
Reaction, by Lesley Choyce, 2010

Refuge Cove, by Lesley Choyce, 2002
Responsible, by Darlene Ryan, 2007
Riley Park, by Diane Tullson, 2009
Rock Star, by Adrian Chamberlain, 2010
Running the Risk, by Lesley Choyce, 2009
Sea Change, by Diane Tullson, 2010
Snitch, by Norah McClintock, 2005
Stuffed, by Eric Walters, 2007

Tell, by Norah McClintock, 2006
Thunderbowl, by Lesley Choyce, 2004
Tough Trails, by Irene Morek, 2003
Viral, by Alex Van Tol, 2011
Wave Warrior, by Lesley Choyce, 2007
Yellow Line, by Sylvia Olsen, 2005
Zee's Way, by Kristin Butcher, 2004

Paulsen, Gary. *Notes from the Dog.* Random House, 2009. 135 p. Grades 5–9.

Fourteen-year-old Finn was hoping to avoid people over the summer but instead meets a neighbor who is struggling with breast cancer. This is another wonderful story from one of our most popular authors. Nominated for multiple state young reader awards.

Potter, Ellen. *Slob.* Philomel, 2009. 199 p. Grades 4–7.

"Picked on, overweight genius Owen tries to invent a television that can see the past to find out what happened the day his parents were killed." LC. Nominated for multiple state young readers awards.

Preller, James. *Bystander.* Feiwel and Friends, 2009. 226 p. Grades 5–9.

"Thirteen-year-old Eric discovers there are consequences to not standing by and watching as the bully at his new school hurts people, but although school officials are aware of the problem, Eric may be the one with a solution." LC

Quintero, Sofia. *Efrain's Secret.* Alfred A. Knopf Books for Young Readers, 2010. 265 p. Grades 8–up.

"Ambitious high school senior and honor student Efrain Rodriguez makes some questionable choices in pursuit of his dream to escape the South Bronx and attend an Ivy League college." LC

Reinhardt, Dana. *The Things a Brother Knows.* Random House, 2010. 256 p. Grades 8–up.

"Although they have never gotten along well, seventeen-year-old Levi follows his older brother Boaz, an ex-Marine, on a walking trip from Boston to Washington, D.C. in hopes of learning why Boaz is completely withdrawn." LC. Starred reviews in *Booklist, School Library Journal,* and *Publishers Weekly.*

Rhuday-Perkovich, Olugbemisola. *8th Grade Superzero.* Scholastic, 2010. 330 p. Grades 5–9.

"After half-heartedly joining his church youth group's project at a homeless shelter near his Brooklyn middle school, eighth-grade "loser" Reggie McKnight is inspired to run for school office on a platform of making a real difference in the community." LC

Roy, Jennifer. *Mindblind.* Marshall Cavendish, 2010. 251 p. Grades 6–10.

Fourteen-year-old Nathaniel, a brilliant scholar who has Asperger's syndrome, attempts to make a contribution to the world in order to truly be a genius. Although he struggles with social relationships, he plays keyboard in a band, has a crush on a girl, and has a friendship with another "Aspie" girl. Outstanding reviews; a fine read.

Sanchez, Alex. *Bait.* Simon & Schuster, 2009. 243 p. Grades 7–up.

"Diego keeps getting into trouble because of his explosive temper until he finally finds a probation officer who helps him get to the root of his anger so that he can stop running from his past." LC

Sanders, Scott. *Gray Baby.* Houghton Mifflin, 2009. 321 p. Grades 7–up.

"Sixteen-year-old Clifton Carlson, emotionally scarred from having seen his father beaten to death by white police officers ten years earlier, grows up without friends or the support of his mother, who has become an alcoholic, but his life is changed when, desperate for friends, he puts messages in bottles and sends them down New River where they are intercepted by Swamper, an elderly man who lives in a shack on the riverbank." LC

Schmidt, Gary D. *Trouble.* Clarion, 2008. 297 p. Grades 5–up.

"Fourteen-year-old Henry, wishing to honor his brother Franklin's dying wish, sets out to hike Maine's Mount Katahdin with his best friend and dog. But fate adds another companion—the Cambodian refugee accused of fatally injuring Franklin—and reveals troubles that predate the accident." LC

Schraff, Anne. *A Boy Called Twister.* Saddleback Educational, 2010. 180 p. Grades 7–10.

"Kevin Walker is determined to be a loner at Tubman High so no one will discover the secret that forced his family to move, but when he becomes the star of the track team, his rising popularity threatens everything." LC

Schraff, Anne. *Dark Secrets.* Saddleback Educational, 2010. 201 p. Grades 7–12.

"Ernesto does not understand why Naomi, the girl who he cares for, puts up with her abusive boyfriend, Clay, but the dark secrets surrounding their relationship are brought to light after Clay hits Naomi in the face during one of their arguments." LC

Seagraves, Doony Bailey. *Gone from These Woods.* Delacorte, 2009. 181 p. Grades 4–7.

When Daniel accidentally shoots and kills his uncle on a hunting trip he did not even want to go on, he has to deal with his feeling that he is a horrible villain and with the way the people in his town treat him.

Senzai, N. H. *Shooting Kabul.* Simon & Schuster, 2010. 262 p. Grades 5–9.

"Escaping from Taliban-controlled Afghanistan in the summer of 2001, eleven-year-old Fadi and his family immigrate to the San Francisco Bay Area, where Fadi schemes to return to the Pakistani refugee camp where his little sister was accidentally left behind." LC

Scrawl **by Mark Shulman. Courtesy of Roaring Book Press, an imprint of the Macmillan Children's Publishing Group.**

Shulman, Mark. *Scrawl.* Roaring Brook, 2010. 234 p. Grades 7–up.

"When eighth-grade school bully Tod and his friends get caught committing a crime on school property, his penalty—staying after school and writing in a journal under the eye of the school guidance counselor—reveals aspects of himself that he prefers to keep hidden." LC. Starred review in *Kirkus.*

Shusterman, Neal. *The Schwa Was Here.* Dutton, 2004. 228 p. Grades 5–9.

Is it possible for a human being to be invisible? Schwa nearly is. When Antsy does notice him, the two boys devise a scheme to make big bucks. Both hilariously funny and poignant, this is a unique and creative novel. The equally good sequel is *Antsy Does Time,* 2008.

Silverberg. Alan. *Milo: Sticky Notes and Brain Freeze.* Aladdin, 2010. 288 p. Grades 5–8.
 "In love with the girl he sneezed on the first day of school and best pals with Marshall, the "One Eyed Jack" of friends, seventh-grader Milo Cruikshank misses his mother whose death has changed everything at home." LC. Includes plenty of Wimpy Kid–like illustrations. Starred review in *School Library Journal.*

Slade, Arthur. *Jolted: Newton Starker's Rules for Survival.* Delacorte, 2009. 321 p. Grades 5–7.
 "Many of Newton Starker's ancestors, including his mother, have been killed by lightning strikes, so when he enrolls at the eccentric Jerry Potts Academy of Higher Learning and Survival in Moose Jaw, Saskatchewan, he tries to be a model student so that he can avoid the same fate." LC. Nominated for multiple state young reader awards.

Author Spotlight: Jordan Sonnenblick

Jordan Sonnenblick, author of *Drums, Girls and Dangerous Pie,* loved reading as a child. Although he mainly writes realistic fiction, as a child he devoured fantasy, science fiction, and comic books. Susan Cooper's *The Dark is Rising* is his all-time favorite book. As an adult he learned how to write funny books about serious topics by reading Kurt Vonnegut and Frank McCourt.

Jordan Sonnenblick Recommends

Rick Riordan

J. K. Rowling

Suzanne Collins

Jeff Kinney

John Flanagan's *Ranger's Apprentice* series

For Boys Willing to Read Realistic Fiction

The Wednesday Wars by Gary Schmidt

Sleeping Freshmen Never Lie by David Lubar

Heat by Mike Lupica

Sonnenblick, Jordan. *After Ever After.* Scholastic, 2010. 260 p. Grades 5–8.
 "Although Jeff and Tad, encouraged by a new friend, Lindsey, make a deal to help one another overcome aftereffects of their cancer treatments in preparation for eighth-grade graduation, Jeff still craves advice from his older brother Stephen, who is studying drums in Africa." LC. This is a fine follow-up to the very popular *Drums, Girls & Dangerous Pie.*

Sonnenblick, Jordan. *Curveball: The Year I Lost My Grip*. Scholastic, 2012. 304 p. Grades 7–9.
After an injury ends his baseball career, Peter develops an interest in photography as he starts high school, worries about his grandfather's health, and meets his first girlfriend.

Sonnenblick, Jordan. *Drums, Girls & Dangerous Pie*. Scholastic, 2004. 182 p. Grades 5–8.
"When his younger brother is diagnosed with leukemia, thirteen-year-old Steven tries to deal with his complicated emotions, his school life, and his desire to support his family" LC. Sonnenblick has successfully written a funny book about cancer. This makes a great read aloud.

Staunton, Ted. *Acting Up*. Red Deer, 2010. 263 p. Grades 7–10.
"Sam Foster is determined to behave maturely enough to convince his parents to leave him home alone for the weekend and to get his learner's permit to drive, but his band, ADHD, his rule-breaking girlfriend, and a teacher who is out to get him make the task nearly impossible." LC

Strasser, Todd. *If I Grow Up*. Simon & Schuster, 2009. 223 p. Grades 7–10.
"Growing up in the inner-city projects, Deshawn is reluctantly forced into the gang world by circumstances beyond his control." LC

Sweeney, Joyce. *The Guardian*. Henry Holt, 2009. 179 p. Grades 7–9.
Hunter, living with an abusive foster mother and three unpleasant foster sisters, needs help desperately. When it suddenly appears, he is mystified. Even reluctant readers enjoy this one.

Sydor, Colleen. *The McGillicuddy Book of Personal Records*. Red Deer, 2010. 221 p. Grades 5–8.
"Thirteen-year-old Lee McGillicuddy begins setting personal records, some bizarre and some very ordinary, in the hopes of proving that he is different from everyone else, but his greatest challenge comes when he must save a friend from certain death." LC

Van Cleave, Ryan G. *Unlocked*. Walker Books, 2011. 160 p. Grades 7–10.
"While trying to impress a beautiful, unattainable classmate, fourteen-year-old Andy discovers that a fellow social outcast may be planning an act of school violence." LC

Volponi, Paul. *Response*. Viking, 2009. 145 p. Grades 6–9.
"Three boys are charged with a hate crime after an African-American high school student is beaten with a baseball bat in a white neighborhood." LC. An ALA Quick Picks for Reluctant Young Adult Readers, 2010.

Volponi, Paul. *Rikers High*. Viking, 2010. 246 p. Grades 8–10.
"Arrested on a minor offense, a New York City teenager attends high school in the jail facility on Rikers Island, as he waits for his case to go to court." LC

Wallace, Rich. *Perpetual Check*. Alfred A. Knopf Books for Young Readers, 2011. 115 p. Grades 8–up.
"Brothers Zeke and Randy participate in an important chess tournament, playing against each other while also trying to deal with their father's intensely competitive tendencies." LC

Wenberg, Michael. *Stringz*. WestSide, 2010. 216 p. Grades 6–9.
Fourteen-year-old Jace's cello helps him survive his rocky life and his fourth new school in two years. Jace is multiracial, with a father who abandoned the family and a mother who

seems to need to keep moving them both, but his playing music in the streets opens up the doors to hope.

Woodson, Jacqueline. *Miracle's Boys.* Putnam Juvenile, 2000. 133 p. Grades 5–up.
    Twelve-year-old Lafayette's close relationship with his older brother Charlie changes after Charlie is released from a detention home and blames Lafayette for the death of their mother. Coretta Scott King Award.

Zadoff, Allen. *Food, Girls, and Other Things I Can't Have.* Egmont, 2009. 314 p. Grades 8–10.
    "Fifteen-year-old Andrew Zansky, the second fattest student at his high school, joins the varsity football team to get the attention of a new girl on whom he has a crush." LC

Chapter ——————— 8

Science Fiction and Fantasy

As you can see by the length of this chapter, science fiction and fantasy books with boy appeal are readily available, and there are many fine writers represented here. It's a genre with wide variety—from fanciful animal stories for young readers to dark dystopian futuristic novels such as *The Hunger Games* by Suzanne Collins and *Unwind* by Neal Shusterman. It can be hard to keep track of some of these series and trilogies, so we hope this chapter will be particularly useful for librarians trying to keep their collections up-to-date.

YOUNGER GUYS

Abbott, Tony. *The Secrets of Droon* series, published by Scholastic, Grades 2–4.
    Three kids cleaning up the basement discover a hidden, magical staircase that takes them into another land filled with danger and excitement. These were originally numbered, but the numbers seem to have disappeared later in the series—which probably means that, at that point, it does not matter that they be read in order.

1. *The Hidden Stairs and the Magic Carpet,* 1999
2. *Journey to the Volcano Palace,* 1999
3. *The Mysterious Island,* 1999

**Journey to the Volcano Palace
by Tony Abbot.**

4. *City in the Clouds*, 1999
5. *The Great Ice Battle*, 1999
6. *The Sleeping Giant of Goll*, 2000
7. *Into the Land of the Lost*, 2000
8. *The Golden Wasp*, 2000
9. *Tower of the Elf King*, 2000
10. *Quest for the Queen*, 2000
11. *The Hawk Bandits of Tarkoom*, 2001
12. *Under the Serpent Sea*, 2001
13. *The Mask of Maliban*, 2001
14. *Voyage of the Jaffa Wind*, 2002
15. *The Moon Scroll*, 2002
16. *The Knights of Silversnow*, 2002

Special Edition #1: The Magic Escapes, 2002
17. *The Dream Thief*, 2003
18. *Search for the Dragon Ship*, 2003
19. *The Coiled Viper*, 2003
20. *In the Ice Caves of Krog*, 2003
21. *Flight of the Genie*, 2003
Special Edition #2: Wizard or Witch? 2004
22. *The Isle of Mists*, 2004
23. *Fortress Of The Treasure Queen*, 2004.
24. *The Race to Doobesh*, 2005
25. *The Riddle of Zorfendorf Castle*, 2005
Special Edition #3: Voyagers of The Silver Sand, 2005
26. *The Moon Dragon*, 2006
27. *The Chariot of Queen Zara*, 2006
28. *In the Shadow of Goll*, 2006
Special Edition #4: Sorcerer, 2006
29. *Pirates of the Purple Dawn*, 2007
30. *Escape from Jabar-loo*, 2007
31. *Queen of Shadowthorn*, 2007
Special Edition #5: Moon Magic, 2008
32. *Treasure of the Orkins*, 2008
33. *Flight of the Blue Serpent*, 2008
34. *In the City of Dreams*, 2008
Special Edition #6: The Crown of Wizards, 2009
35. *Lost Empire of Koomba*, 2009
36. *Knights of the Ruby Wand*, 2010
Special Edition #7: The Genie King, 2010
Special Edition #8: The Final Quest, 2010

Appelt, Kathi. *The Underneath.* Atheneum, 2008. 313 p. Grades 4–up.
Living underneath a ramshackle house in the bayou, an abused, chained, old hound dog acquires an instant family when a pregnant, abandoned cat moves in. The dog's owner is one of the meanest characters in children's books, and this is a story that will stick with you. This is a fine read aloud, incorporating elements of mythology and a lot of suspense.

Applegate, Katherine. *Animorphs* series, published by Scholastic, Grades 3–6.
"Jake and his friends are given the power to morph into animals by a dying alien who tells them the Earth is under attack by the invading Yeerks, and they are called upon to test their new abilities almost immediately when they learn that Vissar Three, deadliest of the Yeerks, is after them." LC. These books were hugely popular in the 1990s, but then went out of print. Now they are being reissued in redesigned format. Five titles came out in 2011.

1. *The Invasion,* 2011
2. *The Visitor,* 2011
3. *The Encounter,* 2011
4. *The Message,* 2011
5. *The Predator,* 2011

Base, Graeme. *The Legend of the Golden Snail.* Abrams, 2010. 48 p. Grades 2–4.
   "Wilbur loves the legend of the Golden Snail, an enchanted galleon, and vows to become its next master." LC

Basye, Dale. *Circles of Heck* series, illustrated by Bob Dob, published by Random House, Grades 4–8.
   "When timid Milton and his older, scofflaw sister Marlo die in a marshmallow bear explosion at Grizzly Mall, they are sent to Heck, an otherworldly reform school from which they are determined to escape." LC

1. *Heck: Where the Bad Kids Go,* 2008
2. *Rapacia: The Second Circle of Heck,* 2009
3. *Blimpo: The Third Circle of Heck,* 2010
4. *Fibble: The Fourth Circle of Heck,* 2011

Beck, Ian. *The Secret History of Tom Trueheart.* Greenwillow, 2007. 341 p. Grades 3–6.
   "When young Tom Trueheart's seven older brothers all go missing during their adventures in the Land of Stories, he embarks on a perilous mission to save them and to capture the rogue story-writer who wants to do away with the heroes." LC

Berkeley, Jon. *Wednesday Tales* trilogy, illustrated by Brandon Dorman, published by HarperCollins, Grades 3–6.
   "Orphaned eleven-year-old Miles Wednesday and his companion, a Song Angel named Little, are helped by a talking tiger as they set off to find a missing Storm Angel and Miles' beloved stuffed bear, ending up in a peculiar circus where the audience cannot stop laughing." LC

1. *The Palace of Laughter,* 2006
2. *The Tiger's Egg,* 2008
3. *The Lightning Key,* 2009

Broach, Elise. *Masterpiece.* Illustrated by Kelly Murphy. Henry Holt, 2008. 291 p. Grades 4–up.
   Marvin, a young beetle, lives with his loving family in the apartment of lonely 11-year-old James Pompaday, whose home is not so loving. When Marvin discovers he has an amazing, and previously unknown, talent, life takes a massive turn for the exciting, mysterious, and adventurous. Marvin cannot talk to human beings, but he figures out a way to communicate with James. This is a memorable and powerful book.

Masterpiece by Elise Broach. Courtesy of Henry Holt Books for Young Readers, an imprint of the Macmillan Children's Publishing Group.

Buckley, Michael. *The Sisters Grimm* series, published by Magic Carpet Books, Grades 4–6.
Sabrina and Daphne Grimm, in foster care since their parents disappeared two years earlier, go to a strange woman who claims to be their paternal grandmother. Is she, really? She also says fairy tales are true and that the whole Grimm family is descended from one of the Grimm brothers. Nonstop action and quite a bit of mystery make these good read alouds. Although the heroines are two girls, teachers swear to me that boys really like them.

1. *The Fairy-Tale Detectives,* 2005
2. *The Unusual Suspects,* 2006
3. *The Problem Child,* 2006
4. *Once Upon a Crime,* 2007
5. *Magic and Other Misdemeanors,* 2007
6. *Tales from the Hood,* 2008
7. *The Everafter War,* 2009
8. *The Inside Story,* 2010

Byrd, Tim. *Doc Wilde and the Frogs of Doom.* Putnam, 2009. 186 p. Grades 4–6.
"Twelve-year-old Brian, ten-year-old Wren, and their father, Doc Wilde, risk their lives in a South American rain forest as they seek the eldest member of their famous family of adventurers, Grandpa, amidst a throng of alien frogs." LC

Collins, Suzanne. *The Underland Chronicles*, published by Scholastic, Grades 4–8.
Eleven-year-old Gregor follows his toddler sister through a vent in the laundry room into another world: the Underland, where rats, spiders, insects, bats, and human beings all live together in a unique and unusual kingdom underneath New York City. This is a real page-turner and cliffhanger. A heck of a good read!

Gregor the Overlander, 2003
Gregor and the Prophecy of Bane, 2004
Gregor and the Curse of the Warmbloods, 2005
Gregor and the Marks of Secret, 2006
Gregor and the Code of Claw, 2007

Coville, Bruce. *Moongobble and Me* series, illustrated by Katherine Coville, published by Simon & Schuster, Grades 2–4.
When Moongobble, an aspiring and pretty incompetent magician, moves nearby, Edward's life becomes exciting.

1. *The Dragon of Doom,* 2003
2. *The Weeping Werewolf,* 2004
3. *The Evil Elves,* 2004
4. *The Mischief Monster,* 2007
5. *The Naughty Nork,* 2008

Cowell, Cressida. *The Heroic Misadventures of Hiccup Horrendous Haddock II* series, published by Little, Brown, Grades 3–6.
Though his dad is the chief, Hiccup is a kid who doesn't really quite cut it in the Viking World. Even the dragon he selects for his own is more than a bit of a wimp—until a

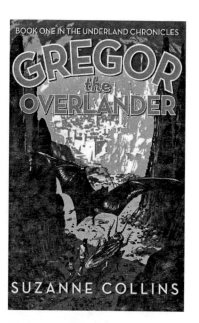

Gregor the Overlander by **Suzanne Collins.**

terrible moment comes and the two of them working together manage to pull off and defeat two enormous dragons determined to kill them all. Filled with gross and funny bits, this series is a winner. It became an even bigger winner when the movie was released. A school librarian told me that if you could get one boy to read the first book, none of the series would ever sit on the shelf again.

1. *How to Train Your Dragon,* 2004
2. *How to be a Pirate,* 2005
3. *How to Speak Dragonese* 2006
4. *How to Cheat a Dragon's Curse,* 2007
5. *How to Twist A Dragon's Tale,* 2008
6. *A Hero's Guide to Deadly Dragons,* 2008
7. *How to Ride a Dragon's Storm,* 2008
8. *How to Break a Dragon's Heart,* 2009

Crum, Shutta. *Thomas and the Dragon Queen.* Alfred A. Knopf Books for Young Readers, 2010. 272 p. Grades 3–5.
"When the princess is kidnapped by a dragon queen, thirteen-year-old Thomas, a new—and very small—squire-in-training boldly sets out on a quest to rescue her." LC. Starred review in *School Library Journal.*

Dashner, James. *The 13th Reality* series, illustrated by Bryan Beus, published by Shadow Mountain /Aladdin, Grades 4–7.
"Thirteen-year-old Atticus "Tick" Higginbottom begins receiving mysterious letters from around the world signed only "M.G.," and the clues contained therein lead him on a journey to the perilous 13th Reality and a confrontation with evil Mistress Jane." LC

The Journal of Curious Letters, 2008
The Hunt for Dark Infinity, 2009
The Blade of Shattered Hope, 2011

De Felice, Cynthia. *Signal.* Farrar, Straus & Giroux, 2009. 151 p. Grades 4–8.
"After moving with his emotionally distant father to the Finger Lakes region of upstate New York, twelve-year-old Owen faces a lonely summer until he meets an abused girl who may be a space alien." LC

DiCamillo, Kate. *The Tale of Despereaux: Being the Story of a Mouse, a Princess, Some Soup, and a Spool of Thread.* Candlewick, 2003. 267 p. Grades 3–6.
"The adventures of Despereaux Tilling, a small mouse of unusual talents, the princess that he loves, the servant girl who longs to be a princess." LC. Received the Newbery Medal, 2004.

DiTerlizzi, Tony. *Kenny & the Dragon.* Simon & Schuster, 2008. 151 p. Grades 3–6.
"Book-loving Kenny the rabbit has few friends in his farming community, so when one, bookstore owner George, is sent to kill another, gentle dragon Grahame, Kenny must find a way to prevent their battle while satisfying the dragon-crazed townspeople." LC

DiTerlizzi, Tony, and Holly Black. *The Spiderwick Chronicles,* published by Simon & Schuster, Grades 3–6.
The Grace children, Simon, Jared, and Mallory, move into a decaying old house with their mother and find a field guide to fairyland—which seems to exist quite noticeably in that very house. Fun, and a little scary. This was made into a movie in 2008.

The Field Guide, 2003
The Seeing Stone, 2003
Lucinda's Secret, 2003
The Ironwood Tree, 2004
The Wrath of Mulgarath, 2004
Arthur Spiderwick's Field Guide to the Fantastical World Around You, 2005
The Care and Feeding of Sprites, 2006
The Nixie's Song, 2007
Giant Problem, 2008
The Completely Fantastical Edition, 2009 (the first five books in one volume)
The Wyrm King, 2010

Doyle, Roddy. *The Giggler Treatment.* Scholastic, 2000. 112 p. Grades 4–6.
"A talking dog, the Mack children and the small elf-like Gigglers themselves must try to stop the prank that the Gigglers have mistakenly set in motion to punish Mr. Mack for being mean to his children." LC

DuPrau, Jeanne. *The Books of Ember* series, published by Random House, Grades 4–8.
The first book, about two kids in a post-apocalyptic decaying underground city, is a superb read and won multiple state young reader awards and was made into a movie. The others are sequels and *The Prophet of Yonwood* is a prequel.

1. *The City of Ember,* 2003
2. *The People of Sparks,* 2004
3. *The Prophet of Yonwood,* 2006
4. *The Diamond of Darkhold,* 2008

Durango, Julia. *Sea of the Dead.* Simon & Schuster, 2009. 136 p. Grades 4–6.
"When thirteen-year-old Kehl, fifth son of the Warrior Prince Amatec, is kidnapped by the Fallen King and forced to map the entire Carillon Empire, he also discovers a secret about his own past." LC. Nominated for multiple state young readers awards and received the Parents' Choice Silver Honors.

Epstein, Adam Jay, and Andrew Jacobson. *The Familiars* series, published by HarperCollins, Grades 4–6.
Aldwyn the alley cat has to pretend he has magical powers when he is purchased by a boy wizard who wants a familiar. Reminiscent of Harry Potter, and predictable to those of us who have read a lot of these kinds of stories, this is still an enjoyable read.
The Familiars, 2010
Secrets of the Crown, 2011

Evans, Nate. *Beast Friends Forever* series, illustrated by Vince Evans, published by Sourcebooks Jabberwocky, Grades 2–4.
Zeke and his little sister discover that a smelly little monster hitched a ride to their house on a package their dad mailed from overseas.

Meet the Beast, 2010
The Super Swap-O Surprise, 2011

Feig, Paul. *Ignatius McFarland: Frequenant!* Little, Brown, 2008. 353 p. Grades 4–8.
"Bullied in school and called "Piggy MacFartland," twelve-year-old Iggy longs to travel to another planet and live among extraterrestrials, until an explosion transports him to a scary alternate reality." LC

Fields, Bryan. *Lunchbox and the Aliens.* Illustrated by Kevan Ateberry. Henry Holt, 2006. 166 p. Grades 3–6.

"Lunchbox is an ordinary basset hound until he is abducted by aliens, zapped by a mental enhancer, and sent back to convert Earth's garbage into food—a task that would be easier if he had opposable thumbs, or at least tentacles." LC. The sequel is *Froonga Planet,* 2008.

Funke, Cornelia. *Dragon Rider.* Scholastic, 2004. 523 p. Grades 4–6.

"After learning that humans are headed toward his hidden home, Firedrake, a silver dragon, is joined by a brownie and an orphan boy in a quest to find the legendary valley known as the Rim of Heaven, encountering friendly and unfriendly creatures along the way, and struggling to evade the relentless pursuit of an old enemy." LC. Nominated for many state young reader awards.

Funke, Cornelia. *The Thief Lord.* The Chicken House, 2002. 349 p. Grades 4–8.

Orphaned 12-year-old Prosper and 5-year-old Bo have run away from home to live in the city their mother always talked about, Venice. Their aunt and uncle want to adopt Bo, but not Prosper. They have found shelter with other homeless children, led by a 13-year-old who calls himself The Thief Lord, in an abandoned movie theater. But when the aunt and uncle come to Venice and hire a detective to find them, their adventures become more desperate. A grippingly good read aloud, with much to discuss. Is it ever OK to steal? Moral dilemmas abound. Also, take a look at the map in the endpapers and trace the adventures on the map—a good lesson in geography.

Gaiman, Neil. *Odd and the Frost Giants.* Illustrated by Brett Helquist. HarperCollins, 2009. 118 p. Grades 3–6.

A popular writer scores again in this story about a 12-year-old boy who helps three Norse gods disguised as a bear, a fox, and an eagle.

Gidwitz, Adam. *A Tale Dark & Grimm.* Dutton, 2010. 249 p. Grades 3–up.

"Follows Hansel and Gretel as they walk out of their own story and into eight more tales, encountering such wicked creatures as witches, along with kindly strangers and other helpful folk. Based in part on the Grimms' tales of Faithful Johannes, Hansel and Gretel, The Seven Ravens, Brother and Sister, The Robber Bridegroom, and The Devil and His Three Golden Hairs." LC. Starred reviews in *School Library Journal, Kirkus,* and *Publishers Weekly.*

Gutman, Dan. *The Christmas Genie.* Illustrated by Dan Santat. Simon & Schuster, 2009. 151 p. Grades 3–6.

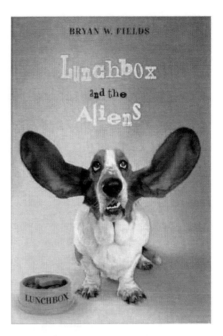

Lunchbox and the Aliens by Bryan Fields. Courtesy of Henry Holt Books for Young Readers, an imprint of the Macmillan Children's Publishing Group.

A Tale Dark & Grimm by Adam Gidwitz. Used by permission of Penguin Group (USA) Inc. All rights reserved.

"The students in a fifth-grade class at Lincoln School in Oak Park, Illinois, must learn to work together quickly when a meteorite crashes into their classroom and the genie inside grants them a Christmas wish—if they can agree on one within an hour." LC

Gutman, Dan. *Nightmare at the Book Fair.* Simon & Schuster, 2009. 231 p. Grades 4–6.
"On his way to lacrosse tryouts, the president of the PTA asks Trip Dinkelman to help her with the book fair, resulting in Trip sustaining a head injury which causes him temporary amnesia and makes for an interesting journey home." LC

Haber, Melissa Glenn. *The Heroic Adventures of Hercules Amsterdam.* Dutton, 2003. 213 p. Grades 4–6.
Hercules Amsterdam's problem is that he is only three inches tall and he lives in a doll house. His parents are sympathetic, but wish he were larger, and when his mother decides to get a job and send him off to public school, he runs away—to the mouse colony he has heard behind the doll house wall. And there he learns that he and his skills are desperately needed. This is a superb adventure for fantasy fans, and works great as a read aloud even for younger children.

Haberdasher, Violet. *Knightley Academy.* Aladdin, 2010. 469 p. Grades 4–7.
"In an alternate Victorian England, fourteen-year-old orphan Henry Grim, a maltreated servant at an exclusive school for the "sons of Gentry and Quality," begins a new life when he unexpectedly becomes the first commoner to be accepted at Knightley Academy, a prestigious boarding school for knights." LC

Haddix, Margaret Peterson. *The Missing* series, published by Simon & Schuster, Grades 4–8.
The first book opens with a compelling story that sets the scene for future chapters. A plane, not on the schedule, arrives at an airport. The gate attendant goes down the jet bridge, opens the door, and sees nothing but babies—one in every seat! Who those babies are and why they are here makes for a great premise.

> *Found,* 2008
> *Sent,* 2009
> *Sabotaged,* 2010
> *Torn,* 2011
> *Caught,* 2012

Haig, Matt. *Samuel Blink and the Forbidden Forest.* Putnam Juvenile, 2007. 316 p. Grades 4–8.
"Samuel and Martha move to Norway to live with their Aunt Edna following the death of their parents and are drawn to the attic and the Shadow Forest behind the house in spite of their aunt's warning to stay away from them." LC. The sequel is *Samuel Blink and the Runaway Troll,* 2008.

Hannan, Peter. *Freddy!* series, illustrated by the author, published by HarperCollins, Grades 2–5.
"Freddy, his jealous sister Babette, and their parents are abducted by slimy aliens and taken to the planet Flurb, where Freddy is made king, much to the dismay of Wizbad." LC

> 1. *Freddy! King of Flurb,* 2011
> 2. *Freddy! Deep-Space Food Fighter,* 2011

Holt, K. A. *Mike Stellar: Nerves of Steel.* Random House, 2009. 263 p. Grades 4–7.
"Mike is suspicious when his family joins an expedition to Mars at the last minute, and his fears are confirmed when all of the adults on the colonizing mission, including his parents, begin to act strangely." LC

Hunter, Erin. *Warriors* **series, published by HarperCollins, Grades 4–8.**

A young orange house cat ventures outside the yard and realizes that there is a world of wild cats out there. There are four clans in the area, and he joins the ThunderClan, becomes an apprentice warrior, and is called Firepaw. Soon he learns that threats come not only from other clans, but also from within his own. Several more series of books have sprung from this original series. It can be hard to keep track of them, but kids seem to have no problem keeping them straight.

1. *Into the Wild,* 2004
2. *Fire and Ice,* 2004
3. *Forest of Secrets,* 2004
4. *Rising Storm,* 2005
5. *A Dangerous Path,* 2005
6. *Darkest Hour,* 2006

Hunter, Erin. *Warriors: Omen of the Stars,* **published by HarperCollins, Grades 4–8.**

1. *Fourth Apprentice,* 2009
2. *Fading Echoes,* 2010
3. *Night Whispers,* 2010
4. *The Sign of the Moon,* 2011
5. *The Forgotten Warrior,* 2011
6. *The Last Hope,* 2012

Hunter, Erin. *Warriors: The New Prophecy,* **published by HarperCollins, Grades 4–8.**

1. *Midnight,* 2005
2. *Moonrise,* 2005
3. *Dawn,* 2006
4. *Starlight,* 2006
5. *Twilight,* 2006
6. *Sunset,* 2007

Warriors Field Guide: Secrets of the Clans, 2007

Hunter, Erin. *Warriors: The Power of Three* **series, published by HarperCollins, Grades 4–8.**

1. *The Sight,* 2008
2. *Dark River,* 2008
3. *Outcast,* 2008
4. *Eclipse,* 2008
5. *Long Shadows,* 2008
6. *Sunrise,* 2009

Hunter, Erin. *Warrior's Field Guides,* **published by HarperCollins, Grades 4–8.**

Secrets of the Clans, 2007
Cats of the Clans, 2008
Codes of the Clans, 2009
Battles of the Clans, 2010

Hunter, Erin. *Warrior's Super Editions,* **published by HarperCollins, Grades 4–8.**

Firestar's Quest, 2008
Bluestar's Prophecy, 2009

SkyClan's Destiny, 2010
Crookedstar's Promise, 2011

Ibbotson, Eva. *The Secret of Platform 13.* Illustrated by Sue Porter. Puffin, 1994. 231 p. Grades 4–6.

Long before Harry Potter was ever published, Eva Ibbotson wrote about a strange platform in King's Cross station in London that opens into a tunnel to an enchanted island for a few days every nine years. Nine years ago, the island's prince, the heir to the throne, and a tiny baby, was kidnapped from his cradle and taken through the tunnel, and now a rescue operation is mounted to bring him back to his home. But when the rescuers arrive, can they find him? Will they like him? Will they want him back? Absolutely delightful and a great read aloud.

Iggulden, Conn. *Tollins: Explosive Tales for Children.* HarperCollins, 2009. 176 p. Grades 3–6.

A fantasy about tiny creatures whose fine existence is horribly changed when a fireworks factory moves in to the nearby village and they are sought to be blown up. *Booklist* called this "a wickedly funny and ingenious read."

Jennewein, James, and Tom S. Parker. *RuneWarriors* **series, published by HarperCollins, Grades 3–6.**

"In an ancient and mystical time, teenaged Dane joins forces with his rival, Jari the Fair, to retrieve the Shield of Odin and Astrid, the girl they love, from the tyrant Thidrek, fulfilling a destiny long foretold." LC

1. *RuneWarriors,* 2008
2. *Shield of Odin,* 2009
3. *Ship of the Dead,* 2010
4. *Sword of Doom,* 2011

Jones, Allan. *Trundle's Quest.* Illustrated by Gary Chalk. Greenwillow, 2011. 176 p. Grades 4–6.

"Trundle Boldoak's simple life as the town lamplighter is turned upside-down the night he meets Esmeralda, a Roamany hedgehog, who whisks him away on a quest to find six fabled crowns and fulfill his role in an ancient prophecy." LC. This is the first in a new series called *Six Crowns.*

Juster, Norton. *The Phantom Tollbooth.* Random House, 1961, 1964. 255 p. Grades 4–7.

This great classic has stood the test of time. "Milo finds a cure for his boredom and discovers the importance of words and numbers on a journey through a fantastical land." LC

Kingsley, Kaza. *Erec Rex* **series, illustrated by Tim Jacobus, published by Simon & Schuster, Grades 4–8.**

"Twelve-year-old Erec Rex stumbles upon a world where magic has not been forgotten, and must survive the ultimate test in order to save the magical kingdom he was born to rule." LC

1. *The Dragon's Eye, 2006,* 2009
2. *The Monsters of Otherness, 2007,* 2009
3. *The Search for Truth,* 2009
4. *The Three Furies,* 2010

Kirov, Erica. *The MagicKeepers* **series, published by Sourcebooks Jabberwocky, Grades 4–6.**

"Living in Las Vegas with his unsuccessful father, Nick Rostov learns on his thirteenth birthday that he is descended from a powerful line of Russian Magickeepers on his dead mother's side, and that the equally powerful but evil Shadowkeepers will stop at nothing to get an ancient relic that his grandfather gave him." LC

The Eternal Hourglass, 2009
The Pyramid of Souls, 2010
The Chalice of Immortality, 2011

Klimo, Kate. *Dragon Keepers* series, published by Random House, Grades 3–6.
   "Cousins Jesse and Daisy always knew they would have a magical adventure, but they are not prepared when the "thunder egg" Jesse has found turns out to be a dragon egg that is about to hatch." LC

   1. *The Dragon in the Sock Drawer,* 2008
   2. *The Dragon in the Driveway,* 2009
   3. *The Dragon in the Library,* 2010
   4. *The Dragon in the Volcano,* 2011

Kloepfer, John. *The Zombie Chasers.* HarperCollins, 2010. 224 p. Grades 4–6.
   "Zack Clarke's sleepover turns into chaos when Zombies invade." LC. The sequel is *Undead Ahead,* 2011.

Knight, Steven. *The Last Words of Will Wolfkin.* WaldenPond, 2010. 384 p. Grades 4–8.
   "Fourteen-year-old Toby, paralyzed since birth and raised in a convent, suddenly finds himself capable of movement and speech when his long-time companion, a cat, takes him on a magical and mysterious journey to Iceland." LC

Knudsen, Michelle. *The Dragon of Trelian.* Candlewick, 2009. 411 p. Grades 4–7.
   "A mage's apprentice, a princess, and a dragon combine their strength and magic to bring down a traitor and restore peace to the kingdom of Trelian." LC

Lasky, Kathryn. *The Guardians of Ga'Hoole* series, published by Scholastic, Grades 4–7.
   A barn owl named Soren, pushed from his nest by his creepy older brother, is captured and taken to a huge prison complex, where baby owls are brainwashed and made into slaves, all in the service of some unknown cause. The first in a popular series, this is a good read, with a lot of action and adventure.

   1. *The Capture,* 2003
   2. *The Journey,* 2003
   3. *The Rescue,* 2004
   4. *The Siege,* 2004
   5. *The Shattering,* 2004
   6. *The Burning,* 2004
   7. *The Hatchling,* 2005
   8. *The Outcast,* 2005
   9. *The First Collier,* 2006
   10. *The Coming of Hoole,* 2006
   11. *To Be a King,* 2006
   12. *The Golden Tree,* 2007
   13. *River of Wind,* 2007
   14. *Exile,* 2007
   15. *War of the Ember,* 2008
   16. *Lost Tales of Ga'Hoole,* 2010

   A Guide Book to the Great Tree, 2007
   Guardians of Ga'Hoole: Lost Tales of Ga'Hoole, 2010

Lizeaux, William. *Clarence Cochran, a Human Boy.* Illustrated by Anne Wilsdorf. Farrar, Straus & Giroux, 2009. 154 p. Grades 4–6.
   When a cockroach finds he has been mysteriously transformed into a human boy, he has a mission to fulfill—to save his cockroach colony from extermination. Fun, with a good message.

Llewellyn, Tom. *The Tilting House.* Tricycle, 2010. 160 p. Grades 4–7.
   "When Josh, his parents, grandfather, and eight-year-old brother move into the old Tilton House, they discover such strange things as talking rats, a dimmer switch that makes the house invisible, and a powder that makes objects grow." LC

Lyga, Barry. *Archvillain.* Scholastic, 2010. 192 p. Grades 4–7.

"Twelve-year-old Kyle Camden develops greater mental agility and superpowers during a plasma storm that also brings Mighty Mike, an alien, to his hometown, but while each does what he thinks is best, Kyle is labeled a villain and Mike a hero." LC

Mason, Timothy. *The Last Synapsid.* Delacorte, 2009. 313 p. Grades 4–8.

When two friends discover two prehistoric (and talking) creatures in their Colorado town, they need to transport both back in time—or humans will not evolve!

McElligott, Matthew, and Larry Tuxbury. *Benjamin Frankenstein Lives!* Putnam Juvenile, 2010. 128 p. Grades 4–7.

"While working on a science fair project, a Philadelphia school boy discovers both a secret laboratory in his basement and Benjamin Franklin, who comes to life after receiving a jolt of electricity." LC

Benjamin Frankenstein Lives! **by Matthew McElligott and Larry Tuxbury. Used by permission of Penguin Group (USA) Inc. All rights reserved.**

Messer, Stephen. *Windblown.* Random House, 2010, 304 p. Grades 4–7.

"Hapless Oliver, who lives in the trees in the town of Windblowne, seeks his eccentric great-uncle Gilbert's help in creating a kite for the all-important kite festival, but when Gilbert suddenly disappears, Oliver is guided by one of Gilbert's kites in a quest through different worlds to find him." LC

Mills, Claudia. *How Oliver Olson Changed the World.* Illustrated by Heather Malone. Farrar, Straus & Giroux, 2009. 104 p. Grades 2–4.

Afraid he will always be an outsider like ex-planet Pluto, nine-year-old Oliver finally shows his helicopter parents that he is capable of doing great things without their help while his class is studying the solar system.

Mills, Claudia. *One Square Inch.* Farrar, Straus & Giroux, 2010. 176 p. Grades 4–6.

"When their mother's behavior changes and she starts to neglect her children, seventh-grader Cooper and his little sister take refuge in Inchland, an imaginary country inspired by deeds to one square inch of land that their grandfather gave them." LC

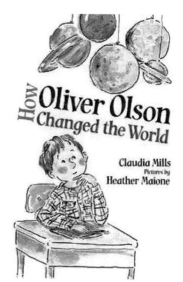

How Oliver Olson Changed the World **by Claudia Mills. Courtesy of Farrar Straus Giroux Books for Young Readers, an imprint of the Macmillan Children's Publishing Group.**

Mull, Brandon. *A World without Heroes.* Aladdin, 2011. 464 p. Grades 4–7.

"Fourteen-year-old Jason Walker is transported to a strange world called Lyrian, where he joins Rachel and a few rebels to piece together the Word that can destroy the malicious wizard emperor, Surroth." LC. The first in the *Beyonders* series.

Nielsen, Jennifer A. *Elliott and the Goblin War.* Sourcebooks Jabberwocky, 2010. 208 p. Grades 3–5.

"Eight-year-old Elliot Penster accidently starts an interspecies war when he stops two goblins, he thought were trick-or-treaters, from chasing a little girl who was actually a brownie." LC

Ogden, Charles. *Edgar & Ellen* **series, illustrated by Rick Carton, published by Simon & Schuster, Grades 4–6.**

Lemony Snicket fans like these stories about 12-year-old twins who cause a lot of mischief in their sweet hometown, Nod's Limbs. This is also a TV series.

1. *Mischief Manual,* 2007
2. *Rare Beasts,* 2003
3. *Tourist Trap,* 2004
4. *Under Town,* 2004
5. *Pet's Revenge,* 2006
6. *High Wire,* 2006
7. *Nod's Limbs,* 2007

The *Edgar & Ellen Nodyssey* **series continues the story**

1. *Hot Air,* 2008
2. *Frost Bites,* 2008
3. *Split Ends,* 2009

Osborne, Mary Pope. *Magic Tree House* **series, published by Random House, Grades 2–4.**

A delightful series of adventures that takes Jack and Annie around the world and throughout time to complete tasks for Merlin the Magician, and Morgan le Fay, the librarian of Camelot. Several titles have nonfiction companions, as well.

1. *Dinosaurs Before Dark,* 1992
2. *The Knight at Dawn,* 1993
3. *Mummies in the Morning,* 1993
4. *Pirates Past Noon,* 1994
5. *Night of the Ninjas,* 1995
6. *Afternoon on the Amazon,* 1995
7. *Sunset of the Sabertooth,* 1996
8. *Midnight on the Moon,* 1996
9. *Dolphins at Daybreak,* 1997
10. *Ghost Town at Sundown,* 1997
11. *Lions at Lunchtime,* 1998
12. *Polar Bears Past Bedtime,* 1998
13. *Vacation Under the Volcano,* 1998
14. *Day of the Dragon-King,* 1998
15. *Viking Ships at Sunrise,* 1998
16. *Hour of the Olympics,* 1998
17. *Tonight on the Titanic,* 1999
18. *Buffalo Before Breakfast,* 1999
19. *Tigers at Twilight,* 1999
20. *Dingoes at Dinnertime,* 2000
21. *Civil War on Sunday,* 2000
22. *Revolutionary War on Wednesday,* 2000
23. *Twister on a Tuesday,* 2001
24. *Earthquake in the Early Morning,* 2001
25. *Stage Fright on a Summer Night,* 2002
26. *Good Morning, Gorillas,* 2002
27. *Thanksgiving on Thursday,* 2002
28. *High Tide in Hawaii,* 2003
29. *Christmas in Camelot,* 2003
30. *Haunted Castle on Hallows Eve,* 2003
31. *Summer of the Sea Serpent,* 2004
32. *Winter of the Ice Wizard,* 2004
33. *Carnival at Candlelight,* 2005
34. *Season of the Sandstorms,* 2005
35. *Night of the New Magicians,* 2006
36. *Blizzard of the Blue Moon,* 2006
37. *Dragon of the Red Dawn,* 2007
38. *Monday with a Mad Genius,* 2008

39. *Dark Day in the Deep Sea*, 2008
40. *Eve of the Emperor Penguin*, 2009
41. *Moonlight on the Magic Flute*, 2009
42. *Good Night for Ghosts*, 2009
43. *Leprechaun in Late Winter*, 2010
44. *Ghost Tale for Christmas Time*, 2010
45. *Crazy Day for Cobras*, 2010
46. *Dogs in the Dead of Night*, 2011
47. *Abe Lincoln at Last!* 2011
48. *A Perfect Time for Pandas*, 2012

Paratore, Colleen Murtagh. *The Funeral Director's Son.* Simon & Schuster, 2008. 136 p. Grades 4–6.

"The last thing twelve-year-old Christopher 'Kip' Campbell wants is to take over the funeral business that has been in his family for generations, but he is the only Campbell heir and seems to have a calling to help the dead and their survivors in a most unusual way." LC. Sequel is *Kip Campbell's Gift*, 2009.

Pearson, Ridley. *Muddle Earth.* Delacorte, 2007. 450 p. Grades 4–9.

"Joe Jefferson suddenly turns into a fearless warrior-hero while walking his dog one night, and is summoned by Muddle Earth's leading wizard to slay ogres, wrestle dragons, and bravely confront villains." LC. A fun parody of *Lord of the Rings*.

Prevost, Guillaume. *The Book of Time* trilogy, translated by William Rodarmor, published by Scholastic, Grades 4–8.

Fourteen-year-old Sam Faulkner travels through time and space as he searches for his father.

1. *The Book of Time*, 2007
2. *The Gate of Days*, 2008
3. *The Circle of Gold*, 2009

Prineas, Sarah. *The Magic Thief series,* illustrated by Antonio Javier Caparo, published by HarperCollins, Grades 4–8.

Conn is a pickpocket, a street kid, a thief—until the day he steals something powerful from a wizard and his life changes dramatically. This is a fun fantasy, lots of action and never a dull moment.

The Magic Thief, 2008
Lost, 2009
Found, 2010

Reeve, Philip. *No Such Thing as Dragons.* Scholastic, 2010. 192 p. Grades 4–7.

"A young, mute boy who is apprenticed to a dragon-slayer suspects that the winged beasts do not exist, until he—and his master—learn the truth." LC. Philip Reeve always delivers a great story.

Reisman, Michael. *Simon Bloom* series, published by Dutton, Grades 4–7.

"Sixth-grader Simon Bloom finds a book that enables him to control the laws of physics; but when two thugs come after him, he needs the formulas in the book to save himself." LC

1. *Simon Bloom, the Gravity Keeper,* 2008
2. *Simon Bloom, the Octopus Effect,* 2009

Rodda, Emily. *Rondo* series, published by Scholastic, Grades 3–6.

"Through an heirloom music box, Leo, a serious, responsible boy, and his badly-behaved cousin Mimi enter the magical world of Rondo to rescue Mimi's dog from a sorceress, who wishes to exchange him for the key that allows free travel between worlds." LC

1. *The Key to Rondo,* 2008
2. *The Wizard of Rondo,* 2009
3. *The Battle for Rondo,* 2009

Service, Pamela F. *Alien Agent* series, published by Darby Creek (Lerner), grades 3–6.

Ordinary American kid Zack is astounded to learn that he is actually an alien secret agent.

1. *My Cousin the Alien,* 2008
2. *Camp Alien,* 2009
3. *Alien Expedition,* 2009
4. *Alien Encounter,* 2010
5. *Alien Contact,* 2010

Skelton, Matthew. *The Story of Cirrus Flux.* Delacorte, 2010. 304 p. Grades 4–7.

Fantasy fans will enjoy this story of a kid who has a mysterious trinket that a lot of other people want to steal. Why? What is in the trinket that they want? Set in an alternate 1783 London.

Sniegoski, Tom. *Billy Hooten, Owlboy* series, illustrated by Eric Powell, published by Random House, Grades 3–6.

"Billy Hooten, a weird kid who likes comic books and monster movies, hears a cry for help coming from the cemetery, and soon finds himself trying to decide if he is up to the task of being Owlboy, a superhero in charge of the safety of the residents of Monstros City, an underground world below his hometown of Bradbury, Massachusetts." LC

1. *Owlboy,* 2007
2. *The Girl with the Destructo Touch,* 2007
3. *Tremble at the Terror of Zis-Boom-Bah,* 2007
4. *The Flock of Fury,* 2008

Sonnenblick, Jordan. *Dodger and Me* series, published by Feiwel and Friends, Grades 4–6.

"Miserable because his only friend moved away and he has once again caused his baseball team to lose a game, fifth-grader Willy Ryan's life suddenly becomes a lot more interesting when he finds Dodger, a furry, blue chimpanzee that only he can see, and he has to decide what he really wishes for in life." LC

Dodger and Me, 2008
Dodger for President, 2009
Dodger for Sale, 2010

Soup, Cuthbert. *A Whole Nother Story.* Illustrated by Jeffrey Stewart Timmins. Bloomsbury, 2009. 264 p. Grades 3–6.

"Ethan Cheeseman and his children, ages eight, twelve, and fourteen, hope to settle in a nice small town, at least long enough to complete work on a time machine, but spies and government agents have been pursuing them for two years and are about to catch up." LC. Fans of Lemony Snicket love this. The sequel is *Another Whole Nother Story*, 2010.

Sparkes, Ali. *Frozen in Time*. Egmont, 2010. 312 p. Grades 4–7.
"In England, thirteen-year-old Ben and his twelve-year-old sister Rachel find two children who have been cryogenically frozen in a bomb shelter since 1956, and must prevent them from being discovered while helping them adjust to modern life." LC.

Stevermer, Carolyn. *Magic Below Stairs*. Dial, 2010. 199 p. Grades 4–7.
Plucked from a horrible orphanage, 10-year-old Frederick Lincoln, accompanied by a brownie named Billy Bly, becomes a footman in the cursed house of the wizard Thomas Schofield. How can they get rid of the curse? Delightful.

Stewart, Paul, and Chris Riddell. *The Edge Chronicles* series, published by Fickling, Grades 4–6.
This first title in this British series tells us the story of Twig, a human child raised by a family of wood trolls in a fantastic world called The Edge. There are some amazingly inventive creatures in this fast-moving story, with many excellent illustrations.

1. *Beyond the Deepwoods*, 2004
2. *Stormchaser*, 2004
3. *Midnight over Sanctaphrax*, 2004
4. *The Curse of the Gloamglozer*, 2005
5. *The Last of the Sky Pirates*, 2005
6. *Vox*, 2005
7. *Freeglader*, 2006
8. *Winter Knights*, 2007
9. *Clash of the Sky Galleons*, 2007
10. *The Immortals*, 2010

Tan, Shaun. *The Haunted Playground*. Stone Arch Books, 2007. 73 p. Grades 3–8.
Gavin's new metal detector works great in playgrounds. When he takes it to one he's never been to before, he is surprised to find that a number of rather strange children come out after dark—and that playing with them is a lot of fun. Slowly, he begins to realize that they are all ghosts—and they want him to join them.

Teague, Mark. *The Doom Machine*. Scholastic, 2009. 343 p. Grades 4–7.
"When a spaceship lands in the small town of Vern Hollow in 1956, juvenile delinquent Jack Creedle and prim, studious Isadora Shumway form an unexpected alliance as they try to keep a group of extraterrestrials from stealing eccentric Unclebud's space travel machine." LC. Received Parents' Choice Silver Honors.

Toft, Di. *Wolven*. The Chicken House, 2010. 325 p. Grades 4–8.
"Twelve-year-old Nat, with help from family, friends, and his 'pet' Woody, a wolf that turns into a boy, must face werewolves that have been altered as part of a dastardly plan." LC

The Haunted Playground by Shaun Tan.

Townley, Roderick. *The Blue Shoe: A Tale of Thievery, Villainy, Sorcery, and Shoes.* Illustrated by Mary GrandPre. Alfred A. Knopf Books for Young Readers, 2009. 207 p. Grades 4–6.

A fun fantasy about a kid who is arrested and exiled, finds his father in the process, and participates in a prisoner's revolt. Nominated for several state young reader awards.

Vande Velde, Vivian. *The Rumpelstiltskin Problem.* Scholastic, 2001. 116 p. Grades 4–7.

This amazingly clever concept makes a fine writing starter. The author thinks the story of Rumpelstiltskin makes no sense at all. If a miller were poor, why would his daughter be able to spin straw into gold? Why would the king believe that? Why would Rumpelstiltskin take as payment small gold pieces when he could make all the gold he wanted? Why would he want a baby? The author rewrites the story six different ways so it makes more sense. Can you come up with any other ways? Are there other folk and fairy tales that are as illogical as this one? Funny, and each version is short and makes a fairly quick read aloud.

Waugh, Sylvia. *Space Race.* Delacorte, 2000.

"When he learns that he and his father must soon leave Earth, eleven-year-old Thomas Derwent is upset, but a terrible accident that separates the two of them makes Thomas's situation much worse." LC. This is a real thriller. Try it as a read aloud. Sequel is *Earthborn*, 2002.

Williams, Tad. *The Dragons of Ordinary Farm.* Illustrated by Greg Swearingen. HarperCollins, 2009. 412 p. Grades 4–8.

"After their great-uncle Gideon invites Tyler and Lucinda to his farm for the summer, they discover his animals are extremely unusual." LC

Wilson, N. D. *The 100 Cupboards* trilogy, published by Random House, Grades 4–7.

"Twelve-year-old Henry York and his cousin Henrietta discover 100 hidden portals to other worlds in the bedroom wall of his aunt and uncle's house." LC

1. *100 Cupboards,* 2007
2. *Dandelion Fire,* 2009
3. *The Chestnut King,* 2010

OLDER GUYS

Alexander, Lloyd. *The Golden Dreams of Carlo Chuchio.* Holt, 2007. 305 p. Grades 5–8.

When Carlo finds a treasure map hidden in the binding of an ancient, mysteriously acquired book, he takes off for action and adventure in an Arabian Nights sort of a story that has a completely satisfactory ending!

Almond, David. *The Savage.* Candlewick, 2008. 79 p. Grades 5–9.

"After his father dies and the town bully Hooper begins to target him, Blue starts to write and illustrate a graphic novel full of blood, guts, and adventures; but after one of Blue's characters pays Hooper a nighttime visit, Blue wonders if the lines of reality have blurred." LC

Almond, David. *Skellig.* Delacorte, 1999. 208 p. Grades 5–8.

Michael and his friend Mina find a strange, mysterious man in the ramshackle garage of the house Michael's family moves into. Who—and what—is Skellig?

Augarde, Steve. *X-Isle.* Random House, 2010. 477 p. Grades 7–up.

"Baz and Ray, survivors of an apocalyptic flood, win places on X-Isle, an island where life is rumored to be better than on the devastated mainland, but they find the island to be a violent place ruled by religious fanatic Preacher John, and they decide they must come up with a weapon to protect themselves from impending danger." LC

Avi. *Murder at Midnight.* Scholastic, 2009. 254 p. Grades 5–8.
"Falsely accused of plotting to overthrow King Claudio, scholarly Mangus the magician, along with his street-smart servant boy, Fabrizio, face deadly consequences unless they can track down the real traitor by the stroke of midnight." LC. *Booklist* chose this one of the top 10 crime fiction books for youth.

Baccalario, Pierdomenico. *Century Quartet* series, published by Random House, Grades 5–9.
Four kids, all born on February 29, need to band together to save the world in four different cities.

1. *Ring of Fire,* 2010
2. *Star of Stone,* 2010
3. *City of Wind,* 2011

Baciagalupi, Paolo. *Ship Breaker.* Little, Brown, 2010. 326 p. Grades 7–up.
Nailer, a ship breaker, searches ships for copper parts. On one of his expeditions, he discovers a girl on the ship. Should he turn her in or work with her? An exciting story set in a dystopian future, this was one of the best reviewed books of 2010 and won the Printz Award. The companion book is *The Drowned Cities,* 2012.

Baggott, Julianna. *The Prince of Fenway Park.* HarperCollins, 2009. 325 p. Grades 5–8.
"In the fall of 2004, twelve-year-old Oscar Egg is sent to live with his father in a strange netherworld under Boston's Fenway Park, where he joins the fairies, pooka, banshee, and other beings that are trapped there, waiting for someone to break the eighty-six-year-old curse that has prevented the Boston Red Sox from winning a World Series." LC

Barnhouse, Rebecca. *The Coming of the Dragon.* Random House, 2010. 310 p. Grades 5–8.
"A retelling of 'Beowulf' in which Rune, raised on a farm by a wise woman after being rescued as an infant by King Beowulf, goes to the king's hall each winter for weapons training, a skill that comes in handy when a dragon awakes in the mountains." LC

Barrett, Tracy. *King of Ithaka.* Henry Holt, 2010. 261 p. Grades 7–up.
"When sixteen-year-old Telemachos and his two best friends, one a centaur, leave their life of privilege to undertake a quest to find Telemachos's father Odysseus, they learn much along the way about what it means to be a man and a king." LC. Starred reviews in *Kirkus* and *School Library Journal.*

Barron. T. A. *Merlin's Dragon* series, published by Philomel, Grades 5–8.
Part lizard, part bat, little Basil becomes the wizard Merlin's rescuer and friend. Lots of action.

1. *Merlin's Dragon,* 2008
2. *Doomraga's Revenge,* 2009
3. *Ultimate Magic,* 2010

Barry, Dave, and Ridley Pearson. *Starcatchers* series, published by Hyperion, Grades 7–up.
Starts with a prequel to Peter Pan. Exactly where did he come from? How did he meet Captain Hook? Exactly why can he fly? All of these questions and more—including where Neverland got its name—are answered in a thrilling and exciting way! A real page-turner, this is Dave Barry's first children's book, written via e-mail with Ridley Pearson.

Peter and the Star Catchers, 2004
Peter and the Shadow Thieves, 2006
Peter and the Secret of Rundoon, 2007
Peter and the Sword of Mercy, 2009
The Bridge to Never Land, 2011

There are three companion books, also written by Barry and Pearson, called the *Never Land Books.*

Escape from the Carnivale, 2006
Cave of the Dark Wind, 2007
Blood Tide, 2008

Bell, Hilari. *Goblin Wood* trilogy, published by HarperTeen, Grades 6–up.
"A young Hedgewitch, an idealistic knight, and an army of clever goblins fight against the ruling hierarchy that is trying to rid the land of all magical creatures." LC. Nominated for several state young reader awards.

The Golden Wood, 2003
The Golden Gate, 2010

Bell, Hilari. *Knight and Rogue* series, published by Eos, Grades 7–12.
These excellent combinations of fantasy and adventure come highly recommended.

1. *The Last Knight,* 2007
2. *Rogue's Home,* 2008
3. *Player's Ruse,* 2010

Bemis, John Claude. *The Clockwork Dark* series, published by Random House, Grades 7–12.
"Drawn by the lodestone his father gave him years before, twelve-year-old orphan Ray travels south, meeting along the way various characters from folklore who are battling against an evil industry baron known as the Gog." LC. Compelling adventure fantasy.

The Nine Pound Hammer, 2009
The Wolf Tree, 2010
The White City, 2011

Benz, Derek. *Grey Griffins* series, first three published by Scholastic/Orchard, the others published by Little, Brown, Grades 5–8.
"When Max Sumner and three friends play a magical card game called Round Table, they realize that it is up to them to prevent the wicked creatures of the cards from destroying their town, indeed, their world." LC

1. *The Revenge of the Shadow King,* 2006
2. *The Rise of the Black Wolf,* 2007
3. *The Fall of the Templar,* 2008

Grey Griffins Clockwork Chronicles

1. *The Brimstone Key,* 2010
2. *The Relic Hunters,* 2011

Black, Kat. *Book of Tormod* series, published by Scholastic, Grades 6–9.

"A fourteenth-century Scottish boy joins a Templar knight on a quest to locate an ancient relic, while he tries to understand and control his own gift of prophetic visions." LC

 1. *A Templar's Apprentice,* 2009
 2. *A Templar's Gifts,* 2011

Brennan, Herbie. *Faerie Wars* series, published by Bloomsbury, Grades 5–8.

"Troubled by family problems, Henry finds his life taking a whole new dimension when he and his friend, old Mr. Fogarty, become involved with Prince Pyrgus Malvae who has been sent from the faerie world in order to escape the treacherous Faeries of the Night." LC. Nominated for multiple state young reader awards.

 1. *Faerie Wars,* 2003
 2. *Purple Emperor,* 2004
 3. *Ruler of the Realm,* 2006
 4. *Faerie Lord,* 2007
 5. *Faeman Quest,* 2011

Brennan, Herbie. *The Shadow Project* series, published by Balzer and Bray, Grades 5–8.

"A young English thief stumbles on, and subsequently is recruited for, a super-secret operation that trains teenagers in remote viewing and astral projection techniques in order to engage in spying." LC

 1. *The Shadow Project,* 2010
 2. *The Doomsday Box,* 2011

Buckingham, Royce. *The Dead Boys.* Putnam Juvenile, 2010. 203 p. Grades 5–8.

"Timid twelve-year-old Teddy Mathews and his mother move to a small, remote desert town in eastern Washington, where the tree next door, mutated by nuclear waste, eats children and the friends Teddy makes turn out to be dead." LC. Starred review in *Kirkus.*

Buckingham, Royce. *Goblins! An Underearth Adventure.* Putnam Juvenile, 2008. 220 p. Grades 5–8.

"Action and humor fill this story of two boys who discover a lair of goblins.

Carey, Janet Lee. *The Beast of Noor.* Atheneum, 2006. Grades 5–8.

"Fifteen-year-old Miles Ferrell uses the rare and special gift he is given to break the curse of the Shriker, a murderous creature reportedly brought to Shalem Wood by his family's clan centuries before." LC. The sequel is *The Dragon of Noor* (Egmont, 2010).

Carman, Patrick. *Atherton* trilogy, illustrated by Squire Broel, published by Little, Brown, Grades 5–10.

"Edgar, an eleven-year-old orphan, finds a book that reveals significant secrets about Atherton, the strictly divided world on which he lives, even as geological changes threaten to shift the power structure that allows an elite few to live off the labor of others." LC. Nominated for multiple state young reader awards.

 1. *The House of Power,* 2007
 2. *Rivers of Fire,* 2008
 3. *The Dark Planet,* 2009

Carman, Patrick. *Thirteen Days to Midnight*. Little, Brown, 2010. 259 p. Grades 7–10.

"After surviving the accident that killed his father, high school student Jacob Fielding discovers he is indestructible, a burden that soon weighs heavy on Jacob's shoulders." LC. Lots of excitement and action from this popular author.

Carroll, Michael. *Quantum Prophecy* series, published by Philomel, Grades 5–8.

"Ten years after the disappearance of superhumans—both heroes and villains—thirteen-year-olds Danny and Colin begin to develop super powers, making them the object of much unwanted attention." LC

The Awakening, 2008
The Gathering, 2009
The Reckoning, 2009
Super Human, 2010 (a prequel)

Catanese, P. W. *The Books of Umber* series, published by Aladdin, Grades 5–8.

There's action and a great number of close calls in this jolly good read about a boy found in a cavern by Lord Umber, who helps him to escape. Fantasy fans love it. Nominated for a few state young reward awards.

Happenstance Found, 2009
Dragon Games, 2010
The End of Time, 2011

Caveney, Philip. *Sebastian Darke* series, published by Delacorte, Grades 6–8.

He is half elf and half human, but not funny—and Sebastian's goal is to be a court jester like his father. Popular series.

Sebastian Darke, Prince of Fools, 2008
Sebastian Darke, Prince of Pirates, 2009
Sebastian Darke, Prince of Explorers, 2010

Chabon, Michael. *Summerland.* Hyperion, 2002. 500 p. Grades 5–7.

"The ferishers, little creatures who ensure perfect weather for Summerland, recruit Ethan Feld, one of history's worst baseball players, to help them in their struggle to save Summerland, and ultimately the world, from giants, goblins, and other legendary, terrible creatures." LC

Chima, Cinda Williams. *Seven Realms* trilogy, published by Hyperion, Grades 6–11.

An exciting, well-written fantasy series.

The Demon King, 2009
The Exiled Queen, 2010
The Gray Wolf Throne, 2011

Clayton, Emma. *The Roar.* Scholastic, 2009. 484 p. Grades 5–8.

"In an overpopulated world where all signs of nature have been obliterated and a wall has been erected to keep out plague-ridden animals, twelve-year-old Mika refuses to believe that his twin sister was killed after being abducted, and continues to search for her in spite of the dangers he faces in doing so." LC. Nominated for multiple state young reader awards.

Clements, Andrew. *Things Not Seen*. Puffin, 2006. 272 p. Grades 6–up.

Fifteen-year-old Bobby Phillips wakes up one morning and finds he is invisible. He is normal in every way except he cannot see his own body and neither can anyone else. What to do? He tells his parents immediately, and they do their best to help, but everyone realizes that this needs to be a secret. What would happen if the press got a hold of this information? Freaked out, he goes to one of his favorite places, a library, and there meets the only person who can accept him as he is: a blind girl. Riveting reading. Sequel is *Things Hoped For*, 2007.

Cody, Matthew. *Powerless*. Alfred A. Knopf Books for Young Readers, 2009. 281 p. Grades 5–8.

Twelve-year-old Daniel discovers that the reason his new hometown is the safest place on earth is because kid superheroes protect it. Great idea and a well-executed story.

Cole, Steve. *Hunting* series, published by Philomel, Grades 5–9.

"From Santa Fe, New Mexico, to Edinburgh, Scotland, thirteen-year-old Adam Adlar must elude police while being hunted by a dinosaur come-to-life from a virtual reality game invented by his father, who has gone missing." LC

Z. Rex, 2009
Z. Raptor, 2011

Colfer, Eoin. *Artemis Fowl* series, published by Hyperion, Grades 5–8.

This is a fast-paced, action-packed read about a criminal mastermind who is only a kid—and who decides to go to battle with the fairy world. Colfer describes it as "*Die Hard* with fairies."

1. *Artemis Fowl*, 2001
2. *The Arctic Incident*, 2003
3. *The Eternity Code*, 2004
4. *The Opal Deception*, 2005
5. *The Lost Colony*, 2006
6. *The Time Paradox*, 2008
7. *The Atlantis Complex*, 2010

The Artemis Fowl Files, 2008, is a guide to the series

Collins, Suzanne. *The Hunger Games* series, published by Scholastic, Grades 6–up (but younger kids are happily reading them).

Compulsively readable books about a horrifying future society in an area that used to be called the United States. Teenagers are chosen by lottery to fight to the death for the amusement of wealthy citizens in the capitol. Hugely popular with kids and adults alike and getting even more popular with the release of the 2012 movie, *The Hunger Games*.

The Hunger Games, 2008
Catching Fire, 2009
Mockingjay, 2010

Cross, Sarah. *Dull Boy*. Dutton, 2009. 311 p. Grades 7–10.

Fifteen-year-old Avery has amazing strength and can fly, but what do you do when you want to keep this a secret? And then you learn there are other kids who have the same powers. An exciting read!

Crossley-Holland, Kevin. *Arthur* **trilogy, published by Scholastic, Grades 5–up.**
This is an unusual take on the King Arthur story. Filled with fascinating details, it is a fine read.

The Seeing Stone, 2001
At the Crossing Places, 2002
King of the Middle March, 2004

Dakin, Glenn. *The Candle Man* **series, published by Egmont, Grades 5–up.**
"Thirteen-year-old Theo, who has lived in seclusion his entire life, discovers he is the descendant of the Candle Man, a Victorian vigilante with the ability to melt criminals with a single touch." LC

The Society of Unrelenting Vigilance, 2009
The Society of Dread, 2010

Author Spotlight: James Dashner

The Maze Runner by James Dashner captivates middle school boys with its mysterious and deadly setting and its realistic characters trapped in a world they don't understand. Author James Dashner loved to read as a child, and his parents took him to the library often for books by Judy Blume, choose-your-own-adventure stories, and *Hardy Boys* and *Nancy Drew* mysteries. Today he is heavily influenced by Stephen King, J. K. Rowling, and Dean Koontz, as well as by filmmakers such as J. J. Abrams, Christopher Nolan, and Peter Jackson.

James Dashner Recommends

Ender's Game by Orson Scott Card

Superfudge by Judy Blume

A Wrinkle in Time by Madeleine L'Engle

Fablehaven by Brandon Mull

Goose Girl by Shannon Hale

Dashner, James. *The Maze Runner* **series, published by Delacorte, Grades 6–up.**
"Sixteen-year-old Thomas wakes up with no memory in the middle of a maze and realizes he must work with the community in which he finds himself if he is to escape." LC. Nominated for several state young reader awards. Very popular with fans of *The Hunger Games.*

The Maze Runner, 2009
The Scorch Trials, 2010
The Death Cure, 2011

Davis, Bryan. *Dragons of Starlight* series, published by Zondervan, Grades 7–10.
"Jason Masters does not believe that dragons take people to another realm as slaves until his own brother is taken, but once through the portal he meets Koren, a slave struggling to destroy a black egg prophesied to doom all mankind." LC. There are four books planned in this series, which has a slight religious cast. A good fantasy.

1. *Starfighter,* 2010
2. *Warrior,* 2011
3. *Diviner,* 2011

de Alacantara, Pedro. *Backtracked.* Delacorte, 2009. 259 p. Grades 6–11.
"While playing a dangerous subway prank, a fifteen-year-old slacker, who lives a comfortable life in Brooklyn, falls through a time-travel vortex and is transported to different time periods in twentieth-century New York City, where he learns firsthand about hardship." LC

De Fombelle, Timothee. *Toby Alone.* Translated by Sarah Ardizzone. Candlewick, 2009. 384 p. Grades 5–8.
"Tiny Toby Lolness, a member of a civilization of people no taller than two millimeters who live in an enormous oak known as the Tree, embarks on a quest to save himself, his family, and the Tree when corporate interests threaten to destroy them all." LC. Sequel is *Toby and the Secrets of the Tree,* 2010. *Kirkus* starred both books.

Toby Alone **by Timothee De Fombelle.**

De Quidt, Jeremy. *The Toymaker.* David Fickling, 2010. 368 p. Grades 5–8.
"Mathias takes a sheet of paper from a dying conjurer in the circus where he works and finds himself pursued by the dangerous Dr. Leiter, his exquisite, human-like doll, and a malevolent dwarf, all of whom will stop at nothing to keep the paper's secrets hidden." LC. Starred review in *Booklist.*

Detorie, Rick. *The Accidental Genius of Weasel High.* Egmont, 2011. 28 p. Grades 6–9.
"A typical boy in ninth grade draws comics and records his thoughts in his journal, describing life with his two parents, adolescent sister, and a bully." LC

Divakaruni, Chitra. *The Brotherhood of the Conch* trilogy, published by Roaring Brook, Grades 5–8.
"Twelve-year-old Anand is entrusted with a conch shell that possesses mystical powers and sets out on a journey to return the shell to its rightful home many hundreds of miles away." LC

1. *The Conch Bearer,* 2003
2. *The Mirror of Fire and Dreaming,* 2005
3. *Shadowland,* 2009

D'Lacey, Chris. *The Fire Eternal* series, published by Scholastic, Grades 5–8.
College student David Rain boards with a woman and her daughter and discovers that the clay dragons in the house are alive.

1. *The Fire Within*, 2001
2. *Icefire*, 2003
3. *Fire Star*, 2005
4. *The Fire Eternal*, 2007
5. *Dark Fire*, 2009
6. *Fire World*, 2011

Druitt, Tobias. *Corydon* trilogy, published by Alfred A. Knopf Books for Young Readers, Grades 6–9.
Corydon, a shepherd with one goat leg, meets several other "monsters" from Greek mythology and ends up leading them against the revolts. A different look at old stories.

1. *Corydon & the Island of Monsters*, 2005
2. *Corydon & the Fall of Atlantis*, 2007
3. *Corydon & the Siege of Troy*, 2009

Duane, Diane. *Young Wizards* series, published by Harcourt, Grades 6–10.
Science fiction and fantasy fans have enjoyed these books for a long time now! Partners Kit and Nita have many adventures.

1. *So You Want to Be a Wizard*, 1983
2. *Deep Wizardry*, 1985
3. *High Wizardry*, 1990
4. *A Wizard Abroad*, 1997
5. *The Wizard's Dilemma*, 2001
6. *A Wizard Alone*, 2002
7. *Wizard's Holiday*, 2003
8. *Wizards at War*, 2007
9. *A Wizard of Mars*, 2010

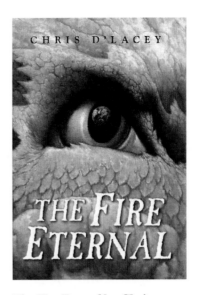

The Fire Eternal by Chris D'Lacey.

Dunkle, Clare B. *The Sky Inside*. Atheneum, 2008. 229 p. Grades 5–8.
Thirteen-year-old artificially engineered Martin lives in a domed city and begins to question the way things are when his six-year-old sister disappears in a product recall. Sequel is *The Walls Have Eyes*, 2009.

Falkner, Brian. *Brain Jack*. Random House, 2010. 349 p. Grades 7–up.
"In a near-future New York City, fourteen-year-old computer genius Sam Wilson manages to hack into the AT&T network and sets off a chain of events that have a profound effect on human activity throughout the world." LC

Falls, Kat. *Dark Life*. Scholastic, 2010. 304 p. Grades 6–9.
Ty, age 15, has always lived at the bottom of the ocean with his pioneer parents. When he meets an orphaned teenage girl looking for her lost brother, the stage is set for a Wild West story set in the future. A winner!

Farmer, Nancy. *The House of the Scorpion*. Simon Pulse, 2002, 2004. 380 p. Grades 7–up.
Raised in a bewildering fashion—sometimes treated lovingly, sometimes like an animal—Matt discovers that he is actually the clone of a 140-year-old drug lord, who had him created for parts. Exciting and what an incredible premise for a story! A challenging book that good readers love.

Farmer, Nancy. *The Land of the Silver Apples.* Illustrated by Rick Sardinha. Atheneum, 2007. 496 p. Grades 5–up.

In this almost-impossible-to-put-down sequel to *The Sea of Trolls*, 13-year-old Jack takes on hobgoblins, the land of the elves, a corrupt monastery and an evil half-kelpie ruler—assisted by none other than a descendant of Lancelot, his old friends Thorgild and the Bard, and a host of new characters. What a wonderful story!

Farmer, Nancy. *The Sea of Trolls.* Simon & Schuster, 2004. 459 p. Grades 5–up.

When Viking raiders capture 11-year-old Jack, a farm boy apprenticed to a Druid bard, and his little sister Lucy, their future looks grim indeed. Both are now thralls, or slaves, to their conquerors, but Jack has a lot of ideas, a lot of intelligence, and a lot of creativity. When he enrages the half-troll Norse queen, she threatens to kill his sister—and he begins a quest into the land of the trolls. This is a real page-turner. You will have a hard time putting it down once you get started.

Feasey, Steve. *Wereling.* Feiwel and Friends, 2010. 288 p. Grades 7–10.

Fourteen-year-old Trey Laporte, having woken up one morning to the discovery that he is a werewolf, finds himself pursued by a psychopathic bloodsucker and in love with an insanely pretty girl who happens to be half vampire. The sequel is *Dark Moon*, 2011.

Fisher, Catherine. *Incarceron.* Dial, 2010. 442 p. Grades 7–up.

An absolutely compelling read about Finn, a prisoner in a horrifying prison, and Claudia, the warden's daughter. Both exist in mystifying and extraordinary worlds, and the final revelation is a stunner. Followed by *Sapphique*, 2011. One of the best reviewed books of 2010.

Flanagan, John. *The Ranger's Apprentice* series, published by Philomel, Grades 5–up.

When 15-year-old Will is rejected by battleschool, he becomes the reluctant apprentice to the mysterious Ranger Halt, and winds up protecting the kingdom from danger. Extremely popular. First published in Australia.

1. *Ruins of Gorlan*, 2006
2. *Burning Bridge*, 2006
3. *Icebound Land*, 2007
4. *Battle for Skandia*, 2008
5. *Sorcerer of the North*, 2008
6. *Siege of Macindaw*, 2009
7. *Erak's Ransom*, 2010
8. *Kings of Clonmel*, 2010
9. *Halt's Peril*, 2010
10. *The Emperor of Nihon-Ja*, 2011

Ranger's Apprentice: The Lost Stories, 2011

Fletcher, Charlie. *Stoneheart* trilogy, published by Hyperion, Grades 5–9.

"Twelve-year-old George breaks the head off a dragon sculpture outside the Natural History Museum in an act of rebellion and soon discovers, to his dismay, that he has reawakened the war between the statues of London." LC

1. *Stoneheart*, 2007
2. *Ironhand*, 2008
3. *Silvertongue*, 2009

Flinn, Alex. *Beastly.* HarperTeen, 2007. 320 p. Grades 7–10.

> Arrogant, popular, and cruel high school student Kyle humiliates Kendra at a school dance and finds himself banished to live as a beast until he can find true love. This take on *Beauty and the Beast* works for boys because the focus is on the "beast."

Flinn, Alex. *Cloaked.* HarperTeen, 2011. 352 p. Grades 6–10.

> "Seventeen-year-old Johnny is approached at his family's struggling shoe repair shop in a Miami, Florida, hotel by Alorian Princess Victoriana, who asks him to find her brother who was turned into a frog." LC

Ford, Michael Thomas. *Z.* HarperTeen, 2010. 276 p. Grades 7–up.

> "In the year 2032, after a virus that turned people into zombies has been eradicated, Josh is invited to join an underground gaming society, where the gamers hunt zombies and the action is more dangerous than it seems." LC

Forman, M. L. *Adventurers Wanted* series, published by Shadow Mountain, Grades 5–8.

> Gamers and fantasy fans will have a grand time with the story of a kid who applies for a job as an adventurer and gets more than he bargained for. Nominated for multiple state young reader awards.

> 1. *Slathbog's Gold,* 2009
> 2. *The Horn of Moran,* 2011

Funke, Cornelia. *Reckless.* Little, Brown, 2010. 394 p. Grades 7–10.

> "Jacob and Will Reckless have looked out for each other ever since their father disappeared, but when Jacob discovers a magical mirror that transports him to a warring world populated by witches, giants, and ogres, he keeps it to himself until Will follows him one day, with dire consequences." LC

Gaiman, Neil. *The Graveyard Book.* Illustrated by Dave McKean. HarperCollins, 2008. 312 p. Grades 5–up.

> "The orphan Bod, short for Nobody, is taken in by the inhabitants of a graveyard as a child of eighteen months and raised lovingly and carefully to the age of eighteen years by the community of ghosts and otherworldly creatures." LC. This scary, hugely popular book won both the Newbery Medal and the UK Carnegie Medal.

Gee, Maurice. *The Salt Trilogy*, published by Orca, Grades 7–up.

> "Hari, a downtrodden underclass boy, and Pearl, a privileged girl, both develop a talent to speak to animals and humans through mind control, and find themselves thrown together on a quest to save mankind from a terrible weapon." LC

> *Salt,* 2009
> *Gool,* 2010
> *The Limping Man,* 2011

Gopnik, Adam. *The King in the Window.* Miramax Books, 2005. 410 p. Grades 5–9.

> "Eleven-year-old Oliver, an American boy residing in Paris, discovers, much to his astonishment, that phantoms live within the windowpanes and have selected Oliver to lead a war against the 'soul-stealers' that inhabit mirrors." LC

Gordon, Roderick, and Brian Williams. *Tunnels* series, published by Scholastic, Grades 5–9.

> Fourteen-year-old Will just loves to dig—and, doing just that, he finds a subterranean colony and learns he was born there. Action and lots of excitement for fantasy fans. Extremely

popular series, though critics criticized the slow start of the first book.

1. *Tunnels,* 2007
2. *Deeper,* 2007
3. *Freefall,* 2010
4. *Closer,* 2010

Grant, Michael. *Gone* series, published by HarperCollins, Grades 6–up.

"In a small town on the coast of California, everyone over the age of fourteen suddenly disappears, setting up a battle between the remaining town residents and the students from a local private school, as well as those who have 'The Power' and are able to perform supernatural feats and those who do not." LC. Nominated for several state young reader awards.

1. *Gone,* 2008
2. *Hunger,* 2009
3. *Lies,* 2010
4. *Plague,* 2011

Tunnels **by Roderick Gordon and Brian Williams.**

Grant, Michael. *The Magnificent 12* series, published by HarperCollins, Grades 5–8.

"Mack Macavoy, a seriously average twelve-year-old boy, is faced with a difficult decision when a three-thousand-year-old man appears in the boys' bathroom and informs him that he is one of the Magnificent Twelve and is needed to find his eleven teammates and save the world." LC

The Call, 2010
The Trap, 2011

Haarsma, P. J. *The Softwire* series, published by Candlewick, Grades 5–9.

"After being orphaned on the seed ship 'Renaissance,' thirteen-year-old Johnny Turnbull and his sister, Ketheria, are forced to work on the Rings of Orbis, where Johnny learns he is the first human Softwire, with a gift to enter any computer via his mind." LC

1. *Virus on Orbis 1,* 2006
2. *Betrayal on Orbis 2,* 2008
3. *Wormhole Pirates on Orbis 3,* 2009
4. *Awakening on Orbis 4,* 2010

Haddon, Mark. *Boom.* Random House, 2010. 208 p. Grades 5–8.

"When Jim and Charlie overhear two of their teachers talking in a secret language and the two friends set out to

Virus on Orbis 1 **by P.J. Haarsma.**

solve the mystery, they do not expect the dire consequences of their actions." LC. What they learn is that aliens are kidnapping science fiction fans!

Halpern, Jake, and Peter Kujawinski. *Book of Dormia* **series, published by Houghton Mifflin, Grades 5–9.**

"After learning of his ancestral ties to Dormia, a hidden kingdom in the Ural Mountains whose inhabitants possess the ancient power of 'wakeful sleeping,' twelve-year-old Alfonso sets out on a mission to save the kingdom from destruction, discovering secrets that lurk in his own sleep." LC

1. *Dormia,* 2009
2. *World's End,* 2010

Hardinge, Frances. *Well Witched.* HarperCollins, 2008. 389 p. Grades 5–8.

When three British kids steal some coins for bus fare from a wishing well, they have no idea that there will be serious repercussions. Each coin has a wish attached to it that must be fulfilled, and there is a witch that lives in the well!

Harland, Richard. *Worldshaker.* Simon & Schuster, 2010. 388 p. Grades 6–10.

"Sixteen-year-old Col Porpentine is being groomed as the next Commander of Worldshaker, a juggernaut where elite families live on the upper decks while the Filthies toil below, but when he meets Riff, a Filthy girl on the run, he discovers how ignorant he is of his home and its residents." LC

Hartinger, Brent. *Shadow Walkers.* Flux, 2011. 214 p. Grades 7–10.

"Zach, living with his grandparents on an island off the coast of Washington State, feels cut off from the rest of the world, but he finds freedom when he discovers how to astral project, a skill that comes in handy when his little brother Gilbert is kidnapped." LC

Haydon, Elizabeth. *The Lost Journals of Ven Polypheme* **series, illustrated by Brett Helquist, published by Starscape, Grades 5–9.**

High fantasy and adventure; not easy reads, but nominated for multiple state young reader awards.

1. *The Floating Island,* 2006
2. *The Thief Queen's Daughter,* 2007
3. *The Dragon's Lair,* 2008

Higgins, F. E. *The Black Book of Secrets.* Feiwel and Friends, 2007. 273 p. Grades 4–8.

"When Ludlow Fitch runs away from his thieving parents in the City, he meets up with the mysterious Joe Zabbidou, who calls himself a secret pawnbroker, and who takes Ludlow as an apprentice to record the confessions of the townspeople of Pagus Parvus, where resentments are many and trust is scarce." LC. Nominated for many state young reader awards. The "paraquel" to this is *The Bone Magician,* 2008.

Higgins, F. E. *The Bone Collector.* Feiwel and Friends, 2008. 272 p. Grades 5–8.

"With his father, a fugitive, falsely accused of multiple murders and the real serial killer stalking the wretched streets of Urbs Umida, Pin Carpue, a young undertaker's assistant, investigates and finds that all of the victims may have attended the performance of a stage magician who claims to be able to raise corpses and make the dead speak." LC

Higgins, F. E. *The Eyeball Collector.* Feiwel and Friends, 2009. 251 p. Grades 5–8.

> Hector Fitbaudly wants revenge on the man who caused his father's death. A shivery, satisfying horror story. This book and *The Bone Collector* are not marketed as a series, but they are related.

Higson, Charlie. *The Enemy.* Hyperion, 2010. 440 p. Grades 6–10.

> "A group of young survivors is offered safety from the roaming packs of zombie-like adults in Buckingham Palace, but, even after they survive their perilous journey through London, the teens arrive only to find their fight is far from over." LC

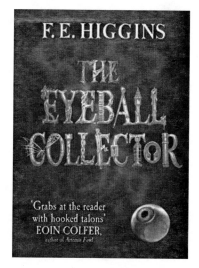

The Eyeball Collector by **Andrew Lane. Courtesy of Feiwel and Friends, an imprint of the Macmillan Children's Publishing Group.**

Horowitz, Anthony. *The Switch.* Philomel, 2009. 162 p. Grades 5–8.

> "Wealthy, spoiled, thirteen-year-old Tad Spencer wishes he were someone else, and awakens as Bob Snarby, the uncouth, impoverished son of carnival workers, and as he is drawn into a life of crime, Tad begins to discover truths about himself and his family." LC

Howe, Norma. *Angel in Vegas: The Chronicles of Noah Sark.* Candlewick, 2009. 247 p. Grades 6–9.

> Noah, a guardian angel, has been demoted after his failure to protect Princess Diana. Having moved to Vegas, he has a new assignment. A fun story.

Hughes, Mark Peter. *A Crack in the Sky.* Delacorte, 2010 416 p. Grades 6–10.

> "Thirteen-year-old Eli Papadopoulos, a member of the family that founded Infinicorp, the massive corporation that runs everything in the domed cities, becomes worried when the sky keeps shorting out, but his questions get him sent away to the Tower where he meets Tabitha, and together they make plans to escape." LC. First in the *Greenhouse Chronicles* series.

Hulme, John. *The Seems* series, published by Bloomsbury, Grades 5–up.

> Becker Drane is recruited by The Seems, a parallel universe that runs everything in our world—and needs him to be a Fixer.

> 1. *The Glitch in Sleep,* 2007
> 2. *The Split Second,* 2008
> 3. *The Lost Train of Thought,* 2009

Hunter, Erin. *Seekers* series, published by HarperCollins, Grades 5–8.

> "Three young bears of different species—one black, one polar, and one grizzly—travel on a perilous quest to the Northern Lights, escorting a shape-shifting grizzly cub whose destiny will affect them all." LC

> 1. *The Quest Begins,* 2008
> 2. *Great Bear Lake,* 2009
> 3. *Smoke Mountain,* 2009
> 4. *The Last Wilderness,* 2010
> 5. *Fire in the Sky,* 2010
> 6. *Spirits in the Stars,* 2011

Jacques, Brian. *Redwall* **series published by Philomel. Grades 5–up.**

Excellent animal fantasy books, full of detail and excellent for proficient readers. As the author died in 2011, this series may be at an end.

Redwall, 1986
Mossflower, 1988
Mattimeo, 1990
Mariel of Redwall, 1992
Salamandastron, 1992
Martin the Warrior, 1994
The Bellmaker, 1995
Outcast of Redwall, 1996
The Great Redwall Feast, 1996
Pearls of Lutra, 1997
The Long Patrol, 1998
Marlfox, 1999
Legend of Luke, 2000
A Redwall Winter's Tale, 2001
Lord Brocktree, 2000
Taggerung, 2001
Triss, 2002
Loamhedge, 2003
Rakkety Tam, 2004
High Rhulain, 2007
Doomwyte, 2008
The Sable Quean, 2010
The Rogue Crew, 2011

Jinks, Catherine. *The Abused Werewolf Rescue Group.* Harcourt, 2011. 416 p. Grades 7–11.

"Tobias Richard Vandevelde wakes up in a hospital with no memory of the night before after being found unconscious in the dingo pen at Featherdale Wildlife Park, and he finds out that he is a werewolf from a group of vampires." LC

Jinks, Catherine. *Living Hell.* Harcourt, 2010. 272 p. Grades 7–10.

A spaceship on a long journey mutates into a living organism when it passes through a radiation field. Seventeen-year-old Cheney leads the fight for survival while machines turn on the passengers, treating all humans as parasites.

Jinks, Catherine. *The Reformed Vampire Support Group.* Harcourt, 2009. 362 p. Grades 7–11.

"Fifteen-year-old vampire Nina has been stuck for fifty-one years in a boring support group for vampires, and nothing exciting has ever happened to them—until one of them is murdered and the others must try to solve the crime." LC

Jones, Diana Wynne. *Enchanted Glass.* Greenwillow, 2010. 304 p. Grades 6–9.

"Andrew Hope inherits a house in an English village from his late grandfather and things are going well until orphan Aidan shows up, trailing a host of magical townsfolk and interlopers in his wake." LC. Diana Wynne Jones never disappoints.

Jones, Diana Wynne. *The Merlin Conspiracy.* Greenwillow, 2004. Grades 5–up.

Told alternately by Roddy and Nick, this complex, riveting fantasy moves swiftly along as the characters combine their newfound magical powers and learn that the actions in one world may have long-reaching effects in other worlds.

Kerr, P. B. *Children of the Lamp* **series, published by Scholastic, Grades 5–9.**

"When twelve-year-old twins Philippa and John discover that they are descended from a long line of djinn, their mother sends them away to their Uncle Nimrod, who takes them to Cairo where he starts to teach them about their extraordinary powers." LC

1. *The Akhenaten Adventure,* 2004
2. *The Blue Djinn of Babylon,* 2006
3. *The Cobra King of Kathmandu,* 2007
4. *The Day of the Djinn Warriors,* 2008
5. *The Eye of the Forest,* 2009
6. *The Five Fakirs of Faizabad,* 2010

Kirk, Daniel. *Elf Realm* **series, published by Amulet, Grades 5–8.**

It's war between the world of humans and the world of elves, and also war between elves themselves, and a 14-year-old human named Matt is at the center of it.

The Low Road, 2008
The High Road, 2009
The Road's End, 2011

Klass, David. *Caretaker* **trilogy, published by Farrar, Straus & Giroux, Grades 6–up.**

Eighteen-year-old Jack is a time traveler, sent from the future to save the world's oceans. Nominated for multiple state young reader awards.

1. *Firestorm,* 2008
2. *Whirlwind,* 2008
3. *Timelock,* 2009

Klass, David. *Stuck on Earth.* Farrar, Straus & Giroux, 2010. 227 p. Grades 6–9.

"On a secret mission to evaluate whether the human race should be annihilated, a space alien inhabits the body of a bullied fourteen-year-old boy." LC

Lake, Nick. *Blood Ninja.* Simon & Schuster, 2010. 371 p. Grades 7–up.

"After his father is murdered and a ninja saves his life, Taro discovers the connection between ninjas and vampires and finds himself being dragged into a bitter conflict between the rival lords ruling Japan." LC

Landon, Kristen. *The Limit.* Aladdin, 2010. 304 p. Grades 6–up.

"When his family exceeds its legal debt limit, thirteen-year-old Matt is sent to the Federal Debt Rehabilitation Agency workhouse, where he discovers illicit activities are being carried out using the children who have been placed there." LC

Langrish, Katherine. *The Shadow Hunt.* HarperCollins, 2010. 336 p. Grades 6–9.

"Wolf, on the run from the monastery where he was raised, rescues a strange child from the moors of Devil's Edge and takes her to a grand castle where he meets Nest, and he is starting to imagine a future there with her until dark forces begin conspiring against them." LC. A medieval fantasy. Starred review in *Booklist.*

LeGuin, Ursula. *Gifts.* Harcourt, 2004. 274 p. Grades 5–up.

Orrec has a terrifying gift, a gift to look at anything and unmake it—turn it into a dead mess. Fearing that he will use it accidentally, he and his father agree to cover up his eyes permanently with a blindfold, at least until he is able to control his gift. Many of the people in the Uplands have unusual gifts that they use primarily to protect and defend themselves—and Gry, the friend and girl whom Orrec loves, supports and sustains him during the family crisis that follows.

Lenahan, John. *Shadowmagic*. Independent Publishers Group, 2010. 278 p. Grades 7–10.
    Fans of light fantasy will enjoy this tale of Conor, who is suddenly kidnapped with his father to Tir na Nog—a place where everyone he meets seems to want to kill him. Actually, that land is his true home—and this is a good read.

Llewellyn, Sam. *Lyonesse* series, published by Orchard, Grades 5–up.
    "Eleven-year-old Idris Limpet, who lives with his family in the once noble island country of Lyonesse, finds his life taking a dramatic turn when, after a near-drowning incident, he is accused of being allied to sea monsters and is rescued from a death sentence by a mysterious stranger." LC

    1. *The Well Between the Worlds,* 2009
    2. *Darksolstice,* 2010

Lupica, Mike. *Hero*. Philomel, 2010. 256 p. Grades 6–9.
    "Fourteen-year-old Zach learns he has the same special abilities as his father, who was the president's globe-trotting troubleshooter until "the Bads" killed him, and now Zach must decide whether to use his powers in the same way at the risk of his own life." LC

Lynch, Chris. *Cybreria* series, published by Scholastic, Grades 5–8.
    Zane can communicate with animals via an inserted chip and can help rescue them from evil scientists—and is continually getting into trouble as a result.

    1. *Cybreria,* 2008
    2. *Monkey See, Monkey Don't,* 2009
    3. *Prime Evil,* 2010

MacDonald, Anne. *Seeing Red*. Kids Can, 2009. 220 p. Grades 5–8.
    "Canadian ninth grader Frankie Uccello, who is extremely normal beside the fact he has the ability to see the future in his dreams, has a premonition that his friend will be injured in a horseback riding accident, and relies on help from the introverted Maura-Lee to stop it from happening." LC

MacHale, D. J. *Morpheus Road* series, published by Aladdin, grades 6–10.
    The series starts out with a bang with a fast-paced fantasy thriller about a high school sophomore threatened by a skeletal character called The Gravedigger.

    The Light, 2010
    The Black, 2011
    The Blood, 2012

MacHale, D. J. *Pendragon* series, published by Aladdin, Grades 5–up.
    Fourteen-year-old Bobby Pendragon's mysterious uncle starts him on an adventure that involves traveling to another earth, battling with dangerous creatures, and trying to save the universe. Bobby looks about eight years old on the cover and this was a tough read for me— no character development at all and completely boring in my opinion. But it's a hot-selling series and the word is that the boys love it, so what do I know?

The Merchant of Death, 2002
The Lost City of Faar, 2003
The Reality Bug, 2003
The Never War, 2003
Black Water, 2005
The Rivers of Zadaa, 2006
The Quillan Games, 2006
The Guide to the Territories of Halla, 2005
The Pilgrims of Rayne, 2007
Raven Rise, 2008
The Merchant of Death: Pendragon Graphic Novel, 2008
Soldiers of Halla, 2010
Pendragon Before the War: Book One of the Travelers, by Carla Jablonski and D. J. MacHale, 2009
Book Two of the Travelers, by Walter Sorrells and D. J. MacHale, 2009
Book Three of the Travelers, by Walter Sorrells and D. J. MacHale, 2009

Mahy, Margaret. *The Magician of Hoad.* McElderry, 2009. 413 p. Grades 7–up.
"A young farm boy who possesses mysterious powers is chosen by the king to be the court's royal magician." LC

McCoy, Chris. *Scurvy Goonda.* Alfred A. Knopf Books for Young Readers, 2009. 327 p. Grades 4–8.
Ted Merritt, now 14 years old, wants to get rid of his imaginary friend, but he learns there is a problem. Imaginary friends everywhere are united and ready to fight back!

McNamee, Eoin. *The Navigator* trilogy, illustrated by Jon Goodell, published by Wendy Lamb Books, Grades 5–8.
"When he receives the cryptic message that 'time is running out,' Owen, known as 'The Navigator,' summons Cati and Dr. Diamond and together they journey to the City of Time in order to discover what has gone wrong." LC

The Navigator, 2007
City of Time, 2008
The Frost Child, 2009

McNamee, Eoin. *The Ring of Five* series, published by Wendy Lamb Books, Grades 5–7.
"Kidnapped on his way to boarding school, Danny Caulfield, who has one blue eye and one brown eye, ends up at a mysterious academy of spies, where he is to be trained in the art of espionage in an effort to keep the Upper and Lower worlds from colliding." LC. Projected to be a trilogy.

The Ring of Five, 2010
The Unknown Spy, 2011

Michaelis, Antonia. *Dragons of Darkness.* Amulet, 2010. 555 p. Grades 7–10.
"Two boys from very different backgrounds are thrown together by magic, mayhem, and a common foe as they battle deadly dragons in the wilderness of Nepal." LC

Moore, James A. *Subject Seven.* Razorbill, 2011. 336 p. Grades 6–9.

    Violence and plenty of action fill this story of five teenagers who are human genetic experiment mistakes—they can change from everyday kids into amazing warriors.

Mull, Brandon. *Fablehaven* series, illustrated by Brandon Dorman, published by Shadow Mountain, then in paperback by Aladdin, Grades 5–9.

    "Kendra and Seth find themselves in the midst of a battle between good and evil when they visit their grandparents' estate and discover that it is a sanctuary for magical creatures." LC. Nominated for several state young reader awards.

1. *Fablehaven,* 2006
2. *Fablehaven: Rise of the Evening Star,* 2007
3. *Fablehaven: Grip of the Shadow Plague,* 2008
4. *Fablehaven: Secrets of the Dragon Sanctuary,* 2009
5. *Fablehaven: Keys to the Demon Prison,* 2010

Myklush, Matt. *Jack Blank and the Imagine Nation.* Aladdin, 2010. 468 p. Grades 5–8.

    "Twelve-year-old Jack, freed from a dismal orphanage, makes his way to the elusive and impossible Imagine Nation, where a mentor saves him from dissection and trains him to use his superpower, despite the virus he carries that makes him a threat." LC

Napoli, Donna Jo. *The Wager.* Henry Holt, 2010. 263 p. Grades 8–up.

    "Having lost everything in a tidal wave in 1169 Sicily, nineteen-year-old Don Giovanni makes a simple-sounding wager with a stranger he recognizes as the devil but, while desperate enough to surrender his pride and good looks for three years, he is not willing to give up his soul." LC

Nateri, Daniel. *Marlowe School* series, published by Candlewick, Grades 6–9.

    "Years after five children mysteriously disappeared from cities across Europe, they reappear at an exclusive party in New York City under the tutelage of a suspicious benefactor, but their unique gifts—reading minds, stopping time, seducing with false beauty, and more—begin to bring them more consequences then benefits." LC

Another Faust, 2009
Another Pan, 2010

Neff, Henry. *Tapestry* series, published by Random House, Grades 5–8.

    "After glimpsing a hint of his destiny in a mysterious tapestry, twelve-year-old Max McDaniels becomes a student at Rowan Academy where he trains in 'mystics and combat' in preparation for war with an ancient enemy that has been kidnapping children like him." LC. Nominated for several state young reader awards.

1. *The Hound of Rowan,* 2007
2. *The Second Siege,* 2008
3. *The Fiend and the Forge,* 2010

Ness, Patrick. *Chaos Walking* series, published by Candlewick, Grades 8–up.

    "Pursued by power-hungry Prentiss and mad minister Aaron, young Todd and Viola set out across New World searching for answers about this space colony's true past and seeking a way to warn the ship bringing hopeful settlers from Old World." LC

The Knife of Never Letting Go, 2009
The Ask and the Answer, 2009
Monsters of Men, 2010

Neumeier, Rachel. *The Floating Islands.* Alfred A. Knopf Books for Young Readers, 2011. 388 p. Grades 6–up.
"The adventures of two teenaged cousins who live in a place called The Floating Islands, one of whom is studying to become a mage and the other one of the legendary island flyers." LC

Nimmo, Jenny. *Children of the Red King* series, published by Orchard, Grades 5–8.
Charlie Bone, age 10, discovers he has magical powers: He can hear people in photographs talking. His control-freak grandmother insists on sending him to Bloor's Academy, which bears a passing resemblance to Hogwarts. There are mysteries in Charlie's life, the most important of which is the disappearance years ago of his father. A good read that Harry Potter fans will enjoy.

The Knife of Never Letting Go **by Patrick Ness.**

1. *Midnight for Charlie Bone,* 2003
2. *Charlie Bone and the Time Twister,* 2003
3. *Charlie Bone and the Invisible Boy,* 2004
4. *Charlie Bone and the Castle of Mirrors,* 2005
5. *Charlie Bone and the Hidden King,* 2006
6. *Charlie Bone and the Beast,* 2007
7. *Charlie Bone and the Shadow,* 2008
8. *Charlie Bone and the Red Knight,* 2010

***Midnight for Charlie Bone* by Jenny Nimmo.**

Nimmo, Jenny. *Chronicles of the Red King* series, published by Scholastic, Grades 5–8.
This new series is about Charlie Bone's ancestor, the Red King.

1. *The Secret Kingdom,* 2011
2. *The Stone of Ravenglass,* 2012

Nix, Garth. *Keys to the Kingdom* series, published by Scholastic, Grades 5–9.
Asthmatic adopted Arthur Penhaligon is given a mysterious object as he lies dying; he immediately stops dying and has the greatest adventure of his life, involving nonstop action and adventure and a promise of much more to come. Very well done.

1. *Mister Monday,* 2003
2. *Grim Tuesday,* 2003
3. *Drowned Wednesday,* 2005
4. *Sir Thursday,* 2006
5. *Lady Friday,* 2007
6. *Superior Saturday,* 2008
7. *Lord Sunday,* 2010

Norcliffe, James. *The Boy Who Could Fly*. Egmont, 2010. 304 p. Grades 5–8.

"Having grown up in a miserable home for abandoned children, a young boy jumps at the chance to exchange places with the mysterious, flying "loblolly boy," but once he takes on this new identity, he discovers what a harsh price he must pay." LC

Nylund, Eric. *The Resisters*. Random House, 2011. 224 p. Grades 5–8.

In this fast-paced and exciting story, 12-year-old Ethan joins a resistance group dedicated to ridding the earth of its mutant insect alien conquerors.

O'Brien, Johnny. *Jack Christie Adventures* series, published by Templar Books, Grades 6–9.

Fifteen-year-olds Angus and Jack become time travelers when they join the VIGIL Society, which has a goal of preventing revisionists from changing the past. Good reads.

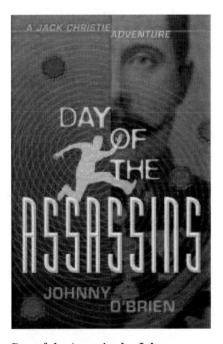

Day of the Assassins by Johnny O'Brien.

1. *Day of the Assassins*, 2009
2. *Day of Deliverance*, 2010
3. *Day of Vengeance*, 2011

Oppel, Kenneth. *Airborn* series, published by Eos, Grades 6–up.

This steam punk series is set in an alternate Victorian world and combines both history and science fiction in a really exciting way. In *Airborn*, Matt Cruse is a cabin boy on the Aurora, a huge airship that carries passengers across the oceans. Matt has dreams of promotions, but he has no money and no prospects, although he has amazing natural gifts. When a wealthy, beautiful young woman befriends him and manipulates him into helping her on a quest, trouble starts. Add pirates to the mix, and it escalates. Fantastic reads!

1. *Airborn*, 2004
2. *Skybreaker*, 2006
3. *Starclimber*, 2009

Owen, James A. *Chronicles of the Imaginarium Geographica* series, published by Simon & Schuster, Grades 6–up.

"Three young men are entrusted with the Imaginarium Geographica, an atlas of fantastical places to which they travel in hopes of defeating the Winter King, whose bid for power is related to the First World War raging in the Real World." LC

1. *Here, There be Dragons*, 2006
2. *The Search for the Red Dragon*, 2008
3. *The Indigo King*, 2008
4. *The Shadow Dragons*, 2009
5. *The Dragon's Apprentice*, 2010

Patneaude, David. *Epitaph Road*. Egmont, 2010. 266 p. Grades 7–up.

"In 2097, men are a small and controlled minority in a utopian world ruled by women, and fourteen-year-old Kellen must fight to save his father from an outbreak of the virus that killed ninety-seven percent of the male population thirty years earlier." LC

Patterson, James. *Maximum Ride* series, published by Little, Brown, Grades 5–9.

Max is part of The Flock—humans genetically altered to be 2 percent bird and 98 percent human. Nonstop action and adventure. Nominated for several state young reader awards.

1. *The Angel Experiment,* 2006
2. *School's Out Forever,* 2006
3. *Saving the World and Other Extreme Sports,* 2008
4. *Final Warning,* 2008
5. *Max,* 2009
6. *Fang,* 2010
7. *Angel,* 2011

Patterson, James. *Witch and Wizard* series, published by Little, Brown, Grades 5–8.

Lots of action fills these thrillers about two sibling teenager resistance fighters with paranormal talents—and an evil man out to stop them or steal their abilities.

1. *Witch and Wizard,* 2009
2. *The Gift,* 2010
3. *The Fire,* 2011

Paulsen, Gary. *White Fox Chronicles.* Delacorte, 2000. 281 p. Grades 5–up.

Having been imprisoned when the Confederation of Consolidated Republics, a foreign power, conquered Los Angeles in 2056, 14-year-old Cody escapes and endures hardship to become the underground hero the White Fox.

Paver, Michelle. *Chronicles of Ancient Darkness* series, published by HarperCollins, Grades 5–up.

Six thousand years ago, 12-year-old Torak promises his dying father that he will go on a confusing quest—and the action begins on page one and never lets up. He bonds with first his guide, a wolf cub, and then a girl from a clan who captures him. I read the first one when a male teacher told me he had to order the next book from England, expensive as that was, because he simply could not stand the wait. The last book in the series won the wildly prestigious Guardian Award in the United Kingdom.

1. *Wolf Brother,* 2005
2. *Spirit Walker,* 2006
3. *Soul Eater,* 2007
4. *Outcast,* 2008
5. *Oath Breaker,* 2009
6. *Ghost Hunter,* 2010

Pearson, Ridley. *Kingdom Keepers* series, published by Hyperion, Grades 5–9.

"Thirteen-year-old Finn Whitman and four other young teens have been transformed into holograms to be guides for visitors to Disney World, but now they must do battle with the evil witch, Maleficent, and her Overtakers to save Walt Disney World." LC

1. *Disney at Dawn,* 2009
2. *Disney after Dark,* 2009
3. *Disney in Shadow,* 2010
4. *Power Play,* 2011
5. *Shell Game,* 2012

Petrucha, Stefan. *Split.* Walker Books, 2010. 272 p. Grades 7–10.

"After his mother dies, Wade Jackson cannot decide whether to become a musician or a scholar, so he does both, splitting his consciousness into two distinct worlds." LC

Philbrick, Rodman. *The Last Book in the Universe.* Blue Sky, 2000. 223 p. Grades 5–up.

After an earthquake has destroyed much of the planet, an epileptic teenager nicknamed Spaz begins the heroic fight to bring human intelligence back to the Earth of a distant future.

Pinkwater, Daniel. *The Neddiad: How Neddie Took the Train, Went to Hollywood, and Saved Civilization.* Houghton Mifflin, 2007. 307 p. Grades 5–9.

"When shoelace heir Neddie Wentworthstein and his family take the train from Chicago to Los Angeles in the 1940s, he winds up in possession of a valuable Indian turtle artifact whose owner is supposed to be able to prevent the impending destruction of the world. " LC

Pinkwater, Daniel. *The Yggyssey: How Iggy Wondered What Happened to All the Ghosts, Found Out Where They Went, and Went There.* Houghton Mifflin, 2009. 245 p. Grades 5–9.

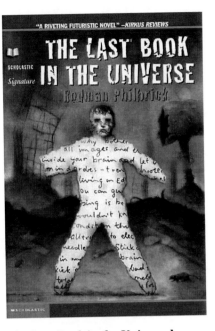

***The Last Book in the Universe* by Rodman Philbrick.**

"In the mid-1950s, Yggdrasil Birnbaum and her friends, Seamus and Neddie, journey to Old New Hackensack, which is on another plane, to try to learn why ghosts are disappearing from the Birnbaum's hotel and other Hollywood, California, locations." LC. Sequel to *The Neddiad.*

Quimby, Laura. *The Carnival of Lost Souls.* Amulet, 2010. 652 p. Grades 5–8.

"Orphaned Jack Carr, tricked into joining a traveling magic show by underworld magician Mussini, finds himself stuck in the Forest of the Dead where souls go before they move on to their final resting place, and must depend on his wits and the help of other kids in the troupe to make his escape." LC

Reeve, Philip. *Art Mumby* series, illustrated by David Wyatt, published by Bloomsbury, Grades 5–8.

These very British funny stories, set in an alternate Victorian England, describe the adventures of a family, living in one of the outer space territories, that uncovers all sorts of dastardly plots. Great fun. (The series doesn't really have an official title.)

1. *Larklight, or, The Revenge of the White Spiders! or, To Saturn's Rings And Back! A Rousing Tale of Dauntless Pluck,* 2006
2. *Starcross, or, The Coming of the Moobs, or, Our Adventures in the Fourth Dimension! A Stirring Adventure of Spies, Time Travel and Curious Hats,* 2007
3. *Mothstorm, or, The Horror From Beyond ~~Uranus~~ Georgium Sidus, or, A Tale of Two Shapers: A Rattling Yarn of Danger, Dastardy and Derring-Do Upon the Far Frontiers of British Space!* 2008

Reeve, Philip. *Here Lies Arthur.* Scholastic, 2008. 338 p. Grades 5–up.

Winner of the UK's Carnegie Medal, their equivalent of our Newbery, this truly is the most unusual version of the King Arthur story you are likely to encounter. It is all a myth, always was a myth, and Arthur himself is no one remotely admirable. A slave girl is taken in by a wily magician named Myrrdin, who aims to make Arthur the king of a united Britain by telling stories about him to all who will listen. Absolutely wonderful.

Reeve, Philip. *Hungry City Chronicles*, **published by Eos, Grades 6–up.**

In this original and fast-paced science fiction series set in a post-apocalyptic future, cities of the world move around on tractor treads pursuing and scavenging each other. A real treat for sci-fi fans.

Mortal Engines, 2004
Predator's Gold, 2006
Infernal Devices, 2006
A Darkling Plain, 2007
Fever Crumb, 2010 (prequel and the beginning of a new trilogy)
A Web of Air, 2011

Revis, Beth. *Across the Universe.* Razorbill, 2011. 400 p. Grades 7–up.

"Amy, having been cryogenically frozen and placed onboard a spaceship which was supposed to land on a distant planet three hundred years in the future, is unplugged fifty years too early and finds herself stuck inside an enclosed world ruled by a tyrannical leader and his rebellious teenage heir and confused about who to trust and why someone is trying to kill her." LC. Science fiction and fantasy fans will love it.

Richards, Douglas. *The Prometheus Project* **series, published by Paragon, Grades 6–9.**

Uprooted to the backwoods of Pennsylvania, a brother and sister discover their scientist parents are part of a mysterious project involving an alien colony. Authentic science fiction.

Trapped, 2005
Captured, 2007
Stranded, 2010

Riordan, Rick. *Heroes of Olympus* **series, published by Hyperion, Grades 5–9.**

Fans of Percy Jackson are thrilled that he and his friends play roles in this new series about more demi-god American kids.

The Lost Hero, 2010
The Son of Neptune, 2011

Riordan, Rick. *The Kane Chronicles* **series, published by Hyperion, Grades 5–8.**

"Brilliant Egyptologist Dr. Julius Kane accidentally unleashes the Egyptian god Set, who banishes the doctor to oblivion and forces his two children to embark on a dangerous journey, bringing them closer to the truth about their family and its links to a secret order that has existed since the time of the pharaohs." LC. Starred reviews in *Booklist* and *Kirkus*.

The Red Pyramid, 2010
The Throne of Fire, 2011
The Serpent's Shadow, 2012

Riordan, Rick. *Percy Jackson and the Olympians* **series, published by Hyperion, Grades 5–up.**

Much to his amazement, Percy Jackson, age 12, learns that his father was a Greek god, and that he is a half-blood god, and that the Greek gods are still around, but now centered in the heart of Western Civilization—the United States. Being a god has both good and bad sides, but the worst is when Percy discovers that he must find and return a lightning bolt stolen from Zeus. Starts out fast and never stops!

The Lightning Thief, 2005
The Sea of Monsters, 2006
The Titan's Curse, 2007

The Battle of the Labyrinth, 2008
The Last Olympian, 2009

Rollins, James. *Jake Ransom* series, published by HarperCollins, Grades 5–9.

"Connecticut middle-schooler Jake and his older sister Kady are transported by a Mayan artifact to a strange world inhabited by a mix of people from long-lost civilizations who are threatened by prehistoric creatures and an evil alchemist, the Skull King." LC

Jake Ransom and the Skull King's Shadow, 2010
Jake Ransom and the Howling Sphinx, 2011

Russell, David O., and Andrew Auseon. *Alienated.* Aladdin, 2009. 344 p. Grades 5–8.

"Santa Rosa, California, junior high school students Gene and Vince try to become famous and popular by publishing a free tabloid about real aliens, but a clash over whether to print a certain story not only damages their friendship, it lands them in the middle of an intergalactic conflict, as well." LC

Sage, Angie. *Septimus Heap*, published by HarperCollins, Grades 5–8.

The poverty-stricken but happy Heap family is devastated when the midwife proclaims that their newborn, Septimus, the seventh son of his father, Silas, also a seventh son, is dead. But is he? Lots of action and adventure, but pretty talky, too. For proficient readers.

1. *Magyk,* 2005
2. *Flyte,* 2006
3. *Physik,* 2007
4. *Queste,* 2008
5. *Syren,* 2009
6. *The Magykal Papers,* 2009

Salmon, Dena K. *Discordia: The Eleventh Dimension.* Hyperion, 2009. 237 p. Grades 5–up. "New York City teenager Lance and his friend, Mrskeller, agree to help a level sixty player of the online game Discordia and are physically transferred into the virtual world where they put their skills to the test as they try to save the dimension and themselves." LC

Salvatore, R. A. *Stones of Tymora* series, published by Mirrorstone, Grades 5–8.

This is the first series of books for children based on the Dungeons and Dragons Forgotten Realms fantasy.

1. *The Stowaway,* 2008
2. *The Shadowmask,* 2009
3. *The Sentinels,* 2010

Sanderson, Brandon. *Alcatraz* series, published by Scholastic, Grades 5–8.

"On his thirteenth birthday, foster child Alcatraz Smedry receives a bag of sand which is immediately stolen by the evil Librarians who are trying to take over the world, and Alcatraz is introduced to his grandfather

Alcatraz Versus the Evil Librarians by Brandon Sanderson.

and his own special talent, and told that he must use it to save civilization." LC. Funny books; nominated for a few state young reader awards.

Alcatraz Versus the Evil Librarians, 2007
Alcatraz Versus the Scrivener's Bones, 2008
Alcatraz Versus the Knights of Crystallia, 2009
Alcatraz Versus the Shattered Lens, 2010

Scott, Michael. *The Secrets of the Immortal Nicholas Flamel* series, published by Delacorte, Grads 6–10.
Fifteen-year-old twins Sophie and Josh find themselves caught up in the deadly struggle between rival alchemists Nicholas Flamel and John Dee over the possession of an ancient book that holds the secret formulas for alchemy and everlasting life. Very well reviewed.

1. *The Alchemyst,* 2007
2. *The Magician,* 2008
3. *The Sorceress,* 2009
4. *The Necromancer,* 2010
5. *The Warlock,* 2011

Scrimger, Richard. *Me and Death: An Afterlife Adventure.* Tundra Books, 2010. 240 p. Grades 7–10.
In this unusual take on *A Christmas Carol,* 14-year-old wannabe gangster, bully, and car thief Jim, having died after being hit by a car and learning about the afterlife, is given the opportunity to return to Earth, where he must face his own demons, which include a violent neighbor and a creepy older sister.

Selznick, Brian. *The Invention of Hugo Cabret.* Scholastic, 2007. 531 p. Grades 5–up.
This unique, original, fascinating book tells the story, part graphically and part in prose, of a boy living on his own in a Paris train station in the 1930s; he gets involved with a girl and her foster father, an old man who runs a toy shop in the station, and makes a wonderful discovery. Hugely popular. Won a Caldecott Medal, 2008.

Shusterman, Neal. *Bruiser.* HarperTeen, 2010. 336 p. Grades 8–12.
"Inexplicable events start to occur when sixteen-year-old twins Tennyson and Bronte befriend a troubled and misunderstood outcast, aptly nicknamed Bruiser, and his little brother, Cody." LC

Shusterman, Neil. *Skinjacker* trilogy, published by Simon & Schuster, Grades 7–up.
"When Nick and Allie are killed in a car crash, they end up in Everlost, or limbo for lost souls, where although Nick is satisfied, Allie will stop at nothing—even skinjacking—to break free." LC. Nominated for multiple state young reader awards.

1. *Everlost,* 2006
2. *Everwild,* 2009
3. *Everfound,* 2011

Shusterman, Neal. *Unwind.* Simon & Schuster, 2007, 2009. 335 p. Grades 8–up.
Three teens embark upon a cross-country journey in order to escape from a society that salvages body parts from children ages 13 to 18. A riveting dystopian novel. The sequel is *Unwholly,* 2012.

Simmons, Michael. *Alien Feast.* Illustrated by George O'Connor. Roaring Brook, 2009. 231 p. Grades 5–8.

"In 2017, human-eating aliens have kidnapped two scientists who might cure the disease that is destroying them, and twelve-year-old William Aitkin, his elderly, ailing Uncle Maynard, and the scientists' daughter, Sophie, set out to rescue them." LC. This is to be the first in the *Chronicles of the First Invasion* series, but is the only one published so far.

Skye, Obert. *Leven Thumps* series, originally published by Shadow Mountain, then by Aladdin, Grades 5–8.

An Oklahoma teenager can find the future—and alter it! A popular series.

1. *Leven Thumps and the Gateway to Foo,* 2005
2. *Leven Thumps and the Whispered Secret,* 2006
3. *Leven Thumps and the Eyes of the Want,* 2007
4. *Leven Thumps and the Wrath of Ezra,* 2008
5. *Leven Thumps and the Ruins of Alder,* 2009

Alien Feast **by Michael Simmons. Courtesy of Roaring Book Press, an imprint of the Macmillan Children's Publishing Group.**

Slade, Arthur. *The Hunchback Assignments* series, published by Random House, Grades 6–10.

"In Victorian London, fourteen-year-old Modo, a shape-changing hunchback, becomes a secret agent for the Permanent Association, which strives to protect the world from the evil machinations of the Clockwork Guild." LC

1. *The Hunchback Assignments,* 2009
2. *The Dark Deeps,* 2011

Smith, Alexander Gordon. *Escape from Furnace* series, published by Farrar, Straus & Giroux, grades 6–9.

"When fourteen-year-old Alex is framed for murder, he becomes an inmate in the Furnace Penitentiary, where brutal inmates and sadistic guards reign, boys who disappear in the middle of the night sometimes return weirdly altered, and escape might just be possible." LC. An ALA Quick Pick for Reluctant Readers.

1. *Lockdown,* 2009
2. *Solitary,* 2010
3. *Death Sentence,* 2011

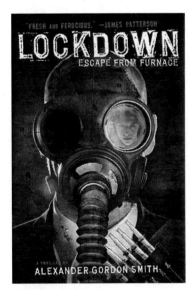

Lockdown **by Alexander Gordon Smith. Courtesy of Farrar Straus Giroux Books for Young Readers, an imprint of the Macmillan Children's Publishing Group.**

Sniegoski, Tom. *Legacy.* Delacorte, 2009. 231 p. Grades 8–up.

"Eighteen-year-old Lucas is left to decide whether to take a stand against his father, who abandoned him, or defend a world that needs him after his mother is killed by mysterious warriors and he learns his superhero father is dying." LC. An ALA Quick Picks for Reluctant Young Adult Readers.

Steer, Donald A. *Dragonology Chronicles* **series, illustrated by Douglas Carrel, published by Candlewick, Grades 5–8.**

This fantasy-adventure series, scheduled to be four books, is about two kids who become assistants to the world's greatest dragon expert.

The Dragon's Eye, 2006
The Dragon Diary, 2009
The Dragon's Apprentice, 2011

Stone, Jeff. *Five Ancestors* **series, published by Random House, Grades 6–9.**

"Five young warrior-monk brothers survive an insurrection and must use the ancient arts to avenge their Grandmaster." LC

1. *Tiger,* 2005
2. *Monkey,* 2006
3. *Snake,* 2007
4. *Crane,* 2008
5. *Eagle,* 2008
6. *Mouse,* 2009
7. *Dragon,* 2010

Stroud, Jonathan. *Bartimaeus* **trilogy, published by Hyperion, Grades 5–up.**

"Nathaniel, a young magician's apprentice, becomes caught in a web of magical espionage, murder, and rebellion, after he summons the djinni Bartimaeus and instructs him to steal the Amulet of Samarkand from the powerful magician Simon Loveland." LC

1. *The Amulet of Samarkand,* 2003
2. *The Golem's Eye,* 2006
3. *Ptolemy's Gate,* 2007

Stroud, Jonathan. *Heroes of the Valley.* Hyperion, 2009. 483 p. Grades 5–up.

This wonderful read about Ragnor, a questioning and adventurous medieval Nordic kid, made many best book lists.

Taylor, Greg. *Killer Pizza.* Feiwel and Friends, 2009. 346 p. Grades 5–8.

"While working as summer employees in a local pizza parlor, three teenagers are recruited by an underground organization of monster hunters." LC. Nominated for multiple state young reader awards.

Testa, Dom. *Galahad* **series, published by Tor, Grades 7–10.**

"Desperate to save the human race after a comet's deadly particles devastate the adult population, scientists create a ship that will carry a crew of 251 teenagers to a home in a distant solar system." LC

1. *The Comet's Curse,* 2009
2. *The Web of Titan,* 2010

Killer Pizza **by Greg Taylor. Courtesy of Feiwel and Friends, an imprint of the Macmillan Children's Publishing Group.**

3. *The Cassini Code,* 2010
4. *The Dark Zone,* 2011

Townley, Roderick. *The Door in the Forest.* Alfred A. Knopf Books for Young Readers, 2011. Grades 5–7.

"While trying to outwit the soldiers who are occupying their small town, fourteen-year-old Daniel, who cannot lie, and Emily, who discovers she has magical powers, are inexplicably drawn to a mysterious island in the heart of the forest where townsfolk have been warned never to go." LC. Set in an alternate 1923.

Turner, Megan Whalen. *The Thief* series, published by various publishers and EOS, Grades 6–up.

Beautifully written, superb reads; excellent for proficient readers. The first book, which has a delightful surprise ending, won a Newbery Honor.

1. *The Thief,* 1996
2. *The Queen of Attolia,* 2000
3. *The King of Attolia,* 2006
4. *A Conspiracy of Thieves,* 2010

Voake, Steve. *The Dreamwalker's Child.* Bloomsbury, 2006. 300 p. Grades 5–up.

British Sam, aged 15, has a terrifying accident and awakens to find himself in a strange otherworld, where insects are bred as airplanes—and where he is a wanted fugitive. There is a lot of action and adventure here.

Wagner, Hilary. *Nightshade City.* Illustrated by Omar Rayyan. Holiday House, 2010. 320 p. Grades 5–8.

"Eleven years after the cruel Killdeer took over the Catacombs far beneath the human's Trillium City, Juniper Belancourt, assisted by Vincent and Victor Nightshade, leads a maverick band of rats to escape and establish their own city." LC

Wallenfels, Stephen. *POD.* Namelos, 2010. 212 p. Grades 6–up.

"As alien spacecraft fill the sky and zap up any human being who dares to go outside, fifteen-year-old Josh and twelve-year-old Megs, living in different cities, describe what could be their last days on Earth." LC

Walsh, Pat. *The Crowfield Curse.* The Chicken House, 2010. 336 p. Grades 5–8.

"In 1347, when fourteen-year-old orphan William Paynel, an impoverished servant at Crowfield Abbey, goes into the forest to gather wood and finds a magical creature caught in a trap, he discovers he has the ability to see fays and becomes embroiled in a strange mystery involving Old Magic, a bitter feud, and ancient secrets." LC. Starred review in *School Library Journal.*

Ward, David. *Grassland Trilogy* series, published by Amulet, Grades 5–8.

"Six young friends, tortured by the Spears and forced to work as slaves in the harsh fields of Grassland, vow to escape to find the freedom that was stolen from them long ago, and their opportunity arises when Outsiders come and wage war against the Spears." LC

1. *Escape the Mask,* 2008
2. *Beneath the Mask,* 2008
3. *Beyond the Mask,* 2010

Wells, Rosemary. *On the Blue Comet.* Candlewick, 2010. 336 p. Grades 5–8.

"When the Depression hits in Cairo, Illinois, and Oscar Ogilvie's father must sell their home and vast model train set-up to look for work in California, eleven-year-old Oscar is left with his dour aunt, where he befriends a mysterious drifter, witnesses a stunning bank robbery, and is suddenly catapulted onto a train that takes him to a different time and place." LC

Westerfeld, Scott. *Leviathan* trilogy, published by Simon Pulse, Grades 6–up.

In an alternate 1914 Europe, 15-year-old Austrian Prince Alek, on the run from the Clanker Powers who are attempting to take over the globe using mechanical machinery, forms an uneasy alliance with Deryn who, disguised as a boy to join the British Air Service, is learning to fly genetically engineered beasts. This is a compelling science fiction/historical/action adventure.

Leviathan, 2009
Behemoth, 2010
Goliath, 2011

Weston, Robert Paul. *Dust City.* Razorbill, 2010. 304 p. Grades 7–10.

"Henry Whelp, son of the Big Bad Wolf, investigates what happened to the fairies that used to protect humans and animalia, and what role the corporation that manufactures synthetic fairy dust played in his father's crime." LC

Wharton, Thomas. *The Shadow of Malabron.* Candlewick, 2009. 382 p. Grades 5–8.

"When Will, a rebellious teen, stumbles from the present into the realm where stories come from, he learns he has a mission concerning the evil Malabron." LC. An excellent quest fantasy and the first in a projected series titled *The Perilous Realm.*

Whitley, David. *The Agora* trilogy, published by Roaring Brook, Grades 7–up.

"In the city of Agora, where everything can be bought and sold, two children stumble upon the mysterious and dangerous Midnight Charter and play their unique part in their society's future as they learn who they can trust." LC

The Midnight Charter, 2009
The Children of the Lost, 2011

Wild, K. *Firefight.* Scholastic, 2009. 339 p. Grades 6–10.

"Freedom Smith, an agent for Phoenix, a black operations unit, investigates a viral video that has made thirteen kids vanish and soon finds himself trapped in a fortress where he must master a fighting technique and battle a supernatural enemy to escape and save his girl, Java." LC

Wilks, Mike. *Mirrorscape* series, published by Egmont, Grades 5–9.

"In a world where all pleasures are severely restricted, Melkin Womper is apprenticed to a master painter when he discovers the Mirrorscape, a world inside paintings, and becomes entangled in a war between the restrictive Fifth Mystery and the rebels fighting to stop them." LC

1. *Mirrorscape,* 2009
2. *Mirrorstorm,* 2012

Williams, Alex. *The Deep Freeze of Bartholomew Tullock.* Philomel, 2008. 298 p. Grades 5–8.
A page-turning fantasy about an inventive family in serious danger of being kicked out of their home and their livelihood by a truly horrendous man.

Wilson, Daniel. *A Boy and His Bot.* Bloomsbury, 2011. 256 p. Grades 5–8.
"When timid young Code falls down a hole into Mekhos, where everything is made of metal and circuitry, he must obtain the legendary Robonomicon from evil Immortalis in order to save the robots of this subterranean world and return home." LC

Wilson, F. Paul. *Jack* series, published by Tor, Grades 7–10.
Jack and his two buddies wander into The Barrens, a wilderness near their suburban home, and discover mysterious objects—including a pyramid and a corpse; fun for science fiction fans.

1. *The Secret Histories,* 2009
2. *The Secret Circles,* 2010
3. *The Secret Vengeance,* 2011

Yep, Laurence. *City* trilogy, published by Starscape, Grades 5–8.
"Twelve-year-old Scirye and her companions travel to Houlani, a new Hawaiian island created by magic, where they enlist the help of volcano goddess Pele in an attempt to stop an evil dragon and a mysterious man from altering the universe." LC

1. *City of Fire,* 2009
2. *City of Ice*, 2011

Chapter —9

Sports Books

Boys cannot get enough of books about sports. And just as with humor books, there seems to be a lack choices for boys who want sports action in their books. Thank goodness for the recent surge in titles by Mike Lupica, Tim Green, and John Feinstein. This chapter will guide you to some great choices to keep your young sports fans reading.

YOUNGER GUYS

Barber, Tiki, and Ronde Barber, with Paul Mantell, published by Simon & Schuster, Grades 4–7.
This series is fiction loosely based on the early lives of the football stars. Though the stories of the famous Barber twins do not really have a series title, they are definitely a series! Well-reviewed books that boys enjoy.

By My Brother's Side, 2004
Game Day, 2005
Teammates, 2006
Kickoff! 2007
Go Long, 2008
Wild Card, 2009
Red Zone, 2010
Game Time, 2010
Goal Line, 2011

Bowen, Fred. *All-Star Sports Story* **series, published by Peachtree, Grades 3–8.**

Fast-moving, entertaining stories for sports fans, including "real story" information at the back of each book. There's a lot of play-by-play information in these. Some are older titles that have been republished. These books read like the sports pages!

Dugout Rivals, 2010
Full Level Fever, 2009
The Golden Glove, 2009
Hardcourt Comeback, 2010
The Kid Coach, 2009
Off the Rim, 2009
On the Line, 2008
Play-Off Dreams, 2009
Soccer Team Upset, 2009
Throwing Heat, 2010
T.J.'s Secret Pitch, 2009
Touchdown Trouble, 2009
Winners Take All, 2009
Hardcourt Comeback, 2010

Christopher, Matt. *Matt Christopher Sports Readers* **series, illustrated by different artists, published by Norwood House, Grades 1–3.**

Thanks to the help of his dog, who can read his thoughts, Mike can perform better at sports. These are older books, newly republished.

The Dog That Stole Football Plays, 1980, 2010
The Dog That Called the Signals, 1982, 2010
The Dog That Pitched a No-Hitter, 1988, 2010
The Dog That Called the Pitch, 1998, 2010
The Dog That Stole Home, 1993, 2010

Christopher, Matt. *New Matt Christopher Sports Library* **series, published by Norwood House, Grades 2–5.**

Winning, enduring, sports stories by a popular author. These are older books, newly republished. Originally published by Little, Brown.

Baseball Flyhawk, 1963, 2010
Dirt Bike Runaway, 1983, 2008
Lacrosse Face-Off (text by Stephanie Peters), 2006, 2010
Return of the Home Run Kid, 1992, 2008
Shoot for the Hoop, 1963, 2010
The Basket Counts, 1968, 2008
The Comeback Challenge, 1996, 2008
The Great Quarterback Switch, 1984, 2008
The Hockey Machine, 1986, 2008
The Team That Couldn't Lose, 1967, 2010
Tough to Tackle, 1971, 2010

Christopher, Matt. *New Peach Street Mudders Library* **series, published by Norwood House, Grades 2–5.**

Newly reissued books popular with young sports fans.

All-Star Fever, 1995, 2009
The Catcher's Mask, 1998, 2009
Centerfield Ballhawk, 1992, 2009
The Hit-Away Kid, 1988, 2009
Man Out at First, 1993, 2009
Shadow Over Second, 1996, 2009
The Spy on Third Base, 1988, 2009
Stranger in Right Field, 1997, 2009
Zero's Slider, 1994, 2009

Coy, John. *4 for 4* **series, published by Feiwel and Friends, Grades 4–6.**

Starting in the fifth grade, each book in this fast-paced sports series covers a different year and a different sport in the lives of four friends. Play-by-play action.

Top of the Order, 2009
Eyes on the Goal, 2010
Love of the Game, 2011

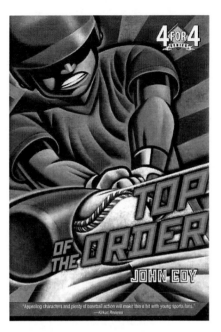

***Top of the Order* by John Coy.**

Author Spotlight: Tim Green

Tim Green, former professional football player and author of *Football Genius* and other popular sports books for boys, knows firsthand what boys like to read about. He loved reading when he was young, especially when a good book took him away to another time and place. His childhood favorites were adventure stories like *The Count of Monte Cristo, Big Red*, and the *Hardy Boys* mysteries. He says that every book that he reads and enjoys has an influence on his writing today.

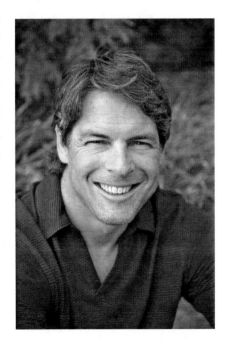

Tim Green Recommends

Maniac Magee by Jerry Spinelli

Bud, Not Buddy by Christopher Paul Curtis

Holes by Louis Sachar

Redwall by Brian Jacques

Mrs. Frisbee and the Rats of NIMH
    by Robert O'Brien

Crispin: Cross of Lead by Avi

Big Red by James Kjelgaard

Watership Down by Richard Adams

Green, Tim. *Baseball Greats* **series, published by HarperCollins, Grades 4–8.**

In the first book, 12-year-old Josh joins a youth championship team and discovers that the unscrupulous coach will do anything to win. Action, suspense, and lots of play-by-play sports make these books a huge hit with boys.

Baseball Great, 2009
Rivals, 2010
The Best of the Best, 2011

Green, Tim. *Football Genius* **series, published by HarperCollins, Grades 4–8.**

Troy's amazing ability to predict football plays is the theme running through these popular titles. Author Tim Green, a former player for the Atlanta Falcons, gives an inside view of professional football.

Football Genius, 2008
Football Champ, 2009
The Big Time, 2010
Deep Zone, 2011

Author Spotlight: Dan Gutman

Dan Gutman relates well to kids who don't like to read because he was one of them when he was young. Even the comic books his mom bought for him didn't get him interested in books. He thought reading was boring and hard to do until age 10 when he became a big sports fan and had to read to learn more about his teams. Today his work is influenced by a range of sources, including *Mad* magazine, *National Lampoon*, Woody Allen, Mel Brooks, *Rowan & Martin's Laugh-In*, *Saturday Night Live*, *Seinfeld*, and more than anything else, the Beatles.

Dan Gutman Recommends

The Invention of Hugo Cabret by Brian Selznick is the Sergeant Pepper of children's books. If I ever created something that good, I would retire happy.

Also books by these authors:

Gary Paulsen

David Lubar

Gordon Korman

Carl Hiaasen

Roland Smith

Peg Kehret

Gutman, Dan. *Baseball Card Adventures* **series, published by HarperTrophy, Grades 4–7.**

Joe Stoshack has the astounding ability to travel through time using baseball cards. He gets the year he wants to go to and travels to that year and that team. Can our Joe change history? These are good reads.

Honus and Me, 1997
Jackie and Me, 1999
Babe and Me, 2000
Shoeless Joe and Me, 2002
Mickey and Me, 2003
Abner and Me, 2005
Satch and Me, 2006
Jim and Me, 2008
Ray and Me, 2009
Roberto and Me, 2010

Heldring, Thatcher. *Roy Morelli Steps Up to the Plate.* Delacorte, 2010. 240 p. Grades 4–8.

"When eighth-grader Roy Morelli's divorced parents find out he is failing history, they ban him from playing on his beloved all-star baseball team, and, even worse, he winds up being tutored by his father's new girlfriend." LC. Lots of baseball action here.

Swimming with Sharks **by Betty Hicks. Courtesy of Roaring Book Press, an imprint of the Macmillan Children's Publishing Group.**

Hicks, Betty. *Gym Shorts* **series, published by Roaring Brook, Grades 2–4.**

Beginning chapter books in which five friends, three boys and two girls, participate in various sports activities and learn a lot of life lessons in the process. Kirkus called the first one "a real score!"

Basketball Bats, 2008
Goof-Off Goalie, 2008
Swimming with Sharks, 2008
Scaredy-Cat Catcher, 2009
Track Attack, 2009
Doubles Troubles, 2010

Kelly, David A. *Ballpark Mysteries***, illustrated by Mark Meyers, published by Random House, Grades 2–4.**

Two nine-year-old detectives solve mysteries in major league ballparks.

1. *The Fenway Foul-Up,* 2011
2. *The Pinstripe Ghost,* 2011
3. *The L.A. Dodger,* 2011

Long, Loren, and Phil Bildner. *Sluggers* **series (formerly** *Barnstormers* **series), published by Aladdin, grades 4–6.**

This is confusing. The series began as *Barnstormers,* but, as Long explains on his website, kids did not know what that word meant. They changed the series title to *Sluggers* in 2009. Quoting Long, the series, which starts in 1899, is about baseball, magic, mystery, action, suspense, family, and American history.

1. *Magic in the Outfield,* 2009
2. *Horsin' Around,* 2009

   3. *Great Balls of Fire*, 2009
   4. *Water, Water Everywhere*, 2009
   5. *Blastin' the Blues*, 2010
   6. *Home of the Brave*, 2010
   7. *Blastin' the Blues*, 2011

Lupica, Mike. *Comeback Kids* **series, published by Philomel, Grades 4–6.**
These popular books about different sports feature ordinary kids working on their problems.

Hot Hand, 2007
Two-Minute Drill, 2007
Safe at Home, 2008
Long Shot, 2008
Shoot-Out, 2010

Markey, Kevin. *Super Sluggers* **series, published by HarperCollins, Grades 3–5.**
Sports fans enjoy these fun reads about kids who play baseball.

Slumpbuster, 2009
Wall Ball, 2010
Wing Ding, 2011

Orca Sports **series, by various authors, published by Orca, Grades 4–8.**
From the publisher's website: "Orca Sports are short high-interest novels with exciting sports action and suspense. Ages 10+." Some well-reviewed titles with boy-friendly topics are:

Absolute Pressure, by Sigmund Brouwer, 2009
All-Star Pride, by Sigmund Brouwer, 2006
Blazer Drive, by Sigmund Brouwer, 2007
Boarder Patrol, by Erin Thomas, 2010
Chief Honor, by Sigmund Brouwer, 2008
Cobra Strike, by Sigmund Brouwer, 2007
Crossover, by Jeff Rud, 2008
Dead in the Water, by Robin Stevenson, 2008
Flying Feet, by James McCann, 2010
Gravity Check, by Alex Van Tol, 2011
Hitmen Triumph, by Sigmund Brouwer, 2007
Hurricane Power, by Sigmund Brouwer, 2007
Jumper, by Michele Martin Bossley, 2006
Kicker, by Michele Martin Bossley, 2007
Maverick Mama, by Sigmund Brouwer, 2008
Oil King Courage, by Sigmund Brouwer, 2009
Paralyzed, by Jeff Rud, 2008
Razor's Edge, by Nikki Tate, 2009
Rebel Glory, by Sigmund Brouwer, 2006
Scarlet Thunder, by Sigmund Brouwer, 2006
Slam Dunk, by Kate Jaimet, 2009
Squeeze, by Rachel Dunstan Miller, 2010
The Drop, by Jeff Ross, 2011
Thunderbird Spirit, by Sigmund Brouwer, 2008
Tiger Threat, by Sigmund Brouwer, 2006
Titan Clash, by Sigmund Brouwer, 2007
Venom, by Nikki Tate, 2009
Winter Hawk Star, by Sigmund Brouwer, 2007

Scaletta, Kurtis. *Mudville.* Alfred A. Knopf Books for Young Readers, 2009. 266 p. Grades 4–8.
"For twenty-two years, since a fateful baseball game against their rival town, it has rained in Moundville, so when the rain finally stops, twelve-year-old Roy, his friends, and foster brother Sturgis dare to face the curse and form a team." LC

Sports Illustrated Kids: Victory School Superstars **series, by various authors, published by Stone Arch Books, Grades 2–4.**
Early chapter books about six friends, students who attend the Victory School for Super Athletes. Titles with particular boy appeal include:

There's No Crying in Baseball
by Anita Yasuda.

Nobody Wants to Play with a Ball Hog, by Julie Gassman, 2010
A Running Back Can't Always Rush, by Nate LeBoutillier, 2010
There Are No Figure Eights in Hockey, by Chris Keie, 2010
There's No Crying in Baseball, by Anita Yasuda, 2011
Who Wants to Play Just for Kicks? by Chris Keie, 2011

Tooke, Wes. *Lucky: Maris, Mantle and My Best Summer Ever.* Simon & Schuster, 2010. 183 p. Grades 4–7.

> "Louis, who loves baseball despite being the worst stickball player in White Plains, New York, sees his opportunity to be bat boy for the 1961 Yankees team as the perfect way to escape the problems of his father's remarriage and moving to the suburbs." LC

Wallace, Rich. *Kickers* series, published by Alfred A. Knopf Books for Young Readers, Grades 2–4.

> Short chapters and plenty of action fill these stories about soccer for young readers.

1. *The Ball Hogs,* 2010
2. *Fake Out,* 2010
3. *Benched,* 2010
4. *Game Day Jitters,* 2011

Wallace, Rich. *Sports Camp.* Alfred A. Knopf Books for Young Readers, 2010. 160 p. Grades 4–6.

> An exciting story about an 11-year-old who goes off to summer camp feeling insecure about his small size and how he will handle the new challenges.

OLDER GUYS

Aronson, Marc, and Charles R. Smith Jr. (editors). *Pick-Up Game: A Full Day of Full Court.* Candlewick, 2011. 176 p. Grades 7–10.

> "A series of short stories by such authors as Walter Dean Myers, Rita Williams-Garcia, and Joseph Bruchac, interspersed with poems and photographs, provides different perspectives on a game of streetball played one steamy July day at the West 4th Street court in New York City known as The Cage." LC

Bloor, Edward. *Tangerine.* Harcourt, 1997, 2006. 294 p. Gr. 5–up.

> When Paul's dysfunctional family, always focused on his hated older brother the football star, moves to Florida, he is determined to play soccer and to make friends in an incredibly weird place, a housing development built on the site of a former tangerine grove. Paul is legally blind, the result of an accident that his brother tells him happened because he gazed too long at a solar eclipse. This combines sports, mystery, and a lot of exciting reading—I stayed up late to finish it!

Coy, John. *Crackback.* Scholastic, 2005. 201 p. Grades 7–up.

> "Miles barely recalls when football was fun after being sidelined by a new coach, constantly criticized by his father, and pressured by his best friend to take performance-enhancing drugs." LC

Deuker, Carl. *Payback Time.* Houghton Mifflin, 2010. 304 p. Grades 7–up.

> Game descriptions, a mystery, and injustice await readers in this well-written story about an aspiring journalist high school senior whose best friend is the star quarterback at a Seattle high school.

Feinstein, John. *Sports Mystery* **series, published by Alfred A. Knopf Books for Young Readers, Grades 5–9.**

Teenage journalists Stevie Thomas and Susan Carol Anderson solve mysteries at sporting events. These have been nominated for several state young reader awards.

Last Shot: A Final Four Mystery, 2005
Vanishing Act: Mystery at the U.S. Open, 2006
Cover Up: Mystery at the Super Bowl, 2007
Change-Up: Mystery at the World Series, 2009
The Rivalry: Mystery at the Army-Navy Game, 2010

Gratz, Alan. *The Brooklyn Nine: A Novel in Nine Innings.* Dial, 2009. 308 p. Grades 5–10.

"Follows the fortunes of a German immigrant family through nine generations, beginning in 1845, as they experience American life and play baseball." LC. Nominated for multiple state young reader awards.

Koertge, Ron. *Shakespeare Makes the Playoffs.* Candlewick, 2010. 176 p. Grades 6–9.

Fourteen-year-old Kevin likes baseball and his girlfriend—until his dad gives him a new journal and he remembers how much he likes writing, too. This is a verse novel, fun and accessible. It is a sequel to *Shakespeare Bats Cleanup,* 2003.

Korman, Gordon. *Pop.* Balzer and Bray, 2009. 180 p. Grades 7–10.

"Lonely after a midsummer move to a new town, sixteen-year-old high-school quarterback Marcus Jordan becomes friends with a retired professional linebacker who is great at training him, but whose childish behavior keeps Marcus in hot water." LC

Lipsyte, Robert. *Center Field.* HarperTeen, 2010. 280 p. Grades 7–12.

"Mike lives for baseball and hopes to follow his idol into the major leagues one day, but he is distracted by a new player who might take his place in center field, an ankle injury, problems at home, and a growing awareness that something sinister is happening at school." LC

Lupica, Mike. *The Batboy.* Philomel, 2010. 256 p. Grades 5–8.

Troubled Brian, whose parents just divorced, gets his dream job of being a batboy for the Detroit Tigers, only to discover that his idol, Hank Bishop, acts like a jerk. Lupica is popular for good reason!

Lupica, Mike. *Heat.* Philomel, 2006. 220 p. Grades 5–8.

A refugee from Cuba, 12-year-old Michael Arroyo, is a pitching prodigy whose right to play Little League baseball is challenged by a hostile coach.

Lupica, Mike. *Million-Dollar Throw.* Philomel, 2009. 252 p. Grades 5–8.

"Eighth-grade star quarterback Nate Brodie's family is feeling the stress of the troubled economy, and Nate is frantic because his best friend Abby is going blind, so when he gets a chance to win a million dollars if he can complete a pass during the halftime of a New England Patriot's game,

he is nearly overwhelmed by the pressure to succeed." LC. Nominated for a few state young reader awards.

McKissack, Frederic. *Shooting Star.* Atheneum, 2009. 283 p. Grades 8–up.
    "Jomo Rogers, a naturally talented athlete, starts taking performance enhancing drugs in order to be an even better high school football player, but finds his life spinning out of control as his game improves." LC

Myers, Walter Dean, and Ross Workman. *Kick.* HarperTeen, 2011. 208 p. Grades 7–up.
    "Told in their separate voices, thirteen-year-old soccer star Kevin and police sergeant Brown, who knew his father, try to keep Kevin out of juvenile hall after he is arrested on very serious charges." LC. This was co-written by Myers and a teenage fan who emailed him!

Ripken, Cal, and Kevin Cowherd. *Hothead.* Hyperion, 2011. 144 p. Grades 5–8.
    "Connor Sullivan, All-Star third baseman on his Babe Ruth League team, has a terrible temper and problems at home, but when the sports editor of the school paper threatens to publish an embarrassing story about his tantrums, Connor must make a change." LC

Ritter, John H. *The Desperado Who Stole Baseball.* Philomel, 2009. 260 p. Grades 5–9.
    "In 1881, the scrappy, rough-and-tumble baseball team in a California mining town enlists the help of a quick-witted twelve-year-old orphan and the notorious outlaw Billy the Kid to win a big game against the National League Champion Chicago White Stockings." LC

Tocher, Timothy. *Bill Pennant, Babe Ruth, and Me.* Cricket Books, 2009. 178 p. Grades 5–9.
    "In 1920, sixteen-year-old Hank finds his loyalties divided when he is assigned to care for the Giants' mascot, a wildcat named Bill Pennant, as well as keep an eye on Babe Ruth in Ruth's first season with the New York Yankees." LC

Tocher, Timothy. *Chief Sunrise, John McGraw, and Me.* Cricket Books, 2004. 154 p. Grades 5–9.
    "In 1919, fifteen-year-old Hank escapes an abusive father and goes looking for a chance to become a baseball player, accompanied by a man who calls himself Chief Sunrise and claims to be a full-blooded Seminole." LC

Volponi, Paul. *Homestretch.* Atheneum, 2010. 151 p. Grades 7–9.
    This story about a kid who finds a job at a horse track was named one of the top 10 youth sports books of the year by Booklist.

Weaver, Will. *Motor* series, published by Farrar, Straus & Giroux, Grades 7–up.
    Trace Bonham, a natural-born racer, works his way up in the world of car racing; kids who love cars will have a fine time.

    Saturday Night Dirt, 2008
    Super Stock Rookie, 2009
    Checkered Flag Cheater, 2010

Saturday Night Dirt by Will Weaver. **Courtesy of Farrar Straus Giroux Books for Young Readers, an imprint of the Macmillan Children's Publishing Group.**

Acknowledgments

The authors and publisher gratefully acknowledge permission for use of the following material.

CHAPTER 1

Cover from *The Karate Mouse* by Geronimo Stilton. Scholastic, 2010. Reprinted with permission.
Cover from *Trackers* by Patrick Carman. Scholastic, 2010. Reprinted with permission.
Cover from *Framed* by Gordon Korman. Scholastic, 2010. Reprinted with permission.
Cover from *Holes* by Louis Sachar. Farrar, Straus & Giroux, 1998. Courtesy of Farrar Straus Giroux Books for Young Readers, an imprint of the Macmillan Children's Publishing Group.
Cover from *Revolver* by Marcus Sedgwick. Roaring Brook, 2010. Courtesy of Roaring Book Press, an imprint of the Macmillan Children's Publishing Group.
Cover from *Malice* by Chris Wooding. Scholastic, 2009. Reprinted with permission.

CHAPTER 2

Cover from *Felix Takes the Stage* by Kathryn Lasky. Scholastic, 2010. Reprinted with permission.
Cover from *The Mammoth Academy* by Neal Layton. Henry Holt, 2008. Courtesy of Henry Holt Books for Young Readers, an imprint of the Macmillan Children's Publishing Group.
Cover from *How I, Nicky Flynn, Finally Get a Life (and a Dog)* by Art Corriveau. Amulet, 2010. Used with permission of Amulet Books, an imprint of Abrams.

CHAPTER 3

Cover from *Claws in the Snow* by Michael Dahl. Stone Arch Books, 2009. Reprinted with permission.
Cover from *Star Wars, Episode I: The Phantom Menace: Volume 1*. ABDO, 2009. Courtesy of ABDO Publishing Group.
Cover from *Journey to the Center of the Earth* by Joeming Dunn. Magic Wagon/Graphic Planet, 2009. Courtesy of ABDO Publishing Group.
Cover from *Big, Hairy Drama* by Aaron Reynolds. Henry Holt, 2010. Courtesy of Henry Holt Books for Young Readers, an imprint of the Macmillan Children's Publishing Group.
Cover from *Ghost of a Chance*. ABDO, 2009. Courtesy of ABDO Publishing Group.
Cover from *Quest for the Silver Tiger* by YoYo. Candlewick, 2009. Reprinted with permission.

CHAPTER 4

Cover from *Resistance* by Ann Jungman. Stone Arch Books, 2006. Reprinted with permission.
Cover from *Journey to the Bottomless Pit: The Story of Stephen Bishop and Mammoth Cave* by Elizabeth Mitchell. Viking, 2004. Used by permission of Penguin Group (USA) Inc. All rights reserved.
Cover from *The Bombing of Pearl Harbor* by Lauren Tarshis. Scholastic, 2011. Reprinted with permission.
Cover from *The Secret Room* by H. Townson. Stone Arch Books, 2006. Reprinted with permission.
Cover from *George Washington's Spy* by Elvira Woodruff. Scholastic, 1991, 2010. Reprinted with permission.

Cover from *Rex Zero, King of Nothing* by Tim Wynne-Jones. Farrar, Straus & Giroux, 2008. Courtesy of Farrar Straus Giroux Books for Young Readers, an imprint of the Macmillan Children's Publishing Group.

Cover from *The Train Jumper* by Don Brown. Roaring Brook, 2007. Courtesy of Roaring Book Press, an imprint of the Macmillan Children's Publishing Group.

Cover from *Al Capone Does My Shirts* by Gennifer Choldenko. Dial, 2004. Used by permission of Penguin Group (USA) Inc. All rights reserved.

Cover from *Owl Ninja* by Sandy Fussell. Candlewick, 2011. Reprinted with permission.

Cover from *The Best Bad Luck I Ever Had* by Kristin Levine. Putnam, 2009. Used by permission of Penguin Group (USA) Inc. All rights reserved.

Cover from *Bloodline* by Katy Moran. Candlewick, 2009. Reprinted with permission.

CHAPTER 5

Cover from *The Strange Case of Origami Yoda* by Tom Angleberger. Amulet, 2010. Used with permission of Amulet Books, an imprint of Abrams.

Cover from *Brains for Lunch: A Zombie Novel in Haiku?!* by K. A. Holt. Roaring Brook, 2010. Courtesy of Roaring Book Press, an imprint of the Macmillan Children's Publishing Group.

Cover from *Diary of a Wimpy Kid* by Jeff Kinney. Amulet, 2007. Used with permission of Amulet Books, an imprint of Abrams.

Cover from *Alien Eraser to the Rescue* by Marissa Moss. Candlewick, 2009. Reprinted with permission.

Cover from *The Adventures Of Ook And Gluk, Kung-Fu Cavemen From The Future* by Dav Pilkey. Blue Sky, 2010. Reprinted with permission.

Cover from *Dragonbreath* by Ursula Vernon. Dial, 2009. Used by permission of Penguin Group (USA) Inc. All rights reserved.

Cover from *Fizzy Whiz Kid* by Maiya Williams. Amulet, 2010. Used with permission of Amulet Books, an imprint of Abrams.

CHAPTER 6

Cover from *The Zombies Who Visited New Orleans* by Steve Brezenoff. Stone Arch Books, 2010. Reprinted with permission.

Cover from *The Curse of the Ancient Mask and Other Case Files* by Simon Cheshire. Roaring Brook, 2009. Courtesy of Roaring Book Press, an imprint of the Macmillan Children's Publishing Group.

Cover from *The Book That Dripped Blood* by Michael Dahl. Stone Arch Books, 2007. Reprinted with permission.

Cover from *Rats on the Page* by Michael Dahl. Stone Arch Books, 2011. Reprinted with permission.

Cover from *The Beasts of Clawstone Castle* by Eva Ibbotson. Dutton, 2006. Used by permission of Penguin Group (USA) Inc. All rights reserved.

Cover from *The Icy Hand* by Chris Mould. Roaring Brook, 2008. Courtesy of Roaring Book Press, an imprint of the Macmillan Children's Publishing Group.

Cover from *The Ransom Note Blues* by Jill Santopolo. Scholastic, 2009. Reprinted with permission.

Cover from *The Game of Sunken Places* by M. T. Anderson. Scholastic, 2005.

Cover from *Eighth Grade Bites* by Heather Brewer. Dutton, 2008. Used by permission of Penguin Group (USA) Inc. All rights reserved.

Cover from *Skeleton Creek* by Patrick Carman. Scholastic, 2009. Reprinted with permission.

Cover from *When I was Joe* by Keren David. Frances Lincoln, 2010. Courtesy of Farrar Straus Giroux Books for Young Readers, an imprint of the Macmillan Children's Publishing Group.

Cover from *Raven's Gate* by Anthony Horowitz. Scholastic, 2005. Reprinted with permission.

Cover from *The Clockwork Three* by Matthew Kirby. Scholastic, 2010. Reprinted with permission.

Cover from *Death Cloud* by Andrew Lane. Farrar, Straus & Giroux, 2011. Courtesy of Farrar Straus Giroux Books for Young Readers, an imprint of the Macmillan Children's Publishing Group.

Cover from *Fear: 13 Stories of Suspense and Horror* by R. L. Stine. Dutton, 2010. Used by permission of Penguin Group (USA) Inc. All rights reserved.

CHAPTER 7

Cover from *Tooth Trouble* by Abby Klein. Blue Apple, 2004. Reprinted with permission.

Cover from *Justin Case: School, Drool, and Other Daily Disasters* by Rachel Vail. Feiwel and Friends, 2010. Courtesy of Feiwel and Friends, an imprint of the Macmillan Children's Publishing Group.

Cover from *Adam Canfield of the Slash* by Michael Winerip. Candlewick, 2005. Reprinted with permission.

Cover from *Flash* by Michael Cadnum. Farrar, Straus & Giroux, 2010. Courtesy of Farrar Straus Giroux Books for Young Readers, an imprint of the Macmillan Children's Publishing Group.

Cover from *Strays* by Ron Koertge. Candlewick, 2007. Reprinted with permission.

Cover from *Secret Saturdays* by Torey Maldonado. Putnam Juvenile, 2010. Used by permission of Penguin Group (USA) Inc. All rights reserved.

Cover from *Scrawl* by Mark Shulman. Roaring Brook, 2010. Courtesy of Roaring Book Press, an imprint of the Macmillan Children's Publishing Group.

CHAPTER 8

Cover from *Journey to the Volcano Palace* by Tony Abbot. Scholastic, 1999. Reprinted with permission.

Cover from *Masterpiece* by Elise Broach. Henry Holt, 2008. Courtesy of Henry Holt Books for Young Readers, an imprint of the Macmillan Children's Publishing Group.

Cover from *Gregor the Overlander* by Suzanne Collins. Scholastic, 2003. Reprinted with permission.

Cover from *Lunchbox and the Aliens* by Bryan Fields. Henry Holt, 2006. Courtesy of Henry Holt Books for Young Readers, an imprint of the Macmillan Children's Publishing Group.

Cover from *A Tale Dark & Grimm* by Adam Gidwitz. Dutton, 2010. Used by permission of Penguin Group (USA) Inc. All rights reserved.

Cover from *Benjamin Frankenstein Lives!* by Matthew McElligott. Putnam Juvenile, 2010. Used by permission of Penguin Group (USA) Inc. All rights reserved.

Cover from *How Oliver Olson Changed the World* by Claudia Mills. Farrar, Straus & Giroux, 2009. Courtesy of Farrar Straus Giroux Books for Young Readers, an imprint of the Macmillan Children's Publishing Group.

Cover from *The Haunted Playground* by Shaun Tan. Stone Arch Books, 2007. Reprinted with permission.

Cover from *Toby Alone* by Timothee De Fombelle. Candlewick, 2009. Reprinted with permission.

Cover from *The Fire Eternal* by Chris D'Lacey. Scholastic, 2007. Reprinted with permission.

Cover from *Tunnels* by Roderick Gordon and Brian Williams. Scholastic, 2007. Reprinted with permission.

Cover from *Virus on Orbis 1* by P. J. Haarsma. Candlewick, 2006. Reprinted with permission.

Cover from *The Eyeball Collector* by Andrew Lane. Feiwel and Friends, 2009. Courtesy of Feiwel and Friends, an imprint of the Macmillan Children's Publishing Group.

Cover from *The Knife of Never Letting Go* by Patrick Ness. Candlewick, 2009. Reprinted with permission.

Cover from *Midnight for Charlie Bone* by Jenny Nimmo. Orchard, 2003. Reprinted with permission.

Cover from *Day of the Assassins* by Johnny O'Brien. Templar Books, 2009. Reprinted with permission.

Cover from *The Last Book in the Universe* by Rodman Philbrick. Blue Sky, 2000. Reprinted with permission.

Cover from *Alcatraz Versus the Evil Librarians* by Brandon Sanderson. Scholastic, 2007. Reprinted with permission.

Cover from *Alien Feast* by Michael Simmons. Roaring Brook, 2009. Courtesy of Roaring Book Press, an imprint of the Macmillan Children's Publishing Group.

Cover from *Lockdown* by Alexander Gordon Smith. Farrar, Straus & Giroux, 2009. Courtesy of Farrar Straus Giroux Books for Young Readers, an imprint of the Macmillan Children's Publishing Group.

Cover from *Killer Pizza* by Greg Taylor. Feiwel and Friends, 2009. Courtesy of Feiwel and Friends, an imprint of the Macmillan Children's Publishing Group.

CHAPTER 9

Cover from *Top of the Order* by John Coy. Feiwel and Friends, 2009. Reprinted with permission.

Cover from *Swimming with Sharks* by Betty Hicks. Roaring Brook, 2008. Courtesy of Roaring Book Press, an imprint of the Macmillan Children's Publishing Group.

Cover from *There's No Crying in Baseball* by Anita Yasuda. Stone Arch Books, 2011. Reprinted with permission.

Cover from *Heat* by Mike Lupica. Philomel, 2006. Used by permission of Penguin Group (USA) Inc. All rights reserved.

Cover from *Saturday Night Dirt* by Will Weaver. Farrar, Straus & Giroux, 2008. Courtesy of Farrar Straus Giroux Books for Young Readers, an imprint of the Macmillan Children's Publishing Group.

Author Index

Title Index

About the Authors

Kathleen A. Baxter is a children's literature consultant. She is the author of six *Gotcha* books, all published by Libraries Unlimited, recommending nonfiction books to young readers. She has written "The Nonfiction Booktalker" column for *School Library Journal* since 1996 and she has presented at hundreds of national and state library and reading conferences all over the country. Kathleen has also taught classes in children's literature, served on the 2001 Newbery Committee, consults for publishers, and has presented all-day seminars on children's books for the Bureau of Education and Research. She served as the Coordinator of Children's Services in the Anoka County Library in suburban Minneapolis for over 25 years. She is a huge fan of Maud Hart Lovelace, author of the *Betsy-Tacy* books, and was the co-founder and first president of the Maud Hart Lovelace Society. Visit her online at http://www.kathleenbaxter.com.

Kathy Baxter's Can't Miss Fiction for Boys Grades 3–5

Angleberger, Tom. *The Strange Case of Origami Yoda*
Clements, Andrew. *Frindle*
Collins, Suzanne. *The Underland* series
Cowell, Cressida. *The Heroic Misadventures of Hiccup Horrendous Haddock III* series
Gutman, Dan. *My Weird School* series
Kerrin, Jessica. *Martin Bridge* series
Kinney, Jeff. *Diary of a Wimpy* kid series. Even the first graders want to read it.
Klein, Abby. *Ready, Freddy!* series
Lubar, David. *Weenies* series
McDonald, Megan. *Stink* series
Nesbo, Jo. *Doctor Proctor's Fart Powder*
Sciezska, Jon. *Time Warp Trio* series
Vernon, Ursula. *Dragonbreath* series

Marcia Agness Kochel has been a school media specialist in grades K–12 in North Carolina, Indiana, Minnesota, and Georgia. She is currently the head librarian at The Galloway School in Atlanta where she works with middle and high school students. She reviews nonfiction books for *School Library Journal*, served on the 2006 Sibert Award Committee, and blogs about young adult books at http://omsbookblog.blogspot.com. She is the author of five other books published by Libraries Unlimited. She has an undergraduate degree from The College of William and Mary in Virginia and a master's degree in Library Science from The University of North Carolina at Chapel Hill.

Marcia Kochel's Can't Miss Fiction for Middle School Boys

Alex Rider series by Anthony Horowitz. Reading these books is like watching an action movie.

Cirque du Freak series by Darren Shan. Boys go crazy for these horror books.

Ender's Game by Orson Scott Card. This is the gateway to science fiction books for many boys.

Hungry City Chronicles by Philip Reeve (beginning with *Mortal Engines*). Give this to boys after they read *Ender's Game*.

Gordon Korman books—*Swindle, Schooled, No More Dead Dogs, Son of the Mob*, and many more. School libraries could not survive without the humor books by Gordon Korman.

Drums, Girls and Dangerous Pie and *After Ever After* by Jordan Sonnenblick. Everyone should read these books.

Unwind by Neal Shusterman. Give this to eighth graders; it's guaranteed to blow their minds.

Private Peaceful by Michael Morpurgo. A beautiful, haunting book about Irish brothers fighting in World War I.

Soldier X by Don Wulffson, *Soldier Boys* by Dean Hughes, and *Fallen Angels* by Walter Dean Myers. Boys love books about war and these are three of my favorites.

For sports fans: anything by Tim Green or Mike Lupica.

Edwards Brothers Malloy
Thorofare, NJ USA
September 11, 2012